26/3/80.

AUTHOR'S NOTE

'The time has come,' the Walrus said,
'To talk of many things:
Of shoes – and ships – and sealing-wax –
Of cabbages – and kings –

LEWIS CARROLL

THE title of *The Time Has Come* . . . is not altogether in-appropriate in view of the fact that:

I spent four years of my youth in a *ship* and later, in others, voyaged in Arctic Waters and the South Seas.

I have many times taken off my *shoes*, in order to admire the magnificent interiors of most of the finest mosques in the world.

During the three years that I was a member of the Joint Planning Staff of the War Cabinet I sent and received scores of top-secret documents in envelopes fastened down with red *sealing wax*.

After the war, as a part-time occupation to assist food supplies, I ran an amateur's market garden, and grew even *cabbages*.

For a part of my life I was the wine-merchant to three *kings*.

THE YOUNG MAN SAID

Dennis Wheatley occupies a unique position among contemporary authors. His superb narrative skill, his creation of so many well-loved characters, the meticulous authenticity of his backgrounds – these are qualities which have earned him a very special relationship with his readers throughout the world.

Now 'The Time Has Come' for Mr Wheatley to unfold the story of his own many-faceted life. The quotation from Lewis Carroll he has chosen as the cumulative title of his autobiography is curiously apt. For he is not merely able to 'talk of many things', he is also the possessor of special affinities with shoes and ships and sealing-wax – with cabbages and kings!

In this first volume, Mr Wheatley portrays the years of childhood and early youth, from his birth in the year of Queen Victoria's Diamond Jubilee to the eve of the First World War. It is a basically suburban scene: the socially secure South London of Edwardian Streatham and Brixton Hill, evoked with a remarkable feeling that reflects the wider ambience of a whole era. With the same acute observation, he brings to life holidays and schooldays passed at Margate, his often sterner experiences as a cadet aboard H.M.S. *Worcester,* his first venture into Europe where he spent nine months living in the Rhineland, learning his first lessons about the wine trade, and a great deal more about the Imperial Germany of 1913.

This is a memoir of rare enchantment, but far from being yet another nostalgic recollection of times past. The Wheatley family had its trials and tribulations, its conflicts of personality. The young Dennis quickly revealed himself as the possessor of a strongly independent spirit, not yielding readily to unjust authority. It is perhaps in following this development of an integrity of mind and purpose, which would later bring its own rich harvest, that the greatest attraction of this book may lie.

BY DENNIS WHEATLEY

NOVELS

The Launching of Roger Brook
The Shadow of Tyburn Tree
The Rising Storm
The Man Who Killed the King
The Dark Secret of Josephine
The Rape of Venice
The Sultan's Daughter
The Wanton Princess
Evil in a Mask
The Ravishing of Lady Mary Ware
The Irish Witch*
Desperate Measures*

The Scarlet Impostor
Faked Passports
The Black Baroness
V for Vengeance
Come Into My Parlour
Traitors' Gate
They Used Dark Forces

The Prisoner in the Mask
The Second Seal
Vendetta in Spain
Three Inquisitive People
The Forbidden Territory
The Devil Rides Out
The Golden Spaniard
Strange Conflict
Codeword—Golden Fleece
Dangerous Inheritance

Gateway to Hell

The Quest of Julian Day
The Sword of Fate
Bill for the Use of a Body

Black August
Contraband
The Island Where Time Stands Still
The White Witch of the South Seas

To the Devil—a Daughter
The Satanist

The Eunuch of Stamboul
The Secret War
The Fabulous Valley
Sixty Days to Live
Such Power is Dangerous
Uncharted Seas
The Man Who Missed the War
The Haunting of Toby Jugg
Star of Ill-Omen
They Found Atlantis
The Ka of Gifford Hillary
Curtain of Fear
Mayhem in Greece
Unholy Crusade
The Strange Story of Linda Lee*

SHORT STORIES

Mediterranean Nights

Gunmen, Gallants and Ghosts

HISTORICAL

'Old Rowley': A Private Life of Charles II (*Illustrated by Frank C. Pape*)
Red Eagle (*The Story of the Russian Revolution*)

AUTOBIOGRAPHICAL

Stranger than Fiction* (*War Papers for the Joint Planning Staff*)
Saturdays with Bricks*

SATANISM

The Devil and All His Works* (*Illustrated in colour*)

All these books, with the exception of those
marked*, are available in The Lymington Edition

As a cadet on H.M.S. Worcester

THE TIME HAS COME . . .

The Memoirs of
Dennis Wheatley

The Young Man Said

1897–1914

HUTCHINSON OF LONDON

Hutchinson & Co (Publishers) Ltd
3 Fitzroy Square, London W1

London Melbourne Sydney Auckland
Wellington Johannesburg and agencies
throughout the world

First published 1977
© Dennis Wheatley Ltd 1977

Set in Monotype Baskerville

Printed in Great Britain by
The Anchor Press Ltd and bound by
Wm Brendon & Son Ltd
both of Tiptree, Essex

ISBN 0 09 127890 2

I dedicate these
five volumes of my memoirs
to

My father, my grandfathers and
to my great friend in the First
World War, Gordon Eric Gordon-Tombe,
who, between them, made me what I am.

CONTENTS

ILLUSTRATIONS

I

'READY MONEY WHEATLEY'

THE person who had the largest share in the formation of my character was a brother officer with whom I shared a room for some months in 1917, and who later became, for several years after the First World War, my boon companion.

His name was Gordon Eric Gordon-Tombe. He was a laughter-loving, woman-loving, wine-loving pagan. He was also very well read, highly intelligent, forceful, unscrupulous and so clever a criminal that he was never even suspected by the police. In due course I shall relate how he was murdered and I mention him here only because he always maintained that I must be a bastard.

Gordon Eric's grounds for this were that physically I bore no resemblance whatever to my father and that our mentalities and whole attitude to life were utterly different. Superficially that was true; yet now, nearly sixty years later, I realise that basically we had certain characteristics in common, such as persistence and the aspiration to better our position in life. These could hardly have been the result of imitation, as it was not until the last few years of his life that I felt any affection for him, and one does not copy a father whom one actively dislikes during one's formative years; it therefore seems that these traits in common must have been inherited.

Moreover, my mother and father were a most devoted couple, their marriage was a love match, and I was their first child; so I think there is little doubt about my right – for what it is worth – to bear the name of Wheatley.

Although I can claim no ancestors of distinction, that it is an English name of some antiquity pleases me. The principal monument in the little church at Pevensey is the alabaster figure of an Elizabethan gentleman. He lies upon his side, apparently in acute discomfort, his head supported only by a ruff like a thick cartwheel round his neck and looking as if he might roll out of his niche in the wall onto the ancient flagstones of the church at any moment. Underneath the figure is the simple inscription *John Wheatley*.

Occasionally during the winter my father and mother used to spend a long weekend at the Grand at Eastbourne, and it was during a drive one afternoon in 1922 that they discovered John.

An enquiry of the vicar elicited the legend that John Wheatley had assisted in financing Queen Elizabeth to equip the fleet that defeated the Spanish Armada. Nothing else was known of him and no descendants of his still lived in the neighbourhood.

This monetary transaction, however patriotic in view of Elizabeth's known reputation for failing to pay her debts, made John a far less glamorous figure than he would have been had he commanded even the smallest vessel of her fleet, but at least the monument proved that we bore the name of a person of quality who had lived three hundred and fifty years ago; and from that day on my father adopted him as our ancestor.

The fact that there was not a single link to connect the sixteenth-century courtier with the twentieth-century wine-merchant troubled my father not at all. He was a serious man, little given to humour and had an immense capacity for believing anything he wanted to believe. On the rare occasions in later years when the subject of ancestry cropped up, he would state with rather ponderous gravity that we were an old Sussex family and that the fleet that defeated the Armada had been equipped by one of our forebears at his own cost.

How he squared this in his own mind with the knowledge that his own father had come from Cambridgeshire, and the family tradition that the Wheatleys had been yeoman farmers there for many generations, none of us ever had the temerity to enquire.

It was typical of his many unscrupulous, but for the most part quite harmless, distortions of fact, which I am convinced arose from a certain simplicity of mind. He never paused to analyse an impulse to the point of discovering that it might be based on a questionable motive but acted on it right away, secure in the conviction that he was an upright man and that whatever he did was beyond reproach.

My mother also adopted John Wheatley, but she had a much more subtle brain and practised this mild deception consciously; led to it by two of her principal characteristics – laziness and snobbery. It was far easier to agree with my father than to question his assertions, because he was incapable of carrying on a logical argument. In consequence she nearly always supported him, and she was ever ready to fasten eagerly upon anything which might testify to her superiority over her middle-class friends.

It is, of course, possible that I am a descendant of the wealthy Elizabethan; but, if so, as we are separated by sixteen generations, a simple calculation shows that no fewer than 65,532 other people have also since contributed to my blood – which clearly demonstrates how pointless such claims really are.

The furthest that I can trace my family with any certainty is to my grandfathers, both of whom, when their recorded history begins about the year 1850, would have been boys of about twelve. Neither of them then owned much more than the clothes he stood up in and, far from helping to finance fleets, it is doubtful if the parents of either could have scraped together two handfuls of sovereigns even had their lives depended upon it.

My paternal grandfather, Dennis Wheatley, was born at St Neots, where his people either had a small farm or were farm workers. In any case, he found life there so hard that at an early age he ran away from home and, sleeping in haystacks and hedgerows by night, walked from Cambridgeshire to London. Another boy, named Charlie Leigh, accompanied him and on arriving in the capital the two spent their first night curled up in a baker's van in Bruton Mews.

We shall never know now if these young Dick Whittingtons displayed remarkable acumen in the choice of their first resting place, or if it was sheer luck. All London must have been equally strange to them; so they might have taken jobs and slaved for a lifetime in a suburb or a slum, but they appear to have made a bee-line for that square quarter mile where beyond all others golden apples could be expected to grow, for they slept in the very heart of Mayfair.

Next morning both boys went in search of work. Charlie Leigh got taken on at D. H. Evans in Oxford Street. He was destined to stay there for many years and the gentle current of time, reinforced by keenness and ability, eventually metamorphosed him into Charles Leigh, Esq., J.P., a director of his firm and the owner of a fine fortune acquired during the building up of that great drapery business.

My grandfather did not walk so far – no more than a hundred paces. Turning out of Bruton Mews he crossed Bond Street, where there flourished until the 1920s the famous grocers and poulterers Cadby and Pratt. There he was taken on as an errand boy. In the years that followed he became a roundsman for his firm and, in time, the best canvasser for business that they had in their employ.

The next scene in his career took place when he was about twenty-four. Walking into his employer's office he respectfully announced his intention of getting married.

One can imagine the partners he confronted, in type at least. As the owners of a prosperous business in Victorian times they would have been somewhat pompous tradesmen; black-coated, side-whiskered, and displaying heavy gold Alberts across well-filled stomachs. The Victorian code encouraged early marriage as the safest means of keeping young people from carnal sin; so they gravely approved the intention of their employee. They were even prepared to subsidise legal wedlock to a limited extent. It was a small premium to pay in order that the Great God Respectability – whose slightest frown had the power to wreck a prosperous business in those days – might have no cause to button up his frock coat and turn the light of his countenance away. In consequence, they at once suggested that a rise in wages would be necessary to assist this young man in meeting his new responsibilities.

'It is that I have come to see you about, gentlemen,' said my grandfather.

The partners proposed an increase of ten shillings a week and – as its equivalent now is in the neighbourhood of five pounds – doubtless felt that they were being generous; but my grandfather replied:

'No, gentlemen. I'm afraid that won't do. As I am getting married, I shall have to provide for two in future, instead of one; so I shall need double the wage that I am getting at present.'

The amazement of the partners at this preposterous demand can better be imagined than described. Yet they were loath to lose an excellent servant; so they pretended to regard his statement as a joke and raised their offer to fifteen shillings.

'No,' said my grandfather. 'It's double what I'm getting now or I must ask you to accept my notice. And, gentlemen, please to remember that I handle all your best accounts. If I leave I shall take most of them with me.'

The response of his masters to this quite justifiable threat was that, even with such accounts as he might remove, no other firm in the West End would pay him as high a salary as they proposed to do if he accepted their last offer. It was then my grandfather threw his final bomb. He told them that unless they agreed to his terms he meant to open on his own in opposition to them.

The partners thought he had taken leave of his senses. They spoke to him gravely of that young wife to be, to whom he owed a solemn duty, and of the children who were so generally a sequel to Victorian marriages, all, perhaps, brought to starvation by such a rash, intemperate decision. They dilated upon the nightmares of a small tradesman unable to meet his debts, and upon the horrors of the workhouse. They appealed to his better feelings and urged loyalty to the firm. Finally they told him that he was both ungrateful and mad, and would be bankrupt within a month.

Unmoved by either blandishments or threats, my grandfather's reply was to walk the same hundred paces that he had walked some twelve years before, but now in the opposite direction. There, on the corner of Bruton Mews, only one door from Bond Street, he opened his first shop.

In view of the pittance which was paid to grocers' roundsmen in those days it is inconceivable that he could have saved any considerable sum of money, and he had no sleeping partner; so how he managed to finance his venture is a mystery.

No doubt he was given long terms by his wholesalers, but to equip and stock the shop would not have been enough, as by far the greater part of his customers were the nobility and gentry of Mayfair. Such households were, of course, fine accounts, as in the 1860s few were staffed by fewer than a dozen servants and some by as many as sixty; but the trades-man who got his money from them regularly every three months could count himself lucky, and many were in the habit of taking a year's credit. In addition to carrying such ever-mounting book debts, as his business increased, my grand-father would have had to pay rent, find stabling for a horse and van, and keep himself, his wife and the young children who soon arrived on the scene.

That he succeeded in keeping his head above water was due in part to a natural business ability but much more to a combination of endeavour and circumstances which could not possibly operate today.

He was off to the poultry market before dawn every morn-ing, opened his shop at eight and for six days a week kept it open till long after dark, then worked on his accounts till midnight. Before going to church on Sunday mornings he did a delivery round, so that his customers might have fresh country butter with their breakfasts, and afterwards, behind closed shutters, did all the odd jobs he had not had time to do during the week. For years, except for bank holidays, he never took a day off. Negligible taxation enabled him, like so many of his contemporaries who made small or large fortunes in Victorian times, to put the bulk of his profits back into his business. His profits were large because he faked his customers' accounts, putting items on their bills that they had never had. Yet we must not condemn him too harshly for this last reprehensible practice. It was universal among the West End tradesmen of his day, and a custom which had grown up through the centuries as their only means of recouping themselves for the long and crippling credit normally taken by the rich.

His wife must, I think, have proved an invaluable help-mate in those early years, despite her frequent pregnancies.

Her name was Sarah Hart, and she came from a Kentish family that lived near Gravesend. I am not certain of it, but have an idea that she was a cook in one of the big houses that my grandfather served.

Physically they were an ill-assorted couple for, as I remember them, he was a short, sturdy little man with a ruddy face, broad forehead, and a pointed grey beard – which gave him the appearance of a typical sea captain; whereas she was a tall, thin, angular, long-faced woman, with thin grey hair scraped back into a small tight bun on the top of her head.

They were also unalike in character. He was easy-going and generous; she was a rigid disciplinarian, strait-laced to the point of fanaticism, and extremely mean. Yet that very meanness, which I so much resented when a boy, probably developed as a result of years of careful managing while her young family grew up and every ha'penny she could save was of help to her husband.

Of their eight children two died in infancy. Those who survived were in order of age: Nell, Jess, Albert David – my father, known as Bert – Dennis junior – known as Den – Charlie and Ettie.

Nell and Jess, poor little devils, were dragged into the business without any schooling, as soon as they were old enough to be made use of; Jess as errand boy and Nell relieving my grandmother at the cash desk. My father fared only slightly better. He had a year or two at a local school in Mayfair, but even while there was pressed into service in the evenings.

The business, like its unwilling parent Cadby and Pratt, was as well as a grocers, a poulterers and pork-butchers. In the 1880s there were no refrigerators, so on Saturday nights anything which might go bad by Monday, and ends of pig saved up during the week, were exposed for sale on trestles out on the pavement. The poor from north of Oxford Street then came down to haggle for these bits and pieces, which were not good enough for the tables of the servants of the nobility, in order to get a tasty meal for Sunday. Right up till midnight, by the light of acetylene flares, while my grandfather wielded the chopper, Jess weighed up the scraps and

Nell took the greasy pennies, poor little Bert, half dead with sleepiness and cold, stood out on the curb endeavouring to attract additional custom by yelling dolefully, 'Buy! Buy! Buy!'

Den was some four years younger than my father. By the time he reached school age the position had much improved; moreover, my grandfather seems to have recognised in this third son signs of an intelligence superior to that of his elder brothers. In any case, he was not only sent to a boarding school but – somewhat surprisingly considering his background – later given a year at school in Paris. Charlie and Ettie were also given good educations, although neither of them was 'finished' abroad.

In what year my grandfather was given the nickname 'Ready Money Wheatley' I do not know, but I gather that it was not very long after he became his own master; which is all the more remarkable considering his original lack of capital. It arose in the following way.

On the sound principle that a seller will always accept a lower price for cash than if he has to give credit, when D.W. drove his van down to the poultry market in Leadenhall at five o'clock in the mornings he took with him a bag of sovereigns. Having inspected the birds offered by the best wholesalers he made his choice, fixed a price, paid and at once had his purchases carried to his van; thus ensuring that no trick of substituting poorer quality birds for these specially low prices, should be played upon him.

No doubt to begin with his dealings were on a modest scale but the time came when 'Ready Money Wheatley' became such a power in the market that no business in first quality goods took place until he made his appearance. If he was late all the finest ducks, chickens, geese, grouse, pheasants, etc. on sale that day were put aside until he had seen them and decided which he would buy for his handfuls of golden coins.

It would have been in the early '80s that my grandfather felt his business to be sufficiently well established for him to take things somewhat easier and provide his family with more comfortable quarters. Hitherto they had lived over the shop, but now he moved the business to better equipped

premises in Mount Street, Park Lane, and took a house in
Boundary Road, St. John's Wood, that had a pleasant
garden. Sundays at last became days of leisure and old
photographs show the young people playing croquet on the
lawn; but 'Ready Money Wheatley' was still only in his
forties and full of drive.

One of the truest sayings is 'Better to be born lucky than
rich.' Both my grandfather and I had this good fortune, and
one of his luckiest breaks occurred on his branching out into
the wine trade. It was occasioned by the peculiar behaviour
of the 1870 clarets.

The '70s were not only the vintage of a generation, they
were the vintage of a lifetime. Even the '74s, '75s, and '78s,
the last of the great vintages before the *phylloxera* attacked and
destroyed the indigenous Bordeaux vines, fine as they were,
could not compete against the truly superb '70s and it seems
unlikely that the disease-resistant vines from California with
which the old stock was replaced will ever yield anything so
fine as their predecessors.

On this I speak with personal knowledge for, God be
praised, these pre-disease giants were still in their prime
when I reached maturity. In the 1920s, as a Mayfair wine-
merchant with ready access to innumerable fine cellars, I
drank with my friends hundreds of bottles of the finest wines
that came from all the greatest vineyards in the world;
'Wines,' as I used to say, 'reserved for wine-merchants and
for kings.' Among them we enjoyed many bottles from the
most famous châteaux of this glorious wine vintaged in the
year that Paris was besieged. Just as Talleyrand said, 'He
who did not live before the Revolution cannot know how
delightful life can be' so one might say 'He who has not drunk
1870 claret cannot know how magnificent Bordeaux can be.'
But when they were young those '70s were the very devil.

At their first showing they were rich beyond belief in fruit
and flavour. In consequence the British wine-merchants went
mad about them. They even sold much of their sacred vintage
ports to buy those 1870 clarets; so virtually put their shirts
upon them.

The wines were duly shipped and binned away; the
merchants awaited with pleasurable anticipation the time

when they should have absorbed their tannin and reach
maturity. All big clarets contain a lot of tannin, so it was
anticipated that the '70s would take longer than most vintages before they would be fit to sell, but as time passed those
who had purchased them became seriously perturbed. Six
years should have been enough, but eight, ten, twelve went
by and still they waited in vain. Every few months they had
a bottle up to try, the bitter taste of the tannin remained as
pronounced as ever, those wonderful '70s which had held so
much promise remained undrinkable.

The merchants who held big stocks were in despair.
Many of them gave it as their opinion that the vintage was
a freak and would never come round at all. Some even began
to unload their holdings for what they would fetch, and in
the middle '80s the wines from the most famous châteaux in
this supreme year were being offered at the price of *vin
ordinaire*.

It was at this juncture that 'Ready Money Wheatley'
appears on the scene as having had some dealings with a firm
of wine-merchants in North Audley Street whose name was,
I think, Davey and Pain. Apparently they owed him a sum
of money which they could not pay, because they had sunk
so much of their capital in a huge stock of the 1870 clarets.
I know no details of the transaction; only that this business
became D. Wheatley and Sons, lock, stock and barrel, overnight. Within a few months the '70s at last began to come
round. Once it became generally recognised that they had
taken a turn their price rose again by leaps and bounds. The
result was that my grandfather acquired a West End wine-
merchants as a going concern for nothing. It was more than
paid for by the 500 per cent profit made on the knock-out
price given for the great stock of 1870s.

The eldest boy, Jess, was put in to run the new business,
while young Den, newly returned from school in Paris, was
placed for a time with Scott and Lofts, wine-merchants in
Davies Street, Grosvenor Square, to learn the vintners'
mysteries. Yet, as it turned out, although my father had no
such training, it was he who became the wine-merchant of
the family. That was a stroke of luck for me, as it led to my
following him into one of the most interesting and delightful

professions in the world, instead of becoming a poultryman and grocer.

Not long after his entry into the wine and spirit trade fortune again smiled on my grandfather. The Grosvenor Estate decided to rebuild a portion of South Audley Street and D.W. applied for a building lease. He was allotted a site in the middle of the proposed block, upon which he no doubt suitably greased the palm of His Grace of Westminster's agent, as he got it changed at no extra cost for the far more convenient and valuable corner plot next to the Grosvenor Chapel, where, incidentally, my father when a boy sang in the choir and as a soloist.

The lease granted to my grandfather entitled him to excavate a single tier basement and build a ground-floor shop with three floors of rooms suitable for a private residence above it. When the builders had gone down the extra few feet below the cellars of the dwelling houses that had stood there previously, to lay the foundations for a modern block, they struck silver sand. Without reference to the Grosvenor Estate, stalwart little 'Ready Money Wheatley' at once ordered his builder to excavate the whole site to the depth of another twelve feet. There was trouble afterwards, of course, but the Surveyor of the Grosvenor Estate was presented with a *fait accompli* and doubtless the matter was smoothed out by a further application of palm oil, as was the happy live and let live custom of those days.

By this transaction my grandfather not only managed to secure for himself an extra eleven hundred square feet of cellarage, through having a double basement; he netted £2,000 by the sale of the silver sand that came out of it, which was enough to pay for the whole building. Henceforth he held the premises known as 26/27 South Audley Street on a ninety-nine year lease at a rental of £375 per annum, and by letting the upper floors had his shop and two-tier cellar for nothing.

With the object of hampering poachers who wished to dispose of their illegal bag in exchange for liquor, a law was long ago passed prohibiting any premises being licensed for the sale of both game and wines and spirits. In consequence, when the new building was completed in 1893, D.W. was debarred from bringing all his departments under one roof. The poultry remained in Mount Street until moved, with the groceries, to No. 65 South Audley Street – a shop in another new block on the opposite side of the road – with Jess in charge. From then on No. 26 supplied only wines, spirits, beers and mineral waters, with my father as its principal and young Dennis as his lieutenant.

Some years later my grandfather bought two other businesses, both north of the Park. Bayswater was then the Mecca of the newly rich Victorians who had made fortunes in commerce and industry. Class distinctions were still so strong that most of them would have thought it presumptuous to take a house in Mayfair or Belgravia, which were almost entirely populated by the aristocracy; but many of the mansions – now hotels and blocks of flats – in the fine terraces and squares between Marble Arch and Paddington were just as large, and hundreds of opulent families lived in the area. It was, therefore, to secure a share of their lavish expenditure that D.W. bought a grocer's in Bathurst Street and another with a wine and spirit licence that did not sell poultry in Spring Street.

By 1900 my grandfather would have been a little over sixty, and half a century of unflagging effort was beginning to tell upon him. His doctor told him that unless his health was to suffer he must take a less active part in business and go to live by the sea. He now owned four shops and had four grown-up sons to run them; so, very sensibly, he took this advice, sold his house in St. John's Wood and bought one at Westgate.

There, for the moment, we will leave him; and turn to my other grandfather, who started life under no less difficult circumstances, made a much larger fortune, and possessed qualities which lifted him far above the level of a successful tradesman.

2

W.Y.B.

WILLIAM YEATS BAKER was born in 1838 at Wandsworth, which at that date was still a country village outside London.

I never heard him, or any member of his family, speak of his father, and I have often wondered if he was illegitimate. Certain facts point to that possibility: his slender, beautifully modelled hands – which both I and my son, Anthony, have had the good fortune to inherit, his small feet, his soft and pleasant voice, his charming courtesy to persons of every condition, his open-handed liberality and his life-long delight in things old, rare or beautiful. Such a combination of physical and mental attributes of aristocracy are rarely found in a man of low birth, however naturally kind at heart he may be or however rich he may become.

Moreover, on one occasion he showed me an envelope which had on its flap a bear holding a ragged staff, and told me that it was the crest of the Earls of Warwick, from whom we were descended.

The only time I used this information was to joke with my second wife, when I learned that she could prove her direct descent from a knight who came over with William the Conqueror, and through her family tree was connected with nearly every royal family in Europe. I said I could do better than that, as one of my ancestors was a King Maker.

Why my grandfather should have had this envelope I have no idea; but it does suggest that he had some connection with the Warwick family and when well past middle age was still corresponding with a member of it. Nevertheless, his childhood was passed in very humble, if not actually poverty-stricken, surroundings.

Another pointer to his father probably having been of the

upper class is that his mother, poor as she was, took great pride in keeping him clean, and as smartly dressed as her means allowed. That was most unusual among the lower classes early in Queen Victoria's reign, for to keep themselves from starvation they were compelled to work appalling hours, so had little leisure to devote to their children. But it might be accounted for by my great grandmother having earlier known better times and, perhaps, for some years been kept in luxury as a rich man's mistress.

In any case, I probably owe my existence to the fact that she clothed her boy in white linen smocks, providing him with a clean one every day and, when laundering them herself, starched them with unusual lavishness.

At that date the River Wandle ran through quiet meadows, and at the age of six it was my grandfather's custom to play with other children of his years beside the river in a field which was leased by a butcher to graze his cattle. One day these children were fishing for tiddlers, the process being that they formed a human chain, the eldest boy clinging to a tree while the youngest – my grandfather in this instance – at the end of a succession of linked arms leaned out over the steep river bank and did the actual fishing.

Suddenly the butcher arrived upon the scene. Furious that his cattle should be disturbed by these small trespassers, he came running, shouting and shaking his fist, towards them. The elder children took fright, unlinked arms and fled helter-skelter. My grandfather pitched forward and fell into the deep pool below the bank.

He could not swim a stroke, but the stiffly starched smock proved his salvation. It bellied out round his small body, taking on the appearance of the top half of a balloon out of which his head and arms were sticking, and in this extraordinary life-belt he floated away on the current down river. Terrified that he would sink, he set up a stupendous howling, but before his smock became sodden the butcher managed to get him out, then led him by the ear back to his mother.

We hear no more of him until he reached the age of twelve. That would be in 1850, and about the time that young Wheatley became an errand boy at Cadby and Pratt's, young Baker became an office boy at the Thames-bank Iron Company, for which he was paid the munificent salary of six shillings a week.

Curiously enough this was exactly the same wage as I was to receive, fifty-three years later, in my first job, as a cellar-hand at a famous wine shippers on the Moselle in Germany. But our circumstances were very different. I had just completed four years as a cadet in H.M.S. *Worcester*, and was sixteen; he was still only a boy of twelve. I was working in an almost honorary capacity, learning the art of wine making; he was a little slave to be kicked around by everybody. My hours were from seven till midday, with every afternoon free to enjoy boating, tennis and bathing; his were from eight in the morning till seven at night, and so poor was his mother that she could not afford to allow him bus fares out of his meagre pay. With a sandwich in his pocket he had to set off at six-thirty every morning to walk the five miles to Blackfriars, then at night walk the five miles back to Wandsworth.

The thought of a child putting in such a fourteen-hour day now appals us; but he took no harm from it. On the contrary, in eighteen years he received promotion after promotion until, recognised as the driving force behind the whole business, at the age of thirty he was made a partner. There then occurs another of those inexplicable hiatuses, comparatively common in Victorian times, after which an employee starting without a penny to bless himself suddenly becomes a man of financial substance. A few years after being made a partner he bought out his co-directors and became the sole owner of the Thames-bank Iron Company.

How was it done? Where did people like him raise the money to perform such amazing feats? By blackmail, forgery, robbery, wild speculation, or by seemingly impossible industry coupled with immense fertility in profitable ideas? In the case of W.Y.B. – as he was affectionately called by his many friends – we shall never know. The fact remains that well before he was forty he had become an iron-master contracting to build gasometers for dozens of towns all over England, and as a hobby buying valuable pictures at Christie's.

He had too, while still in his twenties, acquired a wife. Her maiden name was Herbert, but I know little about her as she died several years before I was born. In a painting of her that I possess she appears as a plump, rather grim-looking middle-aged lady, richly dressed in lace and satin, but at the time he married her he must still have been a clerk on quite a modest salary and I am sure that her social status could have been no more than lower middle class.

My grounds for this are that her sister, whom I knew as Aunt Betsy, survived her for many years and lived with my grandfather as his housekeeper; before which she had been in service as housekeeper with a family of rich merchants named Da Silva, who had a big house in Porchester Square, Bayswater. She was a character, being possessed of a most caustic but kindly wit, and was beloved by all who knew her; but, as the saying goes, she had not an 'H' to her name.

Physically W.Y.B., like D.W., was another short, stalwart man with a slight paunch; which no doubt accounts for my own figure. He too effected a beard, but instead of being pepper and salt and pointed, during the years I knew him it was dead white and cut spade fashion.

His marriage produced three children. The eldest, Willie, was born some years before the other two, and married a South American ballerina. He was said to be like his father: a clever, dapper little man, with a great fondness for smart clothes. As he died in the '90s I never knew him, but I vaguely remember his wife as a dark, glamorous creature decked with valuable jewels.

The second child was my wicked Uncle Johnny, of whose profligate career more anon. I was said to bear such a striking resemblance to him that it greatly perturbed my honest and industrious father. Indeed, my youth provided some grounds for his fears that I might go the same way; but, fortunately, a natural bent to industry, no doubt inherited from my two grandfathers, has done much to counteract my equally strong urge to extravagance; so I have so far escaped the distressing fate that befell my poor uncle.

My mother, Florence Elizabeth Harriet – known as 'Flo' or 'Doll', and later more generally as 'Dolly' – was born in 1875. When I was young I believed her to be beautiful – an assumption about their mothers which is probably common to most children – but I now know that her features, though regular, were too coarse, and her colouring too indeterminate for her ever to have been really lovely. Nevertheless, a good figure, a taste for clothes with plenty of money to indulge it, a lively mind, a sense of humour, a great zest for pleasure and an abundant vitality must have made her when a girl very attractive to the opposite sex. And, indeed, until well advanced in years she continued to charm both sexes by a pleasant manner and vivacious conversation; which led all her acquaintances – other than the few who were capable of detecting her occasional middle-class lapses – to regard her as a polished woman of the world.

Two other relatives resided permanently with my grandfather. They were a Mrs. Nellie Mackie and her son Laurence. She was a dark woman, plump in both face and person and, when young, I imagine her to have been very good-looking. I never heard anything about her husband. In any case my grandfather took her into his family as housekeeper. Why he should have done so when he already had a most capable one in the person of his sister-in-law, Aunt Betsy, one might well wonder. Moreover her father, a Mr. Nelson, who had a fairly prosperous carriage-lamp-making business in Lambeth and lived with his son and two daughters in a sizable house in lower Brixton could, presumably, quite well have given her a home.

However, I have little doubt that the real explanation was that after my grandmother's death W.Y.B. felt the need of younger company in his home and, to save himself much inconvenience, took the practical step of installing this attractive young woman, under the respectable chaperonage of Aunt Betsy. She always called him 'Uncle'; but although the members of her family were frequent visitors he never treated any of them as relatives.

One of his dictums was that a girl should be 'as fresh as a peach and as plump as a partridge', and if that was his taste the young Nellie Mackie may well have been a great source of pleasure to him during his middle age.

Her son Laurie, born about 1892, filled the role of a young brother to my mother and, in due course, an elder brother to myself. He showed infinite patience in playing childish games with me, and when I was older played a valuable part in my education in those tremendously important subjects that Victorian parents and schoolmasters were either too stupid or too cowardly to touch upon. I was devoted to 'Cousin Los' as I now shudder to think I called him; and his mother, Auntie Nell to me, was a sweet-natured woman who spoiled me shockingly. So it was to my great good fortune that these pleasant Mackies came to roost in the Baker nest.

I have no idea where my grandfather lived during the early years of his marriage but in the late '70s or early '80s he bought a property called Aspen House. It stood on the very top of Brixton Hill and had previously been the mansion of the Roupell Park estate.

The Roupell family had been the centre of a Victorian *cause célèbre*. In the '30s and '40s Richard Roupell amassed a considerable fortune as a lead smelter and added to it by a flair for buying properties in South London at a time when they were rapidly increasing in value. But for some inexplicable reason he did not marry the woman with whom he lived, a Miss Crane, until he had had four children by her; they then had a fifth.

He took great pride in his son, William, who was a clever youngster, and having qualified as a solicitor showed remarkable promise in his profession; yet, swayed no doubt by a Victorian regard for property, he made no secret of the fact that he meant to leave his fortune to his youngest, and only legitimate son, Richard.

William appears to have been a more gifted prototype of his successor in the house, my Uncle Johnny; for he indulged in every kind of extravagance. To pay for his dissipations he began to rob his father. This was not difficult as, being a solicitor, he was given the conveyancing of the properties his father bought and sold, and by juggling with the proceeds he diverted several thousand pounds to his own use.

William later became M.P. for Lambeth; but he had to find £10,000 to cover his election expenses, and entertaining his constituents plunged him still further into debt. When his father died very suddenly, he drove down to Aspen House, went to the dead man's room, took his keys, opened the safe, and read the will. As he feared, everything had been left to

Richard. Locking himself in, William sat down beside the corpse and at once forged another will, which left everything to his mother. As she doted on him he knew that he would have no difficulty in getting her to give him money whenever he needed it; and in the years that followed she sold scores of thousands of pounds' worth of property for his benefit.

Yet, eventually, he was seized with remorse and confessed his crimes. As he was a member of Parliament his trial created a great sensation; and from the dock he went to serve a substantial sentence. On his release his friends subscribed a sum sufficient to set him up as a nurseryman with a small market garden only a few hundred yards away from the house in which he had known affluence and committed the worst of his crimes.

In its garden there stood two great mulberry trees. They were said to have been planted by Queen Elizabeth, but it is more probable that they dated from the reign of James I, for it was he who endeavoured to introduce the manufacture of silk into England and subsidised the import of these trees for the silk-worm to feed on, offering them at sixpence a piece to anyone he could induce to plant them. William Roupell and myself were among the many boys who, during the course of three hundred years, must have climbed these trees and enjoyed their luscious fruit. After the one-time M.P.'s release from prison, my grandfather used to allow him to come into the garden every year when the fruit was ripe and pick as much as he liked.

When what William had left of the Roupell Park estate was finally disposed of, the bulk of it was developed into several streets of small to medium-sized houses, my grandfather purchasing the manor house and about three acres to go with it. The house was a square, three-storey block with two lower wings, cream-painted and containing about twenty rooms. There, during the second half of his life, W.Y.B. entertained lavishly, formed his fine art collection and, until his retirement in 1914, was conveyed from it to his office at Blackfriars in the comfort of an elegant brougham.

3

BERT AND DOLLY

As the Wheatleys and the Bakers lived on opposite sides of what was then outer London and the two families had little in common, it is somewhat surprising that they ever became acquainted; but my Uncle Johnny was 'hail fellow well met' with everyone, so no doubt it was he who in the middle '90s invited my father, and a friend of his named Tom Clements, to drive out one Sunday to Aspen House and spend the day there.

My mother must have had a devastating effect on these two young men, for on their way home my father said, 'Tom, I'm going to marry that girl.'

To which Tom replied, 'Well, Bert, I had the very same idea; but as you spoke first I'll stand aside and try my luck only if she won't have you.'

As she did have him, poor Tom had to be content with becoming an honorary 'Uncle' to me; and this large cheerful man generously gave me many expensive toys. He was on the Baltic Exchange, so quite well off, and it may be a further tribute to my mother's powers of fascination that he never married at all. However, later in life he consoled himself by taking as his mistress a smart and intelligent woman who was for many years head-buyer in a West End store. When I was older I lost touch with him, but I was much distressed to hear of his sad end. In, I think, the early '30s, poor Uncle Tom hanged himself in his own lavatory.

My father must have been a young man of considerable determination to fancy his chances with the rich and much spoilt Dolly Baker. His education had been cut short in his early teens and, as he had no natural love of reading, he could have done little since to add to it. He still had to work long hours for an exacting father, so his opportunities for courting a young woman who lived some eight miles from his own home must have been limited. He had few social graces and no sense of humour. His means were too slender for him to give her expensive presents or to offer her as a wife the comforts to which she had been accustomed. He was, if anything, socially her inferior and, above all, he had a most appalling squint.

His assets were that he carried his five feet eleven inches well, had broad shoulders, regular features, fine, light-brown hair and a handsome moustache. He was, I think, the most gentlemanly of the four Wheatley boys and had no trace of a cockney accent. He had a good singing voice and was a very strong swimmer. The latter sport was his only recreation and he had won a number of cups, mostly at the St. George's Baths, Westminster, for fast swimming. As for his squint, my mother insisted that he should have his eye teeth drawn, and this had the happy effect of making his glance normal.

His eyes were brown, completely round and never gave the faintest indication of what was passing in his mind. In consequence, when I was young and had reason to fear that I had been found out in doing something wrong his expressionless stare used to terrify me – generally without reason. Perhaps, by it, he hypnotised my gay mother into marrying him; but, if so, I am certain he was unconscious that he possessed hypnotic powers.

That Dolly was spoilt was due to her having been partially crippled as a child, to having lost her mother while still in her teens, and from over-indulgence by her fond father.

I have a suspicion that my grandmother died of consumption; if so that would account for my mother's hip. Whether or not it was tubercular, when young one of her legs was longer than the other, and for several hours each day she had to lie on a plank with a heavy weight attached to the shorter one. This had the desired effect, for when grown-up she had not even the suggestion of a limp, and it was not until she was over seventy that the hip again gave her any serious trouble. But the disability enabled her to escape many of the disciplines normally imposed on Victorian children.

In the late '80s comparatively few girls were sent to boarding school, but perhaps with the idea that Dolly would

B

acquire more airs and graces than she was likely to do at home, W.Y.B. sent her to Rokesley, on the Kemp Town sea-front at Brighton, an academy for young ladies which can be said to have been the forerunner of Roedean. She had a quick mind and was ambitious; so in addition to mastering such arts as playing the piano well, dancing, singing and decorative needlework, she learned to speak French and German fluently and acquired a very fair knowledge of history, geography and literature.

On her return home at the age of eighteen she was already a young woman of extremely strong character and, with no mother to restrain her, she completely dominated the house-hold. Aunt Betsy's humble origin must have handicapped her in dealing with her well-educated and wilful niece; Nell Mackie was by nature very easy-going and, possibly, felt her own position too precarious to quarrel with the daughter of the house; my grandfather was occupied in making more money, forming his art collections and pottering in his orchid houses. He was, moreover, the most generous of men and from their childhood had spoilt all three of his children.

Willie appears not to have suffered, and is said to have become a very able business man; but the results with Johnny were disastrous. Although nominally employed in his father's office he spent little time there. Dressed in loud checks, a brown billycock hat, and sporting an outsize button-hole, he was a well-known figure on the race courses and in the ringside seats at prize fights. In London and Brighton he hit it up with a rowdy crowd that gambled, drank and frequently entertained ladies of the chorus at private supper parties. Apparently W.Y.B. took no serious steps to curb his extremely costly sowing of wild oats, and only mildly reproved him when one day he came home with the news that, having had one over the odds at lunch, he had afterwards gone to a wine sale at Restalls and bought a hundred dozen bottles of champagne.

In those days, when, apart from railway journeys, horse transport was still the fastest way of getting about, by far the larger part of the population of London lived crammed to-gether in slums, or over their shops, within two and a half miles of London Bridge. To the south of the Thames from

Kennington on, through Brixton and right up the hill, the greater part of both sides of the road was lined with sizable houses each standing in from a half to two acres of garden; while in Streatham there still stood a number of Georgian mansions with fine grounds, and Norbury was mainly open country. As Aspen House was right on the top of the hill the young Bakers had plenty of well-to-do neighbours who entertained as lavishly as they did; so my mother's youth after leaving school was spent almost entirely in one long round of parties.

My father's life in St. John's Wood must have been very different. No doubt 'Ready Money Wheatley' saw to it that the family table was well supplied from his shops and cellars; but old Sarah was a grim disciplinarian and so frugal that one cannot imagine her allowing her children to spend hard-earned money entertaining their neighbours. One can be sure, too, that if the boys ever did get a day's racing it was only once a year on Derby Day, which in those times was regarded by Londoners as almost a national holiday. They would have been at their shops at eight o'clock every morning and not free to amuse themselves, even on Saturdays, until after the same hour at night.

The house, too, was furnished only with what we should now call 'utility' furniture; so my mother, used to living in rooms that held paintings by well-known artists, Buhl cabinets, Dresden china groups, ivories and bronzes, when taken there by her potential fiancé must have found the whole atmosphere of the place in striking contrast to that of her own home. Yet love truly works miracles. In spite of all the odds against him, my father wooed and won her.

W.Y.B. cannot have been pleased. As his only daughter, with Willie dead and Johnny going rapidly to the bad, she was in a fair way to becoming a considerable heiress; and, too, being such an attractive and vivacious young creature, he was entitled to hope that she would have made a much better match. For the only time on record he hardened his heart and put a pistol to her head by declaring that if she persisted in her choice of a husband he would cut off her allowance.

The saying that 'to them that hath shall be given . . .' is a very true one and, alas, it is a sad commentary on human nature that only too often when both families of engaged couples are rich they will vie with one another in contributing lavishly to the establishment of the young people; whereas, if there is money on only one side the parents who could provide it often take the line that it is not for them to make things easy. Yet in this instance I think my grandfather was influenced by the belief that my father was a fortune hunter; so decided to make it clear to him that if he did marry Dolly, instead of benefiting by doing so, he would have to keep her.

They must have been greatly dismayed by this ultimatum, as my father's income was only £200 a year; but united in their love and courage they refused to alter their decision. W.Y.B. then relented to the extent of buying them a house; but he continued to deny my mother a permanent allowance until after her second child was born – although he gave her many presents both in cash and kind.

The marriage took place at Christ Church, which lay only a stone's throw from the back gates of Aspen House garden, where Brixton Hill merges into Streatham Hill. The bride's dress, which my sister and I found laid away in an old chest after my mother's death in 1955, had a waist of only sixteen inches, but the satin was so heavy that we marvelled how a slender girl could have borne its weight for more than an hour; and with its rich trimmings and ten-foot train it must have cost as much as my father was earning in three or four months. As Uncle Johnny acted as master of ceremonies everything else at the wedding was on the same lavish scale.

At about this time he, too, married, leading to the altar a beautiful dark girl named Grace Mitchell. This was another sad disappointment to W.Y.B., because Grace's mother kept a public house at Putney, and I am pretty certain that Grace had played the part of a barmaid there. For some years, believing that she had trapped his son into marrying her, my grandfather received her only occasionally, and with reluctance; but I feel sure that he did her an injustice. She was a little deaf, rather shy, had a deep soft voice, and was altogether too sweet and kind a person for it to be likely that she deliberately ensnared Johnny. In any case, although he was a rich man's son, his dissipated habits made him a dubious

bet as a husband and, in fact, poor 'Auntie Gracie's' marriage
turned out a far from happy one.

Of the young Wheatleys, Nell never married; Jess did so
but I know nothing of his wife Emily's antecedents, as I saw
little of her and remember her only as a short, round-faced,
rather humble woman; Dennis remained a bachelor; Charlie
married a pretty girl named Mabel who, curiously enough,
appeared on my horizon again many years later as a poor
relation of the rich Mrs. Robinson whose youngest daughter
became my first wife; Ettie, like her elder sister, remained a
spinster.

The house bought by W.Y.B. for my parents was No. 10
Raleigh Gardens. It was situated at the bottom of Brixton
Hill, about halfway between Aspen House and the centre of
Brixton, and was a semi-detached in a row of about twenty.
The row was screened from the road by a line of tall trees
and stood about a hundred yards back from it. The major
part of the area in front of the houses consisted of a broad
lawn held in common; but each house had its own small front
garden and a catwalk at the back.

Until my arrival my mother had only one servant, and her
own talents did not include any form of domestic economy.
Indeed, to the day of her death I don't think she ever cooked
anything, and she was hardly capable of boiling a kettle. But
a 'general', as a single servant was called, was in those days
expected to do the work of three. The poor girl had to be up by
six and spent the morning scrubbing, laundering and cleaning; in the afternoons she had to be dressed in cap and stream-
ers ready to attend on visitors, she then cooked the dinner,
waited at table and did the washing up. For this she received
the munificent wage of £12 per annum, and enough material
to make herself a new uniform as a Christmas present.

My parents had married in 1896, my father being twenty-
two and my mother twenty-one years of age. I was their first
child, and was born shortly before 8 o'clock in the evening on
Friday, 8 January, 1897. That was the year of Queen
Victoria's Diamond Jubilee. It was also the year in which
the British Empire reached its greatest extent and the height
of its glory, according to James Morris's fine book *Pax
Britannica – The Climax of an Empire*.

4

RALEIGH GARDENS

My first memory is of an episode in which figured the doctor who brought me into the world. His name was Willie Robertson and he was one of a family of doctors living at Dulwich, his father having attended my mother's birth. This kindly man saw me through all my childhood ailments, and on my marriage showed his good taste in giving me a beautifully bound copy of *Marcus Aurelius*.

I was probably about three, and during an afternoon's walk with my nurse had picked up an acorn which, unperceived by her, I stuffed up my right nostril. It could not be got down, and my parents were away on a holiday; so Nanny and Cook got into a fine state of dither. As that was before the days of telephones somebody must have bicycled off for Dr. Willie, and I recall standing up in my cot while he extracted the offending body from my, by then, much swollen nose.

Another episode of my early childhood, of which I have no memory whatever but affected me all my life, was, so my parents told me later, a nurse having given me some butter that was rancid and forced me to eat it.

In consequence I have never since been able to swallow cold butter, or margarine; even thinly spread in a ham sandwich it makes me sick. It is not the taste but the texture that I find so repulsive. I even dislike the sliminess of cold butter on my fingers. Thank goodness I greatly enjoy it when served hot with asparagus, artichokes or skate. Moreover, I love beef dripping, which is not slimy but granulated and, as long as I lived at home, it was always kept for me as a substitute for butter at breakfast or tea.

One thing I do remember about my day nursery is that the pattern of the wallpaper was khaki on white and consisted of repetitions of several scenes from the Boer War; one, for example, of some Boers shooting down a British soldier who had gone forward holding up a white flag of truce.

Feeling ran very high in both England and Holland at that time and my mother and father were received anything but well when they ill-advisedly spent their summer holiday in The Hague and Amsterdam in 1900.

In London, I am told, there were the wildest scenes of rejoicing when the news of the relief of Ladysmith and Mafeking came through. In the latter case so many healths were drunk to its gallant defender, Colonel Baden-Powell, that my father came home tight; the only recorded instance of his ever having done so.

Inadvertently, Baden-Powell paid a heavy price for one measure that he initiated during the siege. He opened a post office and printed stamps; a 1d one of himself and a 3d one of the sergeant-postman with his bicycle. However, he was apparently unaware that the stamps of any British territory always have in some place on them the sovereign's head. His omission to pay this universally accepted tribute so gravely offended the monarch that she refused to bestow on the defender of Mafeking the reward of a knighthood, which he certainly deserved. The Mafeking stamps are now rare collectors' items of considerable value. But Baden-Powell was not knighted until many years later, and then for his splendid work as the founder of the Boy Scouts.

The houses in Raleigh Gardens, and the streets behind them, had not long been built. Until a few years earlier the area had been a fine private park surrounding a Tudor mansion in which Sir Walter Raleigh had lived. On the opposite side of the High Road to it there still stood when I was a child another ancient house called Ivy Lodge. It had long been empty, its iron gates were padlocked and the garden beyond them was a jungle of weeds and overgrown creepers. Legend had it that Queen Elizabeth used to stay there and that by an underground passage which led from Raleigh's house to it, he used to visit her secretly at night. It was also said to be haunted, so a spot of mystery and awe for a small boy with a highly developed imagination.

The last occupant of Sir Walter's mansion was a Lord

Mayor of London, and it was one of the big houses to which my mother used to go to parties when a girl. It could have been saved from demolition, as in the late '80s the Lambeth Vestry, which then also administered Brixton and Herne Hill, decided to acquire an estate as a public park. The choice lay between Brockwell Park and Raleigh Park. The former was chosen because the land was better wooded; but it is a sad comment on the standard of values general among Victorian Vestrymen that, for the sake of a few additional trees, they should have lost the opportunity of preserving an historical monument of such interest as Sir Walter Raleigh's home.

Our neighbours in Raleigh Gardens were, on one side, a family named Kelly. She was an enormous woman, while her husband, Charlie, was hardly more than a dwarf. He had negroid features, a high falsetto voice and was an artist. Their only child, Norah, my earliest playmate, was an ugly little girl and stupid into the bargain. However, she had a cousin, Reggie, with whom when I was somewhat older I had great fun. Curiously enough his father was a fine-looking man and in no way resembled Charlie. They lived in a big house in Effra Road with a garden of several acres, and among other sports we used to make homemade bombs. Unfortunately one day a china door handle filled with gunpowder went off in Reggie's hand; so that was the end of that. Owing to W.Y.B.'s love of pictures, Charlie Kelly became a great favourite with him, so formed one of the circle that always gathered to drink champagne before lunch on Sunday mornings at Aspen House.

On the other side our neighbour was a Mrs. Mills. She was a widow, comparatively wealthy and most kind-hearted. When my mother came to live next door as a bride, the old lady practically adopted her, and during her pregnancy insisted on feeding her up with every sort of expensive delicacy. Later, she deluged me with lovely toys; among them a set of about thirty knights in armour. I have never seen a similar set, as these were double the size of the average toy soldier, and, mounted, stood a good six inches high. Each differed from the others, all were hand-painted, their horses, shields and plumes in varying colours, and their arms and visors moved. They were really museum pieces and if such a set were procurable today I doubt if its price would be less than £300.

Some fifteen months after I was born a baby brother appeared upon the scene and was christened Jack. I have no memory of him as he died within a year or so of his birth. It was I who inadvertently killed him, as I gave him whooping cough, and the poor mite expired in a fit of convulsions.

I gather that I was not an easy child as, although normally good tempered and affectionate, I was, at times, extraordinarily self-willed and could not be moved by threats, prayers or promises. One instance of this must have been most annoying for my parents. Grandpa Baker had bought for me a beautiful, bright red coat and, apparently, I took an intense dislike to the colour. All efforts to persuade me to wear it were of no avail.

My technique on such occasions was to lie down flat on my back on the floor, refuse to budge, and scream with all the power of my lungs. If the strength of my voice was at all comparable to what it later became, this must have been a truly shattering experience for anyone in the same room with me; for, as an officer, I never had any difficulty in drilling a squad of troops a quarter of a mile distant, and my friends have often been amazed at the way one piercing yell of 'Taxi!' from me can reach a taximan's ear hundreds of yards away along a busy street.

Another episode arose through a man doll, dressed in a blue velvet suit and named Charlie, to whom I was particularly attached. We were about to set off on a holiday. Everyone was dressed for the journey and the trunks were already being loaded onto the roof of the private horse-bus that was to take us to the station. Suddenly I asked, 'Where's Charlie?' I was assured that he had been safely packed; upon which I was seized with awful fears for my favourite. 'Get him out!' I yelled. 'He'll spifflicate! Quick! Quick! Get him out or he'll spifflicate!' Alas, no one could remember which trunk Charlie had been packed in, but nothing short of his immediate rescue could quiet me. Fearful that my screams would lead people in the streets to believe that I was being ill-treated, the assembled females frantically unpacked in the front garden until Charlie was discovered. He travelled to Brighton, or wherever it was, with his head sticking out of my overcoat pocket.

As an alternative to yells I sometimes used quiet but dogged persistence; as on an afternoon when my parents, on another holiday, took me with them for a drive in a carriage. We had not gone more than half a mile when I said, 'I want to get out.' I was told that I couldn't, but a few minutes later I said again, 'Please, I want to get out.' My mother reasoned with me to which my reply was, 'But I *do* want to get out.' Water, it is said, can wear away a stone. Threats of no shrimps for tea, no sandcastles on the beach tomorrow, failed to silence me. Eventually, like prisoners who have been brain-washed under a Communist regime, this awful reiteration of a single sentence got my parents down. The carriage was halted, and for the rest of the afternoon I happily picked wild flowers in a field by the roadside.

These displays of pig-headedness can have taken place only at considerable intervals, as my parents were fond and proud of me. They had several miniatures of me painted and my photograph taken many times. In one that I particularly like I am holding a hoop nearly as high as myself and wearing a three-cornered highwayman's hat trimmed with ostrich feathers.

It was a Mr. Treble who took the photographs, and he had one toy that never failed to hold the smiles of children. It was an affair of wires on each of which was a little bird; when he turned this contraption upside-down, the birds fluttered down the wires, taking just long enough for him to get his picture.

Long after we left Brixton we continued to go to him for our photographs and it was he who first drew my attention to the fact that I had beautiful hands. I went to be photographed in my uniform as a cadet in H.M.S. *Worcester*, and he asked me to pose for a full length with my hand falling naturally down my thigh, so that he could get it against the background of dark trouser.

Most of my waking hours during my early years were spent under a large acacia tree in Raleigh Gardens and, a little later, in shopping expeditions to the centre of Brixton which lay a little under a mile to the north of us. The Bon Marché, our largest local store, always fascinated me, and Quin and Axtens even more so because of the way in which customers' payments were dealt with there. The assistant put the money and the bill in a wooden container, then attached it to a system of overhead wires. A lever was pulled, a bell rang, and the container rocketed away along the wires till it was out of sight. A few minutes later it came rushing back, the assistant unscrewed it and took out the receipted bill with the change. Above all I delighted in Electric Avenue at Christmas time, for this side street was then always decorated with trees, garlands and chains of coloured lights.

When I was a little older my mother used also to take me shopping with her up to the West End. She loved pretty clothes and hats and I often accompanied her to fittings at her dressmakers. I don't suppose that my opinion weighed with her, but she always asked it; and I am sure that these sessions were valuable training which enabled me when older to appreciate good taste in women's clothes. My mother may not have been particularly beautiful, but she was extremely smart, and I admired her enormously.

At the age of five I was sent to a kindergarten run by two sisters named Pierce. It was half a mile away, on the top of Brixton Hill near Aspen House, and it was arranged that an older girl who was also a pupil and a neighbour of ours, should call to take me there every morning. Her name was Dorothy Sharp, and I became very fond of her in the way one is of an elder sister. Her father was an official in the India Office and, as a civil servant, considered to be of some social standing. But I don't think he can really have been much more than a clerk, for the Sharps were always hard up, they could never afford anything better than a young slut as a servant, and kind, generous Mrs. Sharp had to work her fingers to the bone as cook, dressmaker and everything else to her family. Douglas, their only son, was of my own age and in due course became my first great friend.

While still at kindergarten I first experienced the emotions associated with love. In a much higher class than myself there were two sisters named Janie and Honor. The latter was the elder, she had chestnut ringlets falling to her shoul-

ders and I thought her the most lovely person I had ever
seen. My already vivid imagination produced fantastic day-
dreams in which I rescued her from the tyranny of mistresses,
burglars, Red Indians and other evil characters. Perhaps
such mental processes are normal at that age, but they seem
to me surprising in a little boy who, although perfectly
normal physically, was still incapable of doing up his own
boots. That this was so emerges from the following episode.

Dorothy's lessons lasted longer than my own, so my nurse
had to call for me and take me home. Nanny always put my
boots on for me and one day she was late, so I was left sitting
miserably with my coat and cap on, but unable to manage
my boots. My strangely named goddess, happening to notice
this came up to me and, on learning the reason for my distress, promptly knelt down in front of me and laced up my
boots. I don't think I had ever spoken to her before and she
was, of course, entirely unaware of my desperate longing to
be her shining knight; but for me that moment was fraught
with incredible emotion. I could find no words to thank her,
but was struck dumb from a mixture of wonder, embarrassment and shame at my childish helplessness. My small body
must have been one huge blush, and although I was immediately afterwards rescued by the arrival of my nurse, it took
me days to recover from this shattering experience.

I have mentioned rescue from Red Indians as one of my
fantasies in which the lovely Honor was the heroine. This
brings me to an event which was the first – and in spirit
typical of many – that led me in my youth to fear and hate
my father.

Being read to was my greatest delight, and both my mother
and nurse kindly indulged me in it; so, although at that age
I could still read only simple sentences myself, I had already
acquired a rudimentary knowledge of the excitements offered
by books just beyond the fairy-story stage.

My pocket-money was a penny a week and I normally
spent it, after great soul searching, on either some small toy
or sweets. But one day when Nanny and I went to the little
shop where I usually made my purchases, my eye fell on
that week's issue of *Chums*, price 1d. On its front page was a
picture of a Red Indian creeping up behind a Cowboy who

was seated on a fallen tree, and preparing to lasso him. The urge to have this story read to me overcame my craving for sweets and in triumph I carried the paper home.

It must have been a Saturday, as my father was at home when we got back. Taking the paper from me, he upbraided my nurse for allowing me to buy such trash, and there and then thrust it into the sitting-room fire.

In recent years there has been an agitation against the flood of films and television programmes extolling crime and brutality that have found a ready audience among the less literate young. There can be little doubt that these are in part responsible for the great increase in juvenile crime; so I am strongly in favour of their being banned. In my youth we had no cinemas or television, and in magazines like *Chums* there was never anything of that kind. When I was older the annual bound volume of *Chums* was one of my favourite Christmas presents, and I can recall no story in it which did not encourage in young readers an admiration for courage, audacity, loyalty and mercy in the hour of victory; so my father's action can be excused only on the plea that he had a misconception of the paper's contents.

Even so, it is hard to justify and sprung more, I think, from the fact that, even in later life when he had more leisure, he rarely read a book and considered reading, above all fiction, as a waste of time. He made no attempt to explain to me that he thought the story beyond my age, or to look at it himself. He simply burnt it before it could be read to me; and on so young a mind this sudden, harsh and unjustifiable punishment started a festering sore that was not to be healed finally for nearly a quarter of a century.

So ended my first purchase of the printed word, but it did not deter me from making others in due course – scores of cheap reprints in my teens and later beautifully bound editions – so that by now I cannot have spent less than £10,000 on books. As I believe them to be the best value for money that anyone can buy at any age, and that without having read so extensively I should not have been able to make many hundred thousand pounds by writing books, there is in this case something to be said for my streak of obstinacy.

Fortunately my mother's attitude to reading was the opposite of my father's. She did not collect books, but devoured four or five every week from the libraries, and in French as well as English.

Until the 1930s there was a French library in South Audley Street at which I used to change her books for her. The little man who kept it had long black hair, looked a typical Frenchman, spoke French to everyone who understood it, and English with a strong French accent to those who did not. My interest in books and the fact that I was a tradesman in the same street led him one day to confide in me that he was really a cockney, born in the East End, and had never been to France in his life. That is surely an interesting example of how a poor boy with an original idea and plenty of determination can become independent and make a good living for himself.

After Raleigh Gardens, Aspen House figured most prominently in my childhood. We went there for the afternoons and evenings every Wednesday and Saturday, and spent the day there every other Sunday. My grandfather was a true Victorian trencherman. Almost to the end of his life he ate a steak or Dover sole as well as other things for his breakfast. On his return from business there was high tea, with eggs or kippers or crab and masses of strawberries or raspberries and cream when in season. Then for lunch on Sundays, and for dinner every night, chickens, ducks, pheasants, salmon or lobsters, followed by rich puddings, fruit and nuts.

It was no doubt at his table that I acquired my love of good food; for, although we fed quite well at home it was upon much more modest lines. My father and mother were again opposites in that he was a lover of meat, whereas she greatly preferred poultry, game and fish; and I took after her.

In the matter of feeding I think she spoilt me; for as I grew up there were a number of things to which I took a dislike, and I was never made to eat them. It is probable that my obstinacy played a part in this; but I have since often had occasion to regret it, as dislikes which are pandered to all through youth are almost impossible to eradicate later in life, and that at times can make one an awkward guest.

At this time I was too young to appreciate the many

beautiful things in W.Y.B.'s art collections, so I will defer any
mention of the items of more outstanding interest until a
later stage; but I took a great delight in playing in his
garden. To me it was, of course, huge and contained an
endless variety of fascinating places.

Beyond the lawn on which stood the two great mulberry
trees, there were the flower garden, the peach house, the
tomato house, two other hot-houses and two houses which
contained only orchids. Further on came a large two-storey
building with stables and coach-house below and loft above
which contained all sorts of intriguing things to play with.
There were three dark and mysterious potting sheds, a mush-
room house and, down a side alley, a big chicken run in one
part of which bantams were kept so that I might have their
little eggs for tea. Beyond the stables was a big, walled kitchen
garden, two orchards, a summer house, an archery target and
a swing.

What a feast of joys it was for any small boy to roam in on
long summer afternoons! And my cousin Laurie, when on
his holidays from boarding school, displayed an infinity of
patience in playing with me and telling me stories about the
little fairy people who lived in the numerous rockeries.

The four gardeners produced far more vegetables, fruit and
flowers than could possibly be used in the house; but, even
so, I have never known a man who was quite so generous
with his flowers as W.Y.B. He habitually wore the square,
high-crowned bowler of his period and whenever he called
on a friend he always took a spray of orchids for the lady of
the house. But not in his hand; he produced the spray with
a flourish and a courtly little bow from the top of his hat,
inside which it had lain neatly curled in a circle. It was,
though, his flower Sundays that were the high spot of his
generosity.

Against the right side of the house there was a large and
lofty vinery. In autumn scores of pots of chrysanthemums
were brought in to fill the tiers of staging that ran the whole
length of the wall. And in front of the house there were big
beds of tulips and daffodils. On the appropriate Sundays
every year, when the different flowers were at their best, it
was his custom to invite twenty or thirty friends to come in

after church to see them. When his guests had been refreshed with champagne he used to cut the flowers himself until not one was left, giving them to the ladies, who carried them away in huge bunches.

In the garden one incident took place that had an unfortunate after-effect upon me. Someone in the household kept a large bulldog as a pet. The animal was devoted to me and, I am told, I used to play happily with it until one unlucky day when Uncle Johnny and several other people were strolling round the garden. I ran towards him across the grass and, as uncles will, catching me up he gaily swung me high into the air. The bulldog, thinking he meant to harm me sprang straight up under my small legs and fixed its teeth in his chin. As bulldogs are renowned for refusing to leave go, the horrible scene that followed can be imagined. I have no memory of it at all, but it left me with a fear of dogs which it took me many years to get over and still, today, I dislike being licked or pawed by them.

Uncle Johnny and Auntie Gracie had two children, both girls: little Gracie, and Mary, who were one and two years younger than myself. They lived in a largish house with a good garden in the Upper Richmond Road, Putney. Occasionally I went to stay with them for a few nights and I always enjoyed my visits, for my uncle was jolly and generous, my lovely aunt kind, and my cousins gay little companions. One treat I remember was being allowed to gorge myself on strawberry ices made with real cream, as they were then by the best old-fashioned bakers.

To my sorrow, when I was about seven, these visits to Upper Richmond Road ceased, because my uncle's marriage went on the rocks. He must then have been over thirty, but there was no sign of his turning over a new leaf. Aunt Grace divorced him and, wearied at last with his idleness, drunkenness and extravagance, my grandfather decided to pay him a pension providing he lived abroad. He settled in Brittany, married again and had two more children, both boys; but I have never seen them and never saw him again. He had given many people a lot of pleasure and he had had a lot of fun himself; but he had to pay for it and only six or seven years after going into exile he died of dropsy.

Aged three, in my mother's arms

My father in 1913

'Ready Money Wheatley'

William Yeats Baker

My father and mother when engaged, 1895

As a small boy

Aunt Grace and her two girls went to live with her mother, who also had a house at Putney, and now and then I spent a night with my cousins in their new home. One of the last of these occasions was in May, 1910, and memorable as a night of national importance. My aunt took us all to the theatre in Putney to see again the great West End success *Our Miss Gibbs* which by then had gone on tour. Halfway through the second act the curtain was lowered, the manager came on to the stage and in a dramatic silence announced that King Edward VII was dying.

That event marked the beginning of the end of Britain's long era of peace and plenty. It was also a severe blow to my father in his business. The deaths of members of the Royal Family had a much greater effect on the public then than they do now, and particularly on the prosperity of West End tradesmen. That of even a relative of the sovereign could mean a month's Court mourning, during which all social functions were cancelled; while that of the sovereign put an end for three months to every form of social activity and the whole nation went into mourning. That the King's death should have occurred on the 6th of May, at the very beginning of the London season, was little short of disastrous. For that year it meant no Ascot, Lord's, Henley, Goodwood with the big house parties that were given for them, no balls or presentation parties for débutantes; not even small dances. The blinds of the great Mayfair mansions were pulled down and their owners went abroad or to the country, with the result that sales of wine were negligible and what should have been the profit on a year's trading was irretrievably lost.

Of my father's family I saw far less. I do not even know where my uncles Jess, Dennis and Charles lived at this time, although good-looking Dennis, who was my favourite of the three, came out now and then to lunch at Raleigh Gardens on a Sunday. The rest, including Aunt Nell, who had long since been relieved from sitting in a cash desk, lived at Westgate. Very occasionally we went down there for a week-end, but my mother detested the Wheatleys and, as far as my grandmother was concerned, I don't blame her. The elegant Dolly was equally disliked by the Wheatley aunts, who envied her, and at the same time considered her stuck-up, which in their case she was. But the Wheatleys were a quarrelsome lot. The two girls hated their father and one another, and frequently wrote abusive letters to their brothers; while the men were not bound by any tie of strong affection and were inclined to disapprove of each other's way of life.

Jess was proving a problem to the family around 1903–05. He had taken to drink. I gather that he was driven to it through worry over his dealings with the chefs of his principal customers. Up till the First World War, and still to some extent after it, practically everything supplied to any of the stately homes of England and the London houses of the rich was subject to a rake-off.

The chef received a commission on every item that entered the kitchen; the housekeeper on linen, maids' uniforms and flowers; the valet on all his master's clothes; the lady's-maid on her mistress's toilet requisites and the butler on wines and cigars. And the devil of it was that these upper servants had the power to take the account of the household they were in elsewhere if their demands were not satisfied. The chef could refrain from marinading the *tournedos* and send them tough to the table; the butler could serve a less expensive wine than the one his master supposed himself to be drinking. After that sort of thing had happened several times his lordship could usually be induced to try another butcher or wine-merchant.

The French and Italian chefs were by far the most grasping of this below-stairs plutocracy and, not content with five, usually required ten and sometimes fifteen per cent commission. In addition, they frequently insisted that butchers, bakers, fishmongers and grocers should add ten or twenty pounds a month to their bills and split this surplus with them.

This giving of commissions, and charging for goods not supplied as a means of reimbursement for very long credit, were very ancient customs, but that did not make the former any the less questionable or the latter any the less criminal. To pay a fifteen per cent commission, too, the trader had either to charge robbery prices for his goods or resort to adding yet more items to his bill that had not been delivered.

In the old days the nobility had thought it beneath them to examine their accounts, but at the turn of the century, they began to employ secretaries specially charged with supervising their household expenditure. This departure was making the continuance of cheating by tradesmen ever more dangerous, and a court case could have ruined any one of them; so it is not to be wondered at that poor Uncle Jess, caught between the Scylla of rapacious chefs and the Charybdis of inquisitive secretaries, should have taken to the bottle.

The final straw was reached when one night he attempted a flying trapeze act on a chandelier and crashed with it on top of him in the middle of the table. My grandfather came up from Westgate and acted with decision. He sacked him as manager of 65 South Audley Street and sent him into exile; but it was by no means such a leisurely and pleasant exile as that to which Johnny Baker was despatched at about the same period.

Jess was put by his father into a little general shop in the village of St. Margaret's Bay, on the desolate windswept coast the other side of Shakespeare's Cliff from Dover. In this bleak and desolate spot poor Uncle Jess and Aunt Emily eked out a living for the rest of their lives. I saw him only once more and it was there. My grandfather periodically went over to examine his accounts, and on this occasion, as I was staying at Westgate, he took me with him. Jess died about 1920 and his wife survived him by only a few years.

One day in the early '20s I was in my office in South Audley Street when one of the assistants came in to tell me that a woman was asking for my father, who was out, and would neither state her business nor go away. On walking through to the shop I saw a small, faded, seedily dressed woman, and said to her, 'I'm sorry, Madam, but my father really is out, and he may not be back for some time. Can I do anything for you?'

In heart-rending accents she replied, 'Oh, Dennis, don't you know me? I'm your Aunt Emily.'

I have rarely felt so distressed at having hurt anyone, or ashamed of my own lack of perception, as I was after that encounter.

As a result of Jess's dismissal, Dennis was made manager of the grocery and poultry business at No. 65. Young Charles was already running the business at Spring Street, Paddington, and the Bathurst Street shop had by then been sold. Henceforth the wine business at No. 26 had to carry only my father; subject, of course, to continuing to pay tribute to its founder.

'Ready Money Wheatley' used to come up to London to collect his 'rents' in person every three months, and he always insisted on having his money on the date it was due, regardless of any other commitments into which his sons might have entered. Dennis and Charles each paid him £250 per annum and my father £500. Nevertheless, during the early years of the century my father must have been making a very good thing out of wine-merchanting, as when I was seven we moved to a much bigger house, and he spent what was then a considerable sum of money in preparing it for our occupation.

Our new home-to-be was Wootton Lodge, and it again faced the High Road, but was on Streatham Hill about half a mile beyond Aspen House. It was built with stone which had been brought from old London Bridge on its demolition. The central block was roofed with a triangular pediment and it had two slightly lower wings. From two gates a semi-circular drive led up to the front porch, and it contained about sixteen rooms.

My father bought it from two very old spinster ladies, the Miss Hedges, who were daughters of one of the early partners in the famous wine-merchants, Hedges & Butler. They had lived there all their lives and done nothing whatever to modernise the house, so it had not even gas, let alone electricity, and they still carried candles when they went up to bed.

One thing my father did delight in was making a pleasant home, and when he had finished with Wootton Lodge, it certainly did him credit. The whole house was redecorated from top to bottom and electricity installed throughout; the bathroom and plumbing were brought up-to-date; a service lift was installed to carry food up from the basement kitchen to the dining and breakfast rooms, and speaking tubes put into all the principal rooms, so that one could speak to the servants in the basement without ringing for them.

Early in 1904 we said goodbye to Raleigh Gardens and moved to this socially better neighbourhood, Up the Hill.

5

WOOTTON AND SKELSMERGH

An additional joy to the spaciousness of our new home was that it had a good garden. Two verandas at the back overlooked a lawn large enough for a tennis court; on its north side there was a long herbaceous border, and on its south a dense shrubbery inviting games of robbers. Beyond two smaller lawns with flower-beds there was a terrace, pierced in its centre by an arch, on either side of which a tall fence of ornamental iron spears screened off the kitchen garden. There was a big greenhouse in which, among other things, we grew small orange trees, a mysterious potting shed, a summer house with coloured glass windows, a chicken run, stables and various other joys.

The ruler of this small-boy's paradise was a Mr. Gunn, who wore a baize apron and had an inexhaustible fund of fascinating small-talk. He soon became a staunch friend of mine, and made me toy swords, bows of bamboo and arrows tipped for safety with corks. He also showed me how to catch butterflies and moths, and pin them out, when the killing bottle had done its work, on thin sheets of cork so that they showed to the best advantage. Gunn was quite a gifted amateur naturalist, and occasionally I was allowed to go to his home to tea, to see his collection of birds that he had stuffed himself, and butterflies and beetles, all set out in glass cases lined with blue paper. For a long time two such cases of butterflies that he made for me as Christmas presents were among my greatest treasures.

Where, in these days of the Welfare State does one find gardeners like dear old Gunn, who can be happy on a modest wage and will give a part of their leisure to making such presents with loving care for other people's children?

Soon after we had settled in at Wootton Lodge my only

sister, Muriel, was born. It was the poor mite's misfortune
to arrive with several large nevus, the worst of these being on
the hairline of her forehead, on the middle of her spine, and
on her arm. The two first were dangerous; particularly the
former, as it was feared that its roots might grow down into
her brain. They were removed in a very tricky operation
which left her so weak that for some months afterwards it
was feared that she would not survive.

In the summer she was thought well enough to be taken
with us to Folkestone, where we had rooms at a private hotel
on the front. But her state was still so precarious that after
dinner in the evenings my parents used to walk up and down
outside on the Leas, keeping a watch on their bedroom
window. If Nanny switched the light on in their room it was
a signal for them to come in at once because my sister had
taken a turn for the worse. By what was said to be a miracle,
she pulled through and grew up without any ill-effects from
her bad start.

Neither the Wheatley nor the Baker women could make
any claim to beauty and Muriel was not fortunate in that
respect either, but when young she had masses of fine hair
so near the colour of rich gold that my father used to pretend
to lose sovereigns in it. The fact that she was seven years
younger than myself, and my own absence from home at
schools and at the war during the greater part of our youth,
prevented our ever becoming intimates; moreover when
older we had few tastes and no friends in common; but I am
happy to think that although we have seen comparatively
little of one another, we have always got on well together.

It was while we were on holiday at Folkestone that I saw
a sight which I imagine few people have witnessed. I went
with my parents for the afternoon to Hythe, and on coming
out from a visit to the museum in the old Martello Tower,
we saw that a large area of the sky was bright red. With
numerous other people we stared upwards wondering what
this sinister phenomenon could portend. The huge red cloud
descended and swept past us with the effect of catching us
in a storm of scarlet hail. It consisted of millions upon
millions of ladybirds.

Apart from catching a few of the usual child diseases I

have no memory of being ill, or less robust than other little boys. Nevertheless, there must have been grounds for concern about my health, as that autumn Dr. Willie was called in, and he recommended that I should be sent to a boarding school where I would benefit from the sea air.

Margate was chosen – not on account of its proximity to my grandparents at Westgate, but because both my Uncle Johnny and my cousin Laurie had been at Skelsmergh House School there. In consequence, shortly after my eighth birthday, I left home for the first time.

On a grey January day my mother took me to Herne Hill, where the school train stopped on its way from Victoria down into Kent, and I was put aboard among some fifty other small boys, a number of whom were to remain my companions for the next four years. During the journey I made friends with another new boy named Edwards, and I shared with him some chocolate with which my mother had provided me. His mother having been less considerate he was unable to return this courtesy, but he spoke with some pride of a fine cake that was in his luggage and promised that as soon as our tuck boxes were unpacked he would give me a slice of it.

Skelsmergh was a large Victorian house in Dalby Square, one end of which opens onto the front of Cliftonville. Behind it the one-time garden had been turned into a playground for the use of the boys during breaks. It was here that I had my first fight – and that on my very first morning at school. Our tuck boxes having been unpacked I asked Edwards for the promised piece of cake. He refused to give it to me. I had been brought up to regard promises as sacred and insisted that he must keep his. The result was a furious quarrel culminating in blows. We were of the same age so pretty evenly matched; he gave me a black eye and I landed one on his nose that made it bleed. The fight was then stopped and we were taken to matron, who patched us up and read us a lecture.

Skelsmergh had an affiliated school named Lalham, to which in due course most of the senior boys moved up. Lalham was at the extreme end of Cliftonville, a little inland, and on the Broadstairs road. Unlike Skelsmergh, it had been

built as a school, and to seaward there were extensive playing
fields which were used by both schools. Laurie was still at
Lalham for his last term while I was at Skelsmergh for my
first; and, being then a very senior boy, he was allowed once
or twice to take me out.

This 'Educational Establishment for the Sons of Gentlemen',
as such places were called, was run by two brothers, G. N.
and Sam Hester, the former, although the elder, being headmaster of the junior school. There were a great number of
schools in Margate, and it was the most expensive of them;
a fact of which, with the snobbery natural in the young, we
were very proud. But it was very far from being in the class
of Hawtry's, at Westgate, and I think it unlikely that any of
my schoolfellows went on to Eton, Winchester or Harrow.

Headmasters were, in those days, almost always feared;
but G.N. was an exception. He gave instruction in only one
subject, geography, and for this all four classes into which the
school was divided were assembled together. He had travelled
fairly widely and, in particular, as a young man made a
voyage to Australia in a windjammer. His lessons contained
no dreary population figures, heights of mountains and
lengths of rivers, which had to be learned by heart, only to
be forgotten within a year or so. He simply talked to us for
an hour about foreign lands: their climates, scenery, people,
customs and animals.

We listened enthralled while he told us about the ceremony
of Crossing the Line, and how in his ship there had been an
American who had refused to pay homage to Neptune,
locked himself in his cabin, and fired through the door with
a revolver when the sailors tried to break it down; of castles
on the Rhine, of bush rangers, of winter sports in Switzerland; of how in Melbourne his money had been stolen so he
had to pawn his watch; of how terrifying a tempest could be
when in a sailing ship many miles from land; of tea-planting
in Ceylon and wine making in South Africa. This was
education in its best and most valuable sense.

It was also his custom to read to the whole school on
Sunday evenings, but he did not inflict upon us those moral
tales then still considered most suitable to the Sabbath. His
favourite choice was Wilkie Collins. And how impatiently

we waited to hear the next instalment of *The Moonstone*, or *The Woman in White*!

Yet, even under a kind headmaster, and with ample food of reasonably good quality, life was hard at boarding schools in those days. Except in the bathrooms and cloakroom there was no running water. We had basins and ewers in our bedrooms and as there was no heating system at all in the upper part of the house, there were times in winter when we had to break the ice in the jugs for our morning wash.

Before breakfast, too, after only a cup of cocoa, we were taken for our morning walk. On alternate days we went either down to Margate Pier, or along the front in the opposite direction to the flagstaff. Margate may have been healthy but, my God, it could be cold. Margate Pier points due north, and it is a fact that if one went in a ship from it, following its direction, one would not strike any land until one came up against the ice of the Arctic. When a gale was blowing from the north in mid-winter, the effect can be imagined.

We preferred the walk to the pier because it took us through part of the town, and enabled the more adventurous spirits among us to 'do a bunk'. This consisted of slipping away from the straggling procession of twos and threes, into an alley until the master, who brought up the rear, had passed; then rejoining the cavalcade without being observed, on its return. Unless one had a few pennies to spend on tuck, the purchase of which was permitted only on half-holidays, there was no point to this. But it was fun, and 'bunks' were my first essays in pitting my wits against authority.

The pier, too, had on it an intriguing variety of penny-in-the-slot machines which on rare occasions one felt wealthy enough to patronise; and adjacent to it was the harbour. The shipping in it was rarely more than a small tramp and a few fishing smacks or coal barges; but we imagined it to be an important port. At one time it had been. Marlborough sailed from it to Holland on the way to his great campaigns, and right up to the age of steam it was regularly used by rich passengers travelling to the East. They settled themselves in on the run down from Greenwich to Margate, but disembarked there and stayed at hotels, or with friends, in Thanet while waiting, sometimes for several weeks, until the whole convoy of a hundred or more ships had mustered in the Downs off Deal and a favourable wind arisen to carry them on their way to India.

Margate might, for a time, have been as fashionable as Brighton, but for an incredible blunder on the part of its corporation. Brighton, of course, owes its original rise to fame and its beautiful terraces to the patronage of the Prince Regent and his court; but its position as Britain's smartest seaside resort was largely sustained during the latter half of the last century by the frequent visits to it of Edward, Prince of Wales. On one occasion when the Prince had not been well his doctor, the great Sir Frederick Treves, who had a house at Margate, advised him that its air would benefit him more than that of Brighton; so he agreed to go there. After a civic reception at the station, the Prince was driven in an open carriage past the clock tower and up the hill into the centre of the town. As the carriage reached the crossroads the horses took fright and bolted. Despite the coachman's efforts they charged straight through the plate glass window of a drapers. Fortunately the Prince was unhurt, but the draper naturally wanted compensation for the damage and, quite rightly, sent the bill to the corporation. These foolish niggards refused to pay, so the draper then sent his bill to the Prince. Edward paid, but he swore that he would never again set foot in a town so lacking in appreciation of a royal visit. And he never did.

Had the Prince taken to visiting Margate regularly, it is certain that many people in his circle would have followed suit, and that some, liking the place, would have built houses there. This, in turn, would have soon attracted the great moneyed class of late Victorian times, and Northdown might have become another rich residential area similar to those at Bournemouth and Eastbourne. But these fine prospects were thrown away for the price of a plate glass window. I do not think there is a single fine house with a good private garden in the whole area; Margate itself has remained synonymous with bank holiday crowds, while Cliftonville's surrounding fields developed only into ugly seaside suburbs.

There was very little bullying at Skelsmergh, but this may have been due to an equally reprehensible activity – known as mobbing – from which not even the biggest boys were immune. How the victims of mobbing were selected I have no idea, and there never seemed to be any ringleaders who started a mobbing or urged others to participate. It can be likened only to an impulse running through a herd.

Once or twice a term, word spread from mouth to mouth that so-and-so was to be mobbed. The potential victim soon learned of his danger and for a day or two sought desperately to evade it by keeping within sight of a master whenever he could, or locking himself during breaks into a lavatory. But sooner or later he was cornered, either in the playground or in the gloom of a semi-basement room in which our tuck boxes were kept. A score of boys of varying ages fell upon him simultaneously. No holds were barred, and every decent rule of fair play – which we strictly adhered to in straight fights – was ignored. The poor wretch was punched, kicked, thrown down, trampled on, his clothes torn and bits of his hair pulled out.

This horrible practice probably started as a democratic reprisal against big bullies, or as rough justice exercised in cases of sneaking or theft; but the instances I best recall were the mobbing of two top form boys. One, named Harvey, an ugly fellow who wore specs, was admittedly a notorious 'swot'; but the other, Kitchen, a fair-haired, good-looking chap, had been up to the time of his mobbing, and was again after it, the most popular boy in the school. Happily I do not recall any boy having been seriously injured as a result of these savage attacks, and I was lucky enough to escape such an attention.

One very pleasant custom at Skelsmergh was our monthly holiday. From the beginning of the fourth and eighth weeks of each term, every morning on getting out of bed we would run to the window to see what the weather was like. If it was sunny there was a good chance of it being the day on which, after prayers, G.N. would announce a whole holiday. We then set off on a very long ramble in couples or groups, with no restriction about having to keep within sight of the masters. Sometimes we were taken a part of the way by wagonette; but for some of these hours we made our way along the sands and rocks of the shore, or across fields and ditches to the destination we had been given.

These expeditions were usually to Deal, Sandwich, Pegwell Bay, the Reculvers or Sturry Ferry. After a special lunch with lemonade at an hotel, we had the afternoon to romp on the ramparts of one of the Cinque Ports, among the ancient ruins of the Roman lighthouse, or in Sturry Woods. Then there was tea with all the cake we could eat, and the return by train after a long happy day.

Although unaware of it myself, I evidently was delicate, for after my second term I was taken by G.N. into his own house. He lived at some distance from the school in a street of uniform villas on the fringe of Northdown. Three other boys shared with me this special care: Oakes, Leete and Bernie Amendt. The two first were quite a bit older than myself, and Bernie about the same age.

It was Oakes and Leete who instructed me in the 'facts of life', giving for my benefit a demonstration of the normal position in copulation on the floor of our playroom. Leete also taught me how to masturbate, a practice which I indulged in afterwards with considerable frequency.

I do not think it did me any harm, although it is quite possible that my virility in middle life would have remained greater had I exercised more restraint. In any case, I regard it as reprehensible that fathers and masters in those days almost universally shirked the duty of telling children about such matters. As Havelock Ellis and other scientific investigators have shown, masturbation is natural among the young; and in many cases the dangers of excess could be avoided if children of school age were told that no harm would come of it providing they gave way to the temptation only once or twice a week.

Bernie Amendt became a great friend of mine. His father was the head of the catering department of the Great Eastern Railway and their home was a commodious suite in the Great Eastern Hotel, Liverpool Street. Sometimes in the holidays I used to lunch there with Bernie, and it was a great treat to be able to choose one's favourite dishes from the long *carte* of the restaurant, then have them served by waiters in a private room. Mr. Amendt was German; so unhappily lost

his job on the outbreak of war in 1914; but I ran across
Bernie years later as cheerful and well based as ever. He had
become an under-manager at the Berkeley.

Mrs. Hester played no part in the school, except to look
after us four in her own house. At that age I thought of her
as quite elderly, but in reality she can have been little more
than a tall, fair, hoyden of a girl. We did not care for her
particularly but we adored her best friend, Milly Evans, who
came to stay with her for long periods. It was she who provided the clue to one of the most terrifying experiences of my
life.

I made the central figure of this story experience it, in my
book *The Haunting of Toby Jugg,* but I give it again here
because it occurred to myself, and is fact.

The house was separated from its neighbours on either
side by about thirty or forty feet, and behind it had a small
garden. It was a square box, without wings or balconies.
The front door opened onto a narrow hall. Further along it
divided, the left half being a passage to the kitchen, the right
a straight-up flight of stairs. On the first floor there were two
bedrooms on either side of the landing and, over the front
end of the hall, a bathroom. The staircase made a hairpin
bend and continued up to the second floor, which also had
five rooms, immediately above those below.

As the youngest boys, Bernie and I always went up to bed
before the others. Our room was the first on the right on the
first floor. One night we went up side by side, he on the right,
I on the left, next to the banisters. There was no light on the
landing but we could see our way by that which filtered up
from the hall. When we were three steps from the landing I
chanced to glance to my left. At that age my head came up
only to the height of the banister rail. As I looked through
the double row of banisters I found myself staring into
another face within a few inches of my own. Beyond it was
the dark outline of a man's figure. He was crouching low on
the first few steps of the upper flight of stairs, and above his
face one of his hands gripped the rail of the banisters. The
face was round, white and horrible. I was petrified, struck
dumb with fear, and remained rooted to the spot.

Meanwhile Bernie had reached the landing. Opening the

door of our room, he stepped inside and exclaimed, 'Oh, what a lovely moon!'

The sound of his voice released me from the spell. Turning, I gave a terrified yell. As I plunged downstairs, I caught a last glimpse of the figure on the far side of the banisters. It, too, had turned. Swiftly and noiselessly it was gliding up the stairs towards the top floor.

Bernie darted out of our room, saw me tumbling headlong round the lower bend towards the hall, and came pelting after me, crying out 'What happened? What's the matter?'

'A burglar!' I shouted. 'Help! Help! A burglar!'

Mr. and Mrs. Hester, Milly and a man they had asked to dinner all came running out from the sitting-room. While the women sought to pacify me the men seized hockey sticks and went upstairs to tackle the intruder. There was no way out for him: no backstairs, no fire escape, no out-jutting lower roofs onto which he could have jumped, and from the top floor windows it was a thirty-foot drop. They searched every room on both the upper floors, but in vain. The burglar had taken nothing and disappeared without leaving a trace.

They tried to persuade me that my imagination had been playing me tricks, but I was positively convinced that I had seen a man on the stairs and it proved quite a job to quiet me down. I was put to bed, comforted with jelly and cake and eventually read to sleep by Milly. Next morning, as it seemed that the only explanation for the burglar's escape was that he had shinned down a drainpipe, we examined the flower-beds round the house. But there was not even the suggestion of a foot-print; so, for me, how he had managed to get away remained a mystery.

Years later, during the 1914–18 war, I met Milly Evans again. While we were talking over old times, she asked me if I remembered the fright I had given them all by seeing a ghost. I replied that I had never seen a ghost.

Upon which she said, 'Of course you thought it was a burglar. But it wasn't. I remember now that we let you go on thinking it was because we didn't want to frighten you further; but it was some sort of supernatural manifestation that you saw, and from the description you gave us, a pretty nasty one. The Hesters were very keen on spiritualism, and two or three evenings a week we used to practise table-turning, and that sort of thing. As nothing was taken and no man could have got out of that house without our finding some signs of his having been there, we had no doubt at all that our séances had attracted some form of elemental, and it had begun to haunt the place. We were so scared that we gave up spiritualism.'

In view of my complete ignorance of psychic matters at the age of nine, it is quite understandable that I should have taken a ghostly figure for a man of flesh and blood; and *the fact that I did* is irrefutable proof that I – the person who actually saw the ghost – played no part in establishing the intruder as a supernatural apparition. This personal and unsought experience has, in consequence, convinced me beyond all shadow of doubt that there are planes outside our physical world and disembodied intelligences which in certain circumstances impinge upon it.

Unfortunately, from the earliest ages unscrupulous people have sought to make money out of putting bereaved persons into communication with their loved dead, and a very high proportion of them have, sooner or later, been exposed as charlatans. Materialists make much of that, but it really has no bearing on the question, for this is a case in which one swallow *does* make a summer. It needs only a single instance of indisputable communication to prove survival after death, and of the innumerable cases which have been vouched for by reputable people it is difficult to believe that every one of them is founded on either deception, hallucination or lies. My own experience cannot be taken as any proof that on dying the essence of our individualities leave our bodies to continue its activities in some other sphere, but it can be taken as proving the existence of occult manifestations, and the existence of one makes the existence of the other infinitely more plausible.

It was in the bedroom into which Bernie Amendt walked on the night I saw the 'burglar' that my career as a story-teller began. How the custom started I have no idea, but after lights out I used to entertain my three companions with an instalment of an endless serial that I made up as I went along. As I could not have been more than ten it must have been a strange hotch-potch of dragons, robbers, witches, Indians and buried treasure; and, no doubt, most of the episodes were lifted from books that had been read to me in the holidays.

One thing is quite certain – they would not have been about some schoolboy hero performing prodigies on football field or cricket pitch. From the beginning to the end of my school-days, I loathed organised games. Probably, although I never suspected it myself, I was frail and that, coupled with my vivid imagination, made me dread more than most boys getting hurt. Anyhow, I hated the cold, mud and scrums of football, winced at the sting of a cricket ball and became incredibly bored whenever I had to do duty as linesman or waste a good afternoon fielding.

My view was shared by Colonel Sir Rowland Laurence who, while commanding a battalion of the Coldstream Guards between the wars, became a friend of mine. 'Laurie' was a man of both wit and courage, and he told me once that on first reporting to his regiment as an ensign, the adjutant had said to him, 'We like young officers to join the men in their games. I take it, Laurence, that you play footer?' To which Laurie, keeping a perfectly straight face, had had the guts to reply, 'No, sir. Nor do I play cricker or hocker.'

After living for about two years in the Hesters' house I was evidently considered robust enough to be returned to the school, and there my storytelling activities got me into an unusual situation. The masters took it in turns at nights to see that after lights out silence was maintained in the dormi-tories, and the insistence of my companions that I should continue my serial made me a constant offender. One night a young master named Randall was on duty. Catching me out after having warned me several times, he became ex-tremely angry, made me get out of bed and gave me a real dressing down. Probably I was rude to him, although I don't remember being so. Anyway, he lost his temper completely and struck me on the face.

Doubtless in an attempt to evade the blow I stepped back, tripped and fell. The moment I was on the floor I realised that I had him fixed. The blow had not hurt me, but instead

C

of getting up I remained where I was and began to groan. The poor fellow was naturally panic-stricken. Picking me up he carried me from the dormitory down to the linen-room, where the master on duty used to sit till it was time for him to go to bed. There I led him a fine dance. He knew that if it came to G.N.'s ears that he had knocked a boy down he would lose his job, and with the devilishness of youth I played upon his fears.

Despairing of pacifying me he fetched the music-mistress, a Miss Thompson, to whom he was engaged. To their united pleas, coupled with a bribe of cake, I at length relented – as, indeed, I had always intended to do – and promised not to complain to the Head. Afterwards Mr. Randall and I became the best of friends and, of course, whenever he was on duty I was able to regale my companions with my stories up to any hour of the night I liked without fear of interruption by him.

None of us liked Miss Thompson. She was a sulky young woman and made no effort at all to win her young pupils' affections. But fortunately, after my first two terms at Skelsmergh I escaped from lessons with her.

My mother played the piano well, both from music and by ear; so she was naturally eager that I too should have this accomplishment, and started to give me lessons herself as soon as I was old enough to learn simple tunes. Even at that age I appear to have had sufficient cunning to protect myself from assault, as is shown by a story she used to tell of me. Once, when I was practising and giving a particularly bad performance, she rapped me lightly over the fingers with a pencil. I immediately burst into a flood of tears. Puzzled and upset by this, she took me in her arms and said, 'Come, darling, come; I couldn't possibly have hurt you.'

'No,' I sobbed. 'But you hurt my little feelings.'

Miss Thompson's tuition was evidently so inefficient that after two terms with her it was found that instead of progressing I had lost ground. Moreover, my mother reluctantly reached the conclusion that I should never make a good pianist; so, by the Grace of God, I was spared from further hours of torment on the music stool.

That the decision was a right one there can be no shadow

of doubt. Music, like a sense of dress or a way with animals, is a gift, and I have not got it. I love gay tunes of the kind that feature in musical comedies, dance music, marches and, above all, Viennese waltzes, but unhappily I have never been able to derive any pleasure from serious music or the great masters.

In those pre-radio days the most common form of party was the musical evening, and everybody was expected to make some contribution to the entertainment. It may therefore have been my giving up the piano which led to my being given elocution lessons. Possibly W.Y.B. played a part in this, as he too had no musical talent, but provided one of the most popular turns at his own parties by a real gift for recitation. In any case I can never be sufficiently grateful to whoever had the idea, and to my father who paid for me to have these extra lessons in elocution.

Even today my English is very far from perfect, partly perhaps on account of my unmusical ear, but also because during my later teens and early twenties I read scores of weighty books in which words occurred that I had never heard pronounced; so I formed my own ideas of their pronunciation and still, at times, pronounce them incorrectly. But at least my elocution lessons did away with my suburban accent and gave me what may be termed 'an upper-class' voice. And that is an enormous asset to anyone.

For that I have to thank a Miss Lupton. She was not on the staff of the school, but visited several, two or three times a week and in the case of Skelsmergh, gave myself and three other boys these special lessons. As a Royal Academy Gold Medallist she was a real expert at her job and she took infinite pains in coaching us. The culmination of these lessons was four of us giving the duel scene from *Romeo and Juliet* at an end-of-term school concert. In it, as the star pupil, I was given the role of Tybalt, with two duels to fight, first killing Mercutio then being slain myself by Romeo. For our act proper costumes of satin and velvet, complete with swords, were hired from London, and it can be imagined how we revelled in our sword-play.

During my last year at Skelsmergh I got myself into a pretty pickle. With each term some new craze swept the school:

catapults, stamp-collecting, tops and so on. This term it was being robbers; or – to call a spade a spade – theft.

On Wednesdays and Saturday afternoons we went up to the playing fields at Lalham, and on the way back were allowed to spend our pocket money at the shops in the Northdown Road. The procedure adopted was for a gang of us to go into a shop and crowd round the counter. Two or three boys would occupy the attention of the assistants by making purchases. Others watched the doorway to give warning should a master or grown-up customer be about to enter, while two or three more did a light-fingered act with goods they appeared to be examining.

Coombes, the big bakers and confectioners, was the scene of our depredations on this unlucky Wednesday, and I managed to slip what I believed to be a large slab of Cadbury's Milk Chocolate unnoticed into my pocket. We left the shop unchallenged but, either because suspicion had been aroused by our earlier raids, or the assistant having noticed that the pile of slabs had been disturbed, two hundred yards down the street a hurrying master caught up with us. We were searched there and then and – to add insult to injury – my slab of chocolate turned out to be a dummy; which proved conclusively that I could not have paid for it.

That night old G.N. gave me a good leathering with a slipper – the only beating I received while at Skelsmergh. But the talking-to he gave me beforehand shook me more, because I looked up to him with respect and affection, and I felt very ashamed of myself.

I see that I have slipped up in stating that this was the only beating I had at Skelsmergh. I had one other which hurt far more and left me filled with bitter resentment. On joining the school train for my last term but one, I learned to my surprise and distress that G.N. had retired, and a stranger had replaced him as headmaster.

The new Head was a clergyman named Beaumont. He was a powerful-looking, black-haired, sallow-faced man, with a grim expression that boded us no good; and we soon found his harsh rule a sad substitute for that of the benign G.N. No more thrilling geography lessons, no more reading aloud of exciting tales on Sunday evenings. Instead he took us in

Latin; and, probably again owing to my lack of a musical ear, languages are a subject at which I have never been any good.

Our mutual dislike of one another reached a crisis at a time when I was halfway through a book called *Tom Tufton's Toll*. It was about a highwayman, and so exciting that I was rash enough to continue reading snatches of it under cover of the lid of my desk during a Latin lesson. Beaumont caught me, took away the book and ordered me to come to his study that evening. There, he made me take down my trousers and bend over a chair; then he lammed into me with a cane.

It was a vicious beating to inflict on a boy of eleven, and for such a minor offence most masters would have thought an imposition of a hundred lines sufficient. But worse, he confiscated my book permanently, and refused to give it me back even at the end of term. Dear G.N. would, I am sure, have been horrified at the idea of depriving a boy who had been severely punished already from being able to learn the end of an exciting story.

Beaumont was the very worst type of Victorian clergyman, and I am glad to be able to record that he met his just deserts. From a happy school Skelsmergh became an unhappy one, and for that reason, after giving the usual term's notice, my father took me away from it. Many other parents did the same with their boys, and after another few terms the number of Beaumont's pupils was so reduced that he was forced to close down.

Having referred to Victorian clergymen, this is the place to mention why from the day I was old enough to do so I always refused to go to church. At Margate we attended Holy Trinity, the square tower of which provided a well-known landmark for sailors many miles out at sea. In my day its incumbent was a white-haired doctor of Divinity; no doubt a charming gentleman among his friends, but an old fool as far as his congregation was concerned. Many schools attended his church, so much the greater part of the congregation consisted of schoolboys, and on Sunday mornings he never preached for less than forty minutes, sometimes for an hour. For several hundred small boys, the majority of whom were not yet in their teens, to be compelled to sit still pretending to listen to such long sermons, only a small part of which they could be expected to understand, was little less than torture. In me it gradually developed a positive loathing of church.

Fortunately neither of my parents was particularly religious. My father never went to church, devoting his Sunday mornings instead to winding the clocks, doing the wine-cellar, and other little chores; while my mother, although a regular attendant, soon ceased to press me, in the holidays, to accompany her. So, for the greater part of my life, apart from compulsory attendance – also most strongly resented – at military services, my only appearances in church have been at christenings, weddings and funerals.

Turning to more cheerful matters, during two or three weeks of each summer term, I had a specially happy time. W.Y.B. had, many years before, visited Paris with his wife; but she was ill there and it was such an unhappy holiday that it put him off ever again going to the Continent. By my time, he had settled into a routine of going to Brighton every winter, Great Yarmouth in the spring, and Margate in June.

Like many people of his class and age, he preferred rooms in a private house, where his likes and dislikes were known, to going to hotels. At Margate, the best rooms at No. 2 Fort Crescent were always reserved for him, Aunt Betsy and Aunt Nell, and I was allowed to spend my half-holidays and Sundays with them.

This meant not only strawberries and cream galore, washed down with softly fizzy lemonade out of blue-glass syphons, and 'Aspen House food' at meals, but that instead of being tied to a cricket pitch I was free in the afternoons to roam in the arcade.

It formed a short cut from the fort to the pier, and was a favourite place for us to do a bunk into, as its sides were lined with souvenir shops, hoop-la booths, shooting galleries and suchlike. But instead of having to gaze wistfully at these delights, as was the case during most of the year, owing to my grandfather's generosity I could patronise them. It was there, at glass bottles, that I did my first shooting; and although I have never gone in for any contests, I proved a naturally good shot.

This brings me to a feature of my four years at Skelsmergh of which I have as yet said nothing – namely the half-term weekend visits I was allowed to make to my grandparents at Westgate. I suppose I looked forward to them as a change; and anyway, the journey on my own in an old-fashioned single-decker bus with straw on the floor, was an adventure – particularly coming back after dark on Sunday nights in winter – but it was in some ways a gloomy household, and as I spent a good part of my summer holidays there, under 'Holidays' is the place to tell of it.

6

HOLIDAYS

WE were not of the class that has friends to stay with in the country, so from the age of eight to thirteen, except for a few weeks each summer, all my holidays were spent at Wootton Lodge, Streatham Hill.

Its garden provided a delightful playground for me and, in addition, there was that at Aspen House. My twice-weekly afternoons and alternate Sundays at my grandfather's provide my happiest recollections of those years. Old Aunt Betsy and Aunt Nell Mackie spoiled me terribly and Cousin Laurie, who on leaving Lalham had gone into Schroeder's Bank, continued to think up all sorts of exciting games to play with me. There was always lovely food, special toys kept there for me, and as I grew older I was allowed to stay up for parties.

Christmas was, of course, the high spot, and my generous grandfather, not content with giving each of his family one present, always gave them several. In my case they were generally an expensive toy, a new suit of clothes, some small piece of jewellery, such as a tie-pin or pair of cuff-links, and a couple of guineas. Those, of course, were still the days before one-pound notes, and on Christmas mornings he distributed his largess to family, servants and gardeners from a pile of golden sovereigns and another of bright new shillings. He always gave in guineas, never pounds.

Then there was the traditional Christmas dinner with turkey and a flaming pudding that had been soaked in brandy, followed by a wonderful assortment of desserts – crystallised fruits, peel rings, *marrons glacés*, ginger, almonds and raisins, and all sorts of sweets. These always came from Buszards of Oxford Street, from whom in those days all discriminating people bought their wedding cakes, as it was guaranteed by the firm that it never iced a cake that had not been made at least twelve months before.

I have always been a great eater of sweets, so had a special fondness for the goods from Messrs. Buszards under which the sideboard groaned; but alas, one Christmas I was deprived of them.

My mother and father were also generous to me at Christmas, and always provided me with a well-filled stocking. One year, when I was old enough to have learned that Santa Claus was a myth, I remained awake until my father had crept in and tied the stocking to the end of my bed. Having given him time to get to sleep, I switched on the light and eagerly examined the contents of the stocking. Among them was a silver-paper-covered marzipan fish about the size of the average herring. I ate it with relish, there and then, to the last crumb.

In the morning when I had exchanged presents with my parents they asked me what Santa Claus had brought me. I reeled off the list but made no mention of the marzipan fish.

'Didn't he bring you anything else?' they asked.

'No,' I replied, assuming an innocent expression.

'But,' said they, 'he told us he was going to bring you a marzipan fish.'

In vain, I shook my head. Sternly they told me that Santa Claus never lied; and decreed that as I had already eaten half-a-pound of marzipan, I should not be allowed any more sweets that day.

Christmas 1956 was my 59th, and as a change from our usual family party at Grove Place, Lymington, where we then lived, my wife and I spent it at the new house in Chelsea of my eldest step-son, Bill Younger and his wife Poo. His brother and brother's wife, Jack and Marcella, were also there on Christmas morning, and to our amusement and delight Bill and Poo had provided all four of us with stockings. Among the score of presents in mine, what should I find but a marzipan fish! They had remembered my story and had one specially made for me. Next morning I woke about six o'clock and disposed of the fish with as much enjoyment as I had its predecessor fifty years earlier.

Another high spot of Christmas was W.Y.B.'s custom of continuing the old tradition of giving a Twelfth Night party. About fifty people used to come to it and an enormous cold collation was provided, which always included a boar's head, a game pie decked with a stuffed cock-pheasant's head and breast and the feathers of its tail, and a two-foot-high tipsy-cake smothered in cream, crusted with crystallised violets and Jordan almonds.

After the feast the lights were put out and snap dragon brought in – a big dish full of raisins soaked in flaming brandy, which had to be snatched quickly or the penalty was burnt fingers. Then followed the musical evening, the star turn of which were W.Y.B.'s recitations. His favourite pieces were 'The one-legged Goose' which made us roar with laughter, and the famous passage from Shakespeare in which on Bosworth Field King Richard III exclaims 'A horse! My Kingdom for a horse!' and to add to the dramatic effect of that he used the poker as a sword. Among my contributions, when I was old enough to make them, were 'King Robert of Sicily' and 'Little Orphan Annie'. My father had a good voice but as his songs were of the 'Come into the garden Maud' variety, they had little appeal for me. I much preferred little Charlie Kelly's Negro ditties, sung in his extraordinary falsetto.

The Christmas 'hols' were, too, the season for children's parties. I went to two or three every week and my parents always gave one for me with a Christmas tree or lucky tub and a magic lantern show, ventriloquist or conjuror to round off the entertainment. It must have been at one of the earliest that truthfulness still weighed more with me than tact. A conjuror was about to perform the simple feat of changing handkerchiefs from one colour to another. Holding out a white silk handkerchief to me, he asked, 'What colour is this, little man?'

To the poor fellow's confusion I promptly replied, 'Dirty 'ite.'

As I grew older my pronunciation became normal, except for words beginning with 'th', and for years I pronounced three as 'frwe'. In fact, I did not entirely get over this until after the First World War, when I had all my teeth out. They were rotten teeth from the beginning and the worst feature of my holidays was that I never had to have fewer than a couple stopped, which meant several visits to the dentist.

How I dreaded those visits and cringed at the buzzing of the drill! But kind Dr. Willie saved me from more pain than I might have suffered by telling me that when a boy, believing it the commendable thing to do, he had let a dentist drill right through to the nerve of his tooth without protest, until he fainted; and that as a dentist could not know that he was hurting unless he was told, it was stupid to go on enduring pain when it might be avoidable.

All through my teens this constant decaying of my teeth hampered my enjoyment of ices, hot drinks and sweets. By forcing me to go frequently to the dentist my mother did everything possible for me, but as soon as I became my own master, I went only when actually suffering from acute toothache. By 1919 this cowardly neglect resulted in six teeth being too far gone to be repaired and twelve others needing stopping, which would mean at least twenty agonising sessions.

Appalled at this prospect, I said, 'If six must come out anyway, let's get rid of the lot.' The dentist demurred on account of shock to the heart, but my doctor declared that my heart was as strong as a bull's; so I went into a nursing home, was given an anaesthetic, and in six minutes, except for a couple on which to hinge the denture for the lower jaw, the whole lot were gone. It was one of the best day's work that I ever did in my life.

At the time we moved up the hill to Wootton, the Sharps moved too, and to a house in Wavertree Road, which was only just round the corner from us. In consequence our friendship with the family continued and Douglas became my bosom companion.

Most mornings during the holidays we went for a walk together, our favourite ones being across Tooting Bec and Streatham Commons. Soon after we moved up to Streatham, with a great hammering and clanging of rails that disturbed the peace of Wootton for a while, the tramway had been brought up along the main road from Brixton. Occasionally we took it for some distance so that we could explore new ground further south, round Norbury and Thornton Heath which was then still largely fields and orchards.

The tramway had also been brought up on a nearly parallel route past Clapham Common to Balham, and we went to see the opening of the new section. It was performed by the then Prince of Wales, afterwards King George V. A tram had been painted pure white, then garlanded with flags. While it moved at a slow pace between the cheering crowds, the bearded Prince, dressed in a frock coat with shiny silk lapels, and top-hat in hand, stood right at the front of the tram's upper deck, bowing solemnly from side to side.

It was by this road that Londoners drove down to the Derby, and we always went to watch them for an hour or two either going or returning. The endless procession provided a splendid spectacle as, although every sort of vehicle was pressed into service, great numbers of them were either coaches and six, carrying top-hatted gentlemen and lovely ladies, or donkey carts weighed down with costers; the men in suits and caps smothered with pearl buttons and the girls with huge ostrich feathers in their hats.

Another feature of London life which was regarded almost as a bank holiday in those days, was the Boat Race. Practically everybody in both town and suburbs sported a light or dark blue favour. My father and mother were for Cambridge, but I was a passionate partisan of Oxford. Why this choice I have no idea, for none of my family had been to either university, and we did not even know anyone who had.

On Sunday afternoons in summer Grandpa Baker sometimes took us for a drive. Usually it was to Richmond, where we had the famous 'Maid of Honour' tarts for tea, or to Hampton Court, which had the attraction of the lovely garden and its maze; but always once a year it was to Bushey Park, because W.Y.B. liked to see the magnificent avenue of chestnut trees there in the full glory of their blossom.

He also took us every year to the pantomime. It was before the era of plays for children, such as *Peter Pan*, and huge casts still played *Aladdin*, *Red Riding Hood*, or *The Babes in the Wood* on the great stage at Drury Lane. The immortal Dan Leno generally took the role of an old woman, there were wonderful transformation scenes with countless fairies; and, to end up with, the glorious slapstick burlesque of the harlequinade.

My grandfather was a great lover of the theatre, particularly of Shakespeare, and when I was older I was allowed to go with my parents on his theatre parties. What was termed a station bus was hired for these occasions and in it we did the hour's drive up to the West End. Afterwards he used to take us all to supper at Gatti's or Gow's; then there was the long jogging drive home to quiet a little my young mind still vividly picturing scenes of violent passion and sudden death.

But he did not always take us to tragedies. Often it was to the Gaiety, where Gertie Millar and George Grossmith were the leading lights against a background of beautiful chorus girls, many of whom later married into the peerage; or to Drury Lane, where the revolving stage was used in such plays as *The Whip* and *The Hope* to put on race-course scenes with jockeys spurring on real horses against the fast spin of the platform beneath them.

In summer we went for a few weeks to Brighton, Hastings, Margate or Herne Bay. It was at the latter that a confidence trick was played upon me. The tide there goes out for nearly a mile, so the pier is an exceptionally long one. Seeing people fish from it, I wanted to try my hand too. My father bought me the usual beginner's tackle, with a lead, hooks and a square of wood on which was wound a good length of line. That afternoon the tide was in, so I took it halfway along the pier and made a cast. What we then described as 'a common boy' came up to me, said that I was not doing it properly and offered to show me how. I let him; upon which, pretending to bungle matters, he threw the whole caboodle over. When I reported what had happened, my irate parent explained to me that the lead would keep the line from being washed away, and that when the tide went down that evening the common boy would walk out over the sands and collect my brand-new tackle.

I have mentioned that as I grew up I came to dislike and fear my father, but I do not wish to give the impression that he was deliberately unkind to me. It was his lack of humour and Olympian detachment that made the breach. He was devoted to my mother and she was clever enough to get everything she wanted out of him, but he was always spoken of by her to our servants as 'The Master' and that well described his position in the house.

I think his trouble was that, having had very little fun in his own youth, the idea that 'life is grim, life is earnest' had become ingrained in his mentality; and as I grew to know him better I realised that his mind was nearly always preoccupied with thoughts of his business. Only with great difficulty could he be persuaded to have friends to dinner or accept invitations to go out; and he took us to the theatre now and then more as a duty than as a pleasure. But he spared nothing in giving me the best education within his means, and was in fact, although I only realised it later, far more generous than my mother.

He held himself well, so made quite an imposing figure, and always dressed well. This, coupled with my mother's smartness, gave me good reason for being proud of my parents, compared with those of most other boys, whenever they came down to prize-givings, and suchlike, at my schools. Another reason for me to take pride in my father was his efficiency in handling matters whenever we went about as a family.

The sort of thing that impressed me was the way in which he took the lead as if by natural right, wherever he went. My mother and I, with Nanny and little Muriel, generally stayed at the seaside for longer than he did, and he would join us for weekends. He liked the sea, so when we were at Margate he used to come down from London by the *Margate Belle*, or one of her sister ships. My mother and I always met him at the pier and, however crowded the boat, he was always first off it. When I grew up I followed this example, and I found it paid, as whenever there has been a shortage of porters or taxis, it has never been myself and those with me who have had to wait about in the cold and rain.

I enjoyed the Brighton holidays best for several reasons. One was that we always had rooms in the house of a couple named Marchant. He had been a butler and she a cook in a big Mayfair household. They ran their place on lines far superior to those of the usual seaside apartments, and the dishes provided were often new to me. The food I had been accustomed to was the best of meat, fish, poultry and game, but nearly always plain roast, grilled or boiled, and usually followed by simple puddings. Mrs. Marchant was an adept at French sauces, and it must have been in her house that I first knew the delights of soufflés and savouries.

Brighton, too, had an aesthetic appeal to me. Even my unformed mind appreciated its lovely Regency terraces, the small, ancient, bay-windowed shops in the old part of the town and the Royal Pavilion. I was by then already fascinated by history and had begun to devour the novels of Alexandre Dumas *père*.

To his writings I owe an incalculable debt. In addition to the joy I had in reading them, and the fact that they formed my introduction to a life-long pleasure in history, they served as the pattern which brought my own books success. If it can be said that, to write of somewhat similar characters to those already established by an earlier author – although in a different century and country – is plagiarism, then I am guilty of that crime; for those of my first published novel *The Forbidden Territory* were modelled on *The Three Musketeers*. Spiritually the Duke de Richleau is descended from the noble Athos, strong, good-natured Rex Van Ryn from the mighty Porthos, my gentle, clever Jew, Simon Aron, from the subtle Aramis, and Richard Eaton was intended to be a more restrained, English version of the inimitable d'Artagnan.

But there is much more to it than that. It was the atmosphere of Dumas' tales that I endeavoured to get into my own; the blend of desperate deeds, arch plotting and passionate love affairs, against great informative backgrounds often sprinkled with real people. And most important of all, the spirit of his heroes who, although subject to human frailties and, at times, small meannesses, set such a magnificent example to all young readers, of courage, loyalty, endurance and determination to win through, whatever the odds.

It was at Brighton that I first began collecting cheap editions of Dumas, and soon after leaving I might have added a dozen or more to my treasured few but for my father's intervention. George Sadler, the owner of The Old Ship Hotel, and father of my mother's ex-school friend, Jessie Rose, came to the station to see us off. Slipping a coin into my hand, he said, 'Here is something to buy some more Dumas.'

I thought it only a shilling – which was quite a useful tip to a small boy in those days – and, thanking him politely, put it in my pocket. To my amazement, when I got back to London, I found that the generous old gentleman had given me a sovereign. But, equally to my amazement, when my father heard of this he was furious. He declared that I had no business to accept tips from anyone who was not a relation. I had never heard of this strange doctrine and have never subscribed to it myself as far as giving money to the children of my friends is concerned; but he seemed to be under the impression that kind Mr. Sadler had insulted us. Whether he committed the shaming rudeness of sending the money back, I don't know, but I do know that he confiscated it, which made him more than ever an ogre in my eyes.

As the gift had been an unexpected one, being deprived of it did not actually set me back in collecting my favourite author. It was the era in which one could buy cloth-bound reprints of most of the world's masterpieces in sevenpenny and one shilling series; so although my pocket money was only a shilling a week, by the time I was twelve I possessed most of Dumas' best-known romances. Twenty years later I was lucky enough to come across a large bound set of the sixty-volume illustrated edition of Dumas' works, only fifty of which are in existence, and it has since always had an honoured place in my library. Even then – as I was still a wine-merchant – I little thought that yet another twenty years later I would be asked to write an appreciation of Dumas' work as an introduction to a new edition of one of his most famous stories, *The Queen's Necklace*, and myself become known as, 'the modern Dumas'.

During those years I sampled most of the other well-known writers of historical romances and adventure stories. I enjoyed the best of Rider Haggard and Jules Verne, but found Guy Boothby and Henty poor stuff fit only for 'small' boys. On the other hand I was too young to appreciate Scott and Thackeray. Both of them struck me as colossal bores, and as far as the former is concerned I have never seen any reason to alter that opinion. In one of Seton Merriman's books I discovered that he had muddled up two Queens of France, and henceforth I regarded him with contempt. I loved Conan

Doyle's Brigadier Gerard and Professor Challenger stories, but thought Emile Gaboriau's detective Lecoq much more exciting to read about than Sherlock Holmes. So too was E. W. Hornung's Raffles, but all this author's other books proved most disappointing. The same applied to most of Anthony Hope, with the outstanding exception of his two books about Ruritania. The science fiction of H. G. Wells left me cold. As prophetic glimpses of the future they have never been rivalled, but I still find them entirely lacking in excitement. Harrison Ainsworth became a great favourite of mine, but I liked Stanley Weyman even better and I still regard him as the best historical novelist who was writing before the First World War, except for, of course, Dumas.

Most of these authors can only have been sampled by me while I was still at Skelsmergh and the bulk of them read by me in my teens, so in such a résumé I should also include another favourite of mine, Baroness Orczy. I do so particularly because, in my opinion, she gave us with *The Scarlet Pimpernel* one of the three great adventure stories of all time. The other two are Anthony Hope's *Prisoner of Zenda* and, of course, Dumas' *Three Musketeers*. Re-read today the first two are pathetically slender, but the fact remains that their plots were entirely original and set fashions in romance which have since been followed by countless other authors. Dumas gave us the 'devoted friends' theme, Baroness Orczy the gallant rescuer of refugees from the terrors of revolution, and Anthony Hope, court intrigue in an imaginary Balkan State. The three words, Musketeer, Pimpernel and Ruritania, have passed into the English language; each without requiring any context instantly conjures up for us a complete mental picture. To have achieved that is genuine fame, so I would rather have written one of them than any of my own.

I mentioned a few paragraphs back that when I was twelve my pocket money was a shilling a week. It continued to be that sum through my early teens, and by the standard of the times it was not ungenerous. Nevertheless, I was always chronically hard up, and this produced in me a theory with regard to children and money which I later applied to my own son and to my younger step-children with gratifying success.

It is the simple practice of giving youngsters from the earliest age more money than they have any use for. Unless deliberately encouraged to spend, a child of six will find fifty pence a week much more than it needs. In consequence there is no difficulty at all in getting it into the habit of saving money. The sum should, of course, be increased with age and, where parents can afford it, three pounds a week is not too much for a boy or girl of sixteen. By then they will have accumulated quite a useful post-office savings account of their own and take pride in increasing it.

I am by nature extravagant but, even so, I see no reason why this system should not have worked with me. As it was, all through my youth, and right up to the time when I began to earn a considerable income of my own, I have always over-spent myself in advance and was hag-ridden by debt. On the other hand, neither my son, nor the two step-children whom I fathered from the ages of six and ten, have ever been harassed by worry about how they could possibly raise a few shillings to buy something they wanted or to keep their end up with their young friends. They have all had reserves of money from the earliest spending age and, while they have denied themselves nothing within reason, and been very generous about giving presents, they have enjoyed the inestimable blessing of living within their incomes.

I do not suggest that this system will work with every child, but I think it will with most; and at least it is worth the risk. To parents who may hesitate to adopt it on account of the outlay entailed over some twelve years, I would say: is it not better to pay out gradually in advance, saving one's children from financial worry meanwhile, than probably having to pay their debts when they get themselves in a mess later on, as my father had to do on several occasions in my case?

Another thing I believe in is giving generously to the children of relatives, or for that matter, children one comes across casually. A 'silver penny' as I termed half-crowns, or even a pound note, did not mean a very great deal to a grown-up, but to a child or teenager respectively, such sums came as a lovely surprise and meant that some longed for joy could be realised.

Lest it be thought that I am endeavouring to pose as an

unusually generous man, I should add that in some ways I am very mean. During my life I have given practically nothing to organised charity. It is just that I prefer giving to people that I know; and, where children are concerned, have always endeavoured to keep it in mind that the pleasure money can buy is strictly related to age and circumstances.

Having mentioned books, I should not omit to record that I owed my introduction to many of my favourite authors to my father's youngest sister, Aunt Ettie. It was she who read to me Macaulay's *Lays of Ancient Rome* and so aroused my lasting interest in Roman history. Among other thrills that she later produced for me were the early Baroness Orczys and, best of all burglar stories ever written, the first 'Raffles', *The Amateur Cracksman*.

This, of course, was at Westgate, where 'Ready Money Wheatley' had gone to live on his retirement. As my father became better off, he and my mother began to take their summer holiday abroad, and during their absences I was parked with my Wheatley grandparents. In addition, all through the four years I was at Skelsmergh there were my regular half-term weekend visits; so the not very happy household there played a considerable part in the background of my early youth.

The house was called Springfield and was situated some way outside the town on the road to Birchington. It stood on high ground, just beyond the railway bridge, so overlooked the West Bay and the two halves of the golf-course. Architecturally it was a mid-Victorian horror of irregularities crowned with gables. One of them roofed a first-floor excrescence that was the equivalent of a modern sun-parlour. From it there was a fine view of the sea, and one could wave a welcome to anyone in a passing train due into Westgate Station two minutes later. This 'den' as it was called, the fact that the rooms on the upper two floors were on several levels, and that on wet days my grandfather allowed me to play in the cellar – part of which for some strange reason he elected to use as an office – made it rather an intriguing house for a small boy.

It had quite a pleasant garden, although not so big as that of Aspen House, or our own at Wootton Lodge. But my grandfather owned another property, about a quarter of a mile further inland. This was known as Hundreds Gardens, and lay between the convent and the tennis club. It consisted of a very large walled garden and an ugly modern cottage with barns and several yards. Here my grandfather spent most of his mornings, as he had chosen to occupy himself in his retirement by running a market garden and a small poultry farm.

The other residents at Springfield were my grandmother and my Aunt Nell. Both had the misfortune to suffer from deafness, my grandmother being the worse afflicted. Like many deaf people she spoke in a very low voice. She also moved very quietly, and when her tall, gaunt, black-clad figure emerged unexpectedly from round a corner, it could be quite frightening.

On one occasion she came upon me in the morning-room in the act of helping myself to a couple of lumps of sugar from a bowl that was kept in the cupboard under the bookcase. I have often heard modern children say 'No thank you' when offered a sweet, and for one to steal sugar is quite exceptional. Presumably this is because they are given as many sweet things as their young bodies crave, but in Victorian households sweets were doled out very sparingly; hence, no doubt, this lapse of mine into juvenile crime. And it was as crime that my unlovable grandmother regarded it. She told me I was a thief and actually threatened me with a cane – a thing that had never happened to me before. Little wonder that I feared and disliked her.

Aunt Nell was the eldest of the Wheatley children, and, like her mother, tall. It seemed that lean old Sarah's physical ascendancy had gradually been overcome by her more stalwart but shorter husband: for Jess was also very tall, my father and Dennis were of medium height and Charles and Ettie, the youngest, quite short. I don't think Nell cared about children; and for that I do not blame her in the least, but it meant that I never got to know her or regard her with any affection.

Ettie was about ten years younger, and still only in her middle twenties during my years at Skelsmergh. She was a small bird-like creature with very bright eyes, many enthusi-

asms and an intense manner. She was a great champion of
underdogs but invariably marred her case with me by a sort
of jovial 'it is such fun to do good' attitude, which made
many curates of that age quite unbearable. When I was older
she several times gave me a lecture on the theme 'money
does not bring happiness'.

That is most absurd nonsense. It is true enough that the
possession of a fortune and the reinvesting each year of the
bulk of the income it brings in does no-one, except the
Government, much good. But having money and spending
it on oneself and others can bring an infinite variety of
pleasure to its fortunate possessor. The only things one cannot buy outright with money are the love of an individual
woman at a given time, and health; but even the first may
often be gradually won by the tactful use of it, and the second,
if bad, can generally be made endurable.

This 'cheerful martyr' attitude of poor Aunt Ettie's was,
I am sure, the outcome of the old man making her and her
sister only very small allowances. That, I suspect, was not
because he was by nature mean – to me he was certainly the
most open-handed of his family – but because money was his
only weapon in a vendetta with his daughters.

Nell must have been to some pains to educate herself after
her withdrawal from the cash desk in the nineties, and Ettie
had received a good education. Both of them were intelligent, well-spoken women who later travelled fairly frequently
on the Continent and made friends of good social standing.
But they regarded their father as 'common'. By the standards
of Victorian gentility he probably was, although I never
knew him to be rude to anyone and he certainly did not drop
his h's. Yet it was an inescapable fact that he was a retired
retail tradesman, and that my aunts were known as 'the
grocer's daughters'.

In that day and age, in a place like Westgate, this stigma
did, of course, bar them from the entrée to the highest social
circle. They were accepted as members of the tennis club,
but some people would never ask them to make up a set, and
such slights rankled – otherwise I would never have become
conscious of this situation. Moreover, they felt so ashamed of
their father – though why I still do not understand – that

they would never ask the friends they did make to the house. The 'Pater' as they called him, must have been aware of this and, resenting the way they despised him, retaliated by doing no more than keep them and give them enough money only for their bare necessities.

Perhaps it is a little ungenerous to suggest that my spinster Aunt Ettie found in me a stop-gap to her maternal longings, but I am sure she enjoyed mothering me during my long stays at Westgate; and I was willing enough to give a polite ear to her starry-eyed moralising in exchange for fun with which she provided me. At what must have been considerable physical exertion she often took me down to the town and back on the step of her bicycle, and from Arthur Mee's *Children's Encyclopedia* she produced many games for us to play. Best of all, she taught me how to make uncooked sweets.

Once or twice a year, as a very special treat, we would go down to the grocers and buy the ingredients; then in the afternoon take over the kitchen. The process is simplicity itself and should be known to all who may ever have a child left on their hands for the day.

For binding purposes only the white of one or more eggs, mixed with an equal quantity of water, is required. The basis of the sweets is icing sugar, and the first act to roll all the lumps out of it on a pastry board until it is as smooth as flour. For coconut ice you add to the sugar an equal weight of desiccated coconut, tip the whole into a pudding basin, add enough white of egg watered down to make it a sticky paste, mix well with a wooden spoon, then add more sugar gradually until the mixture becomes stiff. Next, mould lumps of it into the shape of eggs pointed at the ends, then roll them in some of the dry coconut. Marzipan – a mixture of two thirds icing sugar and one third ground almonds – is made in the same way. When firm but not yet at the cracking stage, roll lumps between the palms into balls, then flatten each one by pressing a dried walnut down on top of it. Alternatively, to this mixture can be added unsweetened cocoa, which will produce chocolate marzipan. This is best rolled out flat on the pastry board – sprinkle first with icing sugar so that the mixture does not stick – and cut into diamonds, each of which is decorated with a blanched almond.

Peppermint creams require only icing sugar, white of egg water and a few drops of peppermint flavouring to taste. The mixture is then rolled out and cut into circular pieces by putting a 10 penny piece on top and drawing a sharp-pointed knife round its edge.

The above are the basic types which my aunt taught me how to make, but later when making them for my own youngsters, with the aid of a few bottles of flavouring essences and artificial colourings, and a set of tin sweet-cutters, I developed many other varieties. I should add, too, that I have found granulated better than icing sugar for all marzipans as it makes the sweets crisper.

Strawberry and maraschino essence make good alternative flavourings for marzipan. Raspberry noyeau can be made by using that flavour in marzipan, adding chopped nuts, rolled out between two layers of rice paper and cutting into oblongs. The chocolate marzipan mixture is also good if mixed nuts are added. Crystallised cherries can be concealed in a cochineal-coloured coating of marzipan, and dates can be split open, stoned and stuffed with it. Violet, orange and lemon creams can all be made in the same way as peppermint creams, and a variety of shapes and colours adds greatly to the attraction of a box if some of the sweets are given away as Christmas presents.

A tiny dab of white of egg should be given to the top of each sweet before sticking on such decorations as nuts or crystallised violets, otherwise these are liable to come off. The white-of-egg and water mixture can also be used to paint the outsides of sweets when they are finished, as it gives them a shiny appearance, but this should be done only lightly. To harden off, the sweets should be laid out on wire trays or wooden ones that have had a lavish sprinkling of icing sugar to prevent their sticking. They should be given forty-eight hours to dry out a little and are at their best from three to ten days after making, then they gradually lose their crispness and become too hard.

In those years Randall Jackson's concert party was always a feature at Margate during the summer months. It gave performances in turn at the Cliftonville Oval, the Fort, and Westbrook bandstand; and Aunt Ettie and I sometimes took a sandwich lunch and went over in the horse-bus to it. Its biggest draw was the soprano, Carrie Tubb, who had sung before King Edward and Queen Alexandra at Sandringham. Her career was to be as long as it was distinguished. Indeed she lived to celebrate her hundredth birthday and died as recently as September 1976. Not being musical I fear I did not appreciate her singing; but there was a funny man, party ensembles, and a hearty baritone of the 'Devon, Glorious Devon!' type that I enjoyed.

One concert my aunt took me to I shall never forget. It was given by a girls' school on the front at Westgate called, I think, Waterside, and it was the female equivalent of the aristocratic Hawtry's. In the choruses there was a beautiful dark girl of about my age whose name I saw from the programme was Montifiore. One of the very few big properties in Thanet was at Kingsgate, and owned by her family, so no doubt that was her home. I fell desperately in love with her at sight, and although I never saw her again I day-dreamed of her for months afterwards.

During my last two summers at Skelsmergh I enjoyed a different kind of holiday. My father took for us a cottage in Surrey, near Churt. Actually it was next door to the Pride of the Valley Inn, which stands on the crossroads from Milford to Frensham and Farnham to Haslemere, exactly halfway between the two latter and so six miles from the nearest railway station.

Although only thirty-five miles from London, as motoring was then only in its infancy, that part of the world was still entirely unspoilt country. Within the range of a morning's walk there were not more than half a dozen modern houses, all cooking was still done on coal ranges, and a local girl whom we took back to London with us as a nursemaid for my sister had never even seen electric light. Mr. Marshall, the landlord of the Pride of the Valley – who hired us our pony and trap and provided the wagonette in which on Saturdays we drove into Farnham to shop and meet my father's train – habitually wore a yokel's pudding basin hat and a hand-goffered impeccably-white smock. Few, except the better off, of the people who lived in the villages round about had ever been to London. The woods were unfenced and one could

walk for miles through them, or across the heaths that
separated them, without seeing a soul.

Behind our cottage lay a rough lawn, then a little stream
and a small wood. Beyond that lay the road to Churt and
across it more trees surrounding two large lakes from the
further shores of which rose steep heather-covered hills
crowned with a stony outcrop called the Devil's Jumps. The
roads to Milford and Hindhead also ran through deep woods
of pine, fir, birch and oak, carpeted with bracken and blue-
bells, while below Hindhead lay the huge crater known as
the Devil's Punch Bowl, and at about the same distance in
another direction the biggest lake in the district, Frensham
Pond. Thus, by trap, on bicycles or on foot we had an
infinite variety of lovely spots in which to picnic.

By far the greater part of East Kent consists of cultivated
fields and orchards; and during my visits to Westgate, sea,
sand and rocks had been the background against which I
played. Now, at Churt, I was for the first time living in real
country. It was a new world to me and in it I found many
novel delights – the gorgeous dragon-flies flitting above the
bulrushes in the lakes, the deep silence of the woods, the
wild flowers that could be collected, and paddling in the little
stream with its miniature tinkling waterfalls. It was no doubt
these early experiences which later made me regard the
sweep of rolling downs and vistas of waving corn with com-
parative indifference. For me the most lovely thing in nature
is a woodland glade and although I have since travelled in
many countries I still have no memories of the kind which
exceed in beauty those of the Surrey woods before they became a weekend playground for London's millions.

For a month or two during both summers that we had the
cottage the solitude of the woods and lanes was frequently
shattered, but for me in a most exciting manner; the troops
of the Aldershot Command were holding their annual
manoeuvres. To one side of Frensham Pond there lay a wide
expanse of level heath and on it there arose a great tented
camp. For miles around at any moment one might meet a
marching column, or come upon a little group of khaki
figures busy laying a field telephone or stealing through the
undergrowth.

As my favourite recreation in those days was playing with my toy soldiers the delight I took in seeing real ones engaged in mimic warfare can easily be imagined, and from dawn to dusk I hovered eager-eyed in their vicinity.

The high-spot of this treat came on the last day. A line which included the Devil's Jumps was held by a skeleton army and the previous night a brigade of field artillery had dug its guns in along the crest of the range. Early in the day the General of a mock army and his staff took up their position upon the highest stone outcrop. All the morning they sat there with outspread maps, occasionally looking through their field glasses towards the opposite heights of Hindhead, from which, at intervals, little groups of the attacking army could be seen crossing open spaces at the run as they made their way down into the valley. Now and then puffs of white smoke rose from the enemy batteries, and ours ranged along the hilltop discharged their blanks with an answering roar.

At midday an elaborate picnic was laid out on the flat stone and the staff happily set to. As I was not one of a crowd, but the only civilian in sight, no attempt had been made to shoo me away. On the contrary, several of the officers talked to me most kindly, explaining what was happening, and the General even offered me a sandwich. To my great embarrassment I had to refuse it, because it contained butter, which I knew would make me sick.

By the late afternoon the enemy had concentrated in force along the road below the Jumps. Hundreds of them burst through the shallow screen of trees and, flinging themselves flat, opened fire on us with their rifles. For some ten minutes the General and his staff sat unperturbed on their hilltop looking down at the flickering flashes made by thousands of rounds of blanks. Then bugles rang out, the attackers ceased fire, sprang to their feet and charged the steep gorse-covered hill, the officers waving their drawn swords and the sunlight glinting on the innumerable bayonets of the men. Panting and gasping they at last reached the top to fling themselves down exhausted. The great day was over.

It now fills me with amazement that this spectacle I witnessed in my boyhood should have been an earnest military endeavour to practise the art of war. Obviously those who directed it were thinking in terms of their own experiences, less than ten years earlier, when they had fought the Boers, and the fact is that this mock battle differed in no way from the type of conflict that took place in the Napoleonic wars. Guns were still sited on hilltops to enable them to fire point blank on attacking infantry, regardless of the fact that it gave away their position; thus, owing to the greater range of modern artillery, rendering it certain that the enemy guns would blot them out long before any massed assault could develop. The place for a General was on the highest ground in the forefront of the battle, again regardless of the fact that he and his staff, with their gold-peaked scarlet-banded caps, would have been spotted through modern binoculars from miles away and blasted out of existence by one well-aimed salvo. As for the frontal attack up a steep hill, against machine guns and repeating rifles not a man would have survived; but it would then have been thought lacking in courage to take a strong position by outflanking and going round it.

Only five or six years later a great part of those very officers and men must have come face to face with the Germans at Mons. No doubt the General, and he was the same – for it was no less a man than General Sir John French who offered me a sandwich – deployed them in a very similar manner to that I had witnessed. Indeed, it took many of our generals years to learn that with the development of modern fire power and the coming of the aeroplane the days of waging war successfully on the Napoleonic pattern were gone for ever.

Apart from these brief exciting periods when manoeuvres were taking place, most of my days at Churt were spent in rambles which I enjoyed no less because they were solitary. However, my mother's relations with my Wheatley aunts must at this time have improved, as both of them came to stay. During Aunt Ettie's visits she again devoted herself to me and we made a number of long expeditions together on bicycles.

Reverting now to Westgate, ungrateful as it may sound, I think I enjoyed the hours I spent there with my grandfather more than those I spent with my affectionate but goody-goody aunt, in spite of all the trouble she went to in providing amusements for me. He was a rather silent man, but he never moralised and we were very happy companions.

On mornings when the tide was out I usually went to the beach on my own. Fields then ran down to the end of the west bay, which was the furthest from the town, and even in the height of summer it was practically deserted. There was a splendid stretch of golden sand, acres of rocks from the pools in which little crabs, shrimps and pretty seaweeds could be collected and, beyond the end of the promenade, high chalk cliffs with smugglers' caves running up into them. But when the tide was in I used to accompany my grandfather to Hundreds Gardens, where I would help pick the fruit or feed the seven hundred head of poultry. Then in the afternoons he would sometimes take me with him for a round of golf or on expeditions.

In time I learned to play quite a good game of golf with him, but my year in Germany, four years of war and living afterwards in London with no golf-course easily accessible, prevented a continuance of my youthful enthusiasm for the game; and as I have always found more pleasure in mental pursuits I rather doubt if in any case I should have developed into a regular golfer.

The expeditions were mainly for the purpose of visiting the buyers of his market garden produce, and took us to Margate, Ramsgate and Dover. The harbours of the last two had a great attraction for me, particularly the latter, as it was still in use as a full-scale naval base, and my grandfather always allowed ample time for us to walk right to the end of the wharves so as to get a close-up view of the ships.

In Margate, too, he allowed time for us to visit Lord George Sanger's circus in the Hall by the Sea. It had a permanent menagerie and, as he knew the head keeper, I was allowed behind the scenes to handle the lion cubs and other young animals. There was also a rink for roller skating, which was a great craze at that time. He bought me a fine pair of skates, and whizzing round and round on them was a splendid thrill.

Another present he made me at my request was a pair of boxing gloves, but I never got far with the noble art and perhaps because I was rather a puny boy, took up ju-jitsu

instead. I never became an expert in that either, but learned
enough from an illustrated book I bought to master the
principles of the sport, and a few useful grips which came
in handy during rough and tumbles with my schoolfellows.

Other fairly frequent expeditions with my grandfather
were our visits to Quex Park. It was a well-wooded, walled-in
area of many acres and the only big private property for
many miles around. The owner was a Colonel Powell-
Cotton. He was a famous big-game hunter and spent much
of his time abroad, but it was not him we went to see. My
grandfather's friend was the head gardener. Usually we
drove over in the pony and trap and spent an hour or so
going through the beautifully-kept glasshouses; but the high
spot of these expeditions for me was being taken in to see the
museum, a big building adjacent to the house. It contained
scores of heads of lion, hippo, giraffe and other beasts shot
by the Colonel, and also a fine collection of native weapons.

Years later I visited Quex Park again; this time at the
invitation of the Colonel. I was writing a book called *Contraband* and had decided that the tree-screened meadows inside
Quex Park would make a perfect place for aircraft to land
secretly at night. Colonel Powell-Cotton could not have been
kinder. He gave me permission to use his property in my
book, and took me over the several follies and towers scattered about the park which made it even more suitable for
nefarious operations by modern smugglers.

From what I have written it will be seen that I had no
real cause to complain about my parents sending me to
Westgate when they went on holidays abroad. But I was
never happy there in the same way as I was at Aspen House.
Grandpa Baker, always humming a little tune as he moved
among his art treasures and his flowers was a warmer personality than Grandpa Wheatley. The Wheatley aunts, Nell
with her aloofness and Ettie with her do-gooder's attitude to
life, could not compete in my affections with plump, easy-
going Nellie Mackie and jolly old Auntie Betsy. There was
no Cousin Laurie to invent exciting games, and no other
children were ever asked in to play with me. Above all the
grim figure of my deaf and stealthy grandmother dominated
the house.

Both my sister and myself fell foul of old Sarah Wheatley, and both of us on account of pets. Muriel committed her misdemeanour some years later when I was in Germany and she in turn was sent to Westgate for summer holidays. There lived in the house a large grey collie called Don. One day my small sister was left alone in a room with the dog and an open work basket. Taking a pair of scissors from the basket, she cut off the collie's tail.

Since the dog did not attack her and, presumably, the scissors were quite small ones, it may be assumed that all she actually did was to snip off from the tail just a few inches of hair at its end. But there was the dickens of a hullaballoo. Not only was the poor child lectured and punished but my parents were abused for having brought her up to be cruel to animals, and it took her years to live the episode down.

My crime was much more serious, as my grandmother's real love was cats, and she had a very beautiful blue Persian that was the apple of her mean old eye. On this occasion my mother was paying one of her rare visits to Westgate, and with my two aunts was up at the top of the house in a room used for dressmaking. I was outside on the upper landing playing with the cat, and at the same time conducting a one-way conversation with an invisible familiar of mine.

I have since learned that it is not at all unusual for children who have no brothers or sisters near their own age, and are brought up very much alone, to invent imaginary playmates. That being my case, I had thought up 'John'. We always went about together, I frequently asked his opinion and, whenever I was allowed to get away with it, took an extra chocolate which in theory was for him.

Having consulted with John I placed the cat's head between two banisters, then gave it a sudden shove. Turning a succession of somersaults the poor animal hurtled down the well of the staircase from the top of the house to the bottom.

With the extraordinary ability cats possess for breaking their falls, it landed in the hall apparently unhurt, for it scampered off out of sight. But its squawk of terror while it was falling brought everyone running, and there was no disguising what I had done. In answer to a barrage of angry questions I could only reply rather meanly, 'But John told me to.' Naturally, that was not taken as a valid excuse. I was severely punished and, I imagine, only the presence of my mother saved me from being whipped by the old woman.

This incident must have taken place when I was very young, probably before I went to Skelsmergh, but it is one of my most vivid memories of Westgate and brings me to a strange and sinister happening connected with my grand-mother's death.

That my impression of her, as a far from pleasant character, is not solely due to bias, is shown by a pastime of hers well-known to her family; she used deliberately to set her cat on the birds in the garden and take pleasure in seeing it destroy them. At the hour of her death my Aunt Nell was in the hall; the door from it into the morning-room, and from that into the garden both happened to be open. My aunt saw a robin come hopping in from the morning-room, and to her surprise it hopped up the stairs to the first floor. Following it out of curiosity she saw that it had hopped along the landing and was standing still outside the door of the room in which my grandmother lay dying. After remaining there for a few minutes, the robin hopped back along the passage, down the stairs through the morning-room and out into the garden. A few minutes later the nurse came out of my grandmother's room to say that her heart had failed and she was gone. My aunt put forward a theory that the birds, who had good reason to hate old Sarah, had sent the robin to fetch her soul away.

Such a suggestion can hardly be taken seriously, and it is known that many birds, such as vultures, are inexplicably drawn to death from far beyond the sight, sound or smell of it; but it is certainly strange for a robin to enter a house and hop for a considerable distance from room to room without showing the least sign of panic.

Having told how I got into hot water with my grand-mother, with old G. N. Hester for playing robbers, and with that horrid man the Reverend Beaumont, I must now relate how I got myself into really serious trouble less than a year after leaving Skelsmergh.

7

DENNIS IS BELIEVED TO BE A MENACE

At the age of thirteen most boys at Skelsmergh were moved up to its senior sister school, Lalham, where they remained until about eighteen; but, whatever my father's other short-comings, he was anxious to give me the best education within his means, and this entailed my going to a public school.

Those of the first rank were both socially and financially beyond our sphere, but there are three of good repute in London, to any of which I could have been sent at a moderate cost as a day-boy, and Dulwich was chosen, no doubt because it was the nearest. Had the choice fallen on Westminster or St. Paul's matters might have panned out differently; but I rather doubt it.

Possibly my complaints to my parents about the revolting Mr. Beaumont played into the hands of the Fates; since, instead of being left at Margate until I was thirteen, I was removed just before my twelfth birthday (8 January, 1909) and shortly after it began my first term at Dulwich. Probably I would have been just as unhappy there had I gone a year later, but it is at least interesting to note that this period of misfortune occurred during my thirteenth year (4) which was in conjunction with my ruling number (8) the most sinister of all combinations according to the science of astrology, of which something is said in the next chapter.

My removal to Dulwich brought about a revolution in my young life comparable to that in an older person who, by an evil twist of fate, is suddenly snatched from a secure and ·peaceful existence among a friendly community in some place that he has come to know well, and despatched to exile in a foreign land where he finds the population hostile, his lot that of a slave and no possible hope of escape.

To start with it entailed the distresses normal to a boy of

my age changing schools. From a senior I became again a junior, I was friendless among scores of potential enemies, and there were the usual customary taboos, to which all new boys are subject, to be learned. But such matters were only a small part of the miseries which my new status inflicted on me.

At Skelsmergh, as a boarder I had, during four years – an immense period in a child's life – become thoroughly accustomed to the sharp division between hols. and terms; now I was to live permanently at home, yet during term time find myself deprived of nearly all the pleasures associated with my home.

As a boarder I had become accustomed to a curriculum in which certain hours were devoted to lessons and one hour in the evening to prep. The rest of the day was given to recreation. Even allowing for games and walks there were still considerable periods during which one was free to rag, read or cultivate one's hobbies, and at bedtime there was that last jolly hour of companionship in the dorm. before lights out.

As a day-boy my life was utterly different. I had to get up just as early, but instead of a morning walk with friends, I had to push-bike three miles from Streatham Hill to Dulwich. Lessons filled the morning. There was a midday break of an hour and a half – the only really free time in my day – more lessons from two o'clock till five, then three miles on my push-bike home – including two very steep hills up the crests of which I had to walk. The evening went in homework, supper and more homework, as the tasks set were always far more than any boy could have done in a formal hour of prep. And so, without the pleasure of friendly chatter, to a lonely bed.

Even that was not all. At Skelsmergh we had played soccer and, although I could already think of a score of ways of passing my time more pleasantly than participating in ball-games, I had become not a bad little goal-keeper. Now, on Saturday and Wednesday afternoons I was initiated into the mysteries of rugger.

At Dulwich, to us smaller boys, the game appeared to consist of senseless mêlées in which every time anyone touched the ball there was a loud shout of 'Scrum!' Upon

D

this, great loutish prefects wielding short pieces of rope with a knot at the end drove us into two opposing wedges with our heads buried between the shoulders of our companions. There, time after time, we blindly kicked and buffeted one another while squelching about in the slimy mud. After an hour or two of this moronic behaviour we returned muddy, bloody, bruised and exhausted to shiver under the cold showers in the changing rooms.

Add to such jolly recreations that the only masters with whom I came in contact were dull, unsympathetic peda-gogues, obviously concerned only with holding their jobs by dragooning their pupils into learning parrot-fashion enough just to get by in the end-of-term exams, and one has a fair picture of life as a junior scholar at Dulwich College in 1909.

God, how I hated that rotten school!

So overwhelmed and depressed was I by this penal regime that of the two and a half terms that I spent at Dulwich I have only one pleasant memory. During the summer term, by some cunning subterfuge I succeeded in evading cricket. This enabled me on half-holidays, when I could afford it, to take out a skiff on the lake in Dulwich Park. The park is a small but pretty one and in those days was little frequented. To lounge in the shade given by the trees on the island in the middle of the lake while the water gently rippled at the sides of the boat meant solitude in delightful surroundings, and I can think of no way in which I could better have secured all too brief relief from the loathsome round of that uninspired, and at times barbarous, educational establishment.

Yet it must not be thought that I developed into a solitary. To do so would have been entirely contrary to my nature. I made a number of friends, the two closest being a rather bulky, red-faced boy named Springfield, and a deli-cate-looking dark-haired boy named Woods. Between them, unwittingly, they led to my downfall. There were others, too, and again, owing no doubt to my irrepressible vitality and imagination, I became their leader in a gang.

We formed a Secret Society taking frightful oaths not to betray one another – although what there was to betray goodness only knows. Vaguely we had dark plans for rebellion against authority, but they were entirely theoretical and we never even said as much as 'boo' to a prefect.

Nevertheless, the game provided us with a mild excitement during our lunch break – the only time we ever had to really play in. Adjacent to the college there then lay only fields and the grounds of a few large private houses. In them we made several secret hide-outs, to one of which four or five of us would make our separate ways with as much caution as if on being seen or followed we might be seized and subjected to the most ghastly tortures; then, when assembled, converse in whispers while eating the buns and biscuits of which our midday meal consisted.

One such hide-out lay at the bottom of the garden of a charming old Georgian mansion, called Toksowa. It had been for many generations, and was then still, the country residence of the Russian Ambassador. Years later, after the Russian Revolution, it became a private hotel, and for several weeks that winter while my parents were in the South of France I lived there as a boarder. One special attraction of this particular hide-out was that nearby stood a fine mulberry tree which for a while provided us with fun to climb, and delicious fruit with which to round off our picnic lunches. But such brief interludes in long harassing days did little to console me for the loss of sea-bathing all through the summer at Margate, G.N. reading the thrilling tales of Wilkie Collins, jolly rambles on our monthly holidays and feasts in the dormitory at night.

Of course, as several of my elders seemed to take pleasure in pointing out to me later, if I had told my parents of my unhappiness there is little doubt that my father would have anyway taken me away from Dulwich and, perhaps, sent me again to a boarding school. Seeing that all through my boyhood I was on the best of terms with my mother, I could have put my situation to her; but in that day and age the Victorian dictum that in all family matters 'Your Father knows best' was still generally maintained; and, although she was extremely skilful in getting her way in everything that affected her own comfort, in decisions that concerned me she was no exception to that rule. So it would only have meant my having to put my case to him myself afterwards; and, frankly, I was terrified of him. It was his misfortune as well as mine that those round brown eyes of his, which lacked all expression yet seemed to hold a secret knowledge of all one's worst faults, actually masked a kind heart and a considerable affection for me.

The mention of picnic lunches brings me to the genesis of my fall from grace. A dreary lunch of the 'meat and two veg.' variety was supplied in Hall for day-boys at a modest price. For this my father supplied me with lunch-money, but the food was unappetising and ill-served, and I was perpetually hard-up. In consequence I made do on buns and kept the balance of the lunch-money to supplement my meagre finances.

My constant penury was not due to my father giving me less than the average pocket-money, but to my own extravagance. In addition to a larger than average outlay on sweets, which I have always loved, I simply could not resist the temptation to buy such items as new designs in toy pistols, etc., and to add to my fine collection of lead soldiers, with the result that I regularly overspent myself and was never free from worry about small debts.

In the autumn, about halfway through my third term at Dulwich, my financial situation became so acute that I resorted to desperate measures. I needed a new school cap and my father gave me half-a-crown to buy one at the school shop; instead I diverted the money to my own emergencies. After a week or so enquiries about when I was going to get my new cap became persistent. I was at my wits' end and so took the fatal step of stealing one.

My victim, I am ashamed to relate, was my friend Woods. It so happened that he had just bought one and his school locker was next to mine. I did not plan the theft; the opportunity arose, and a cap I had to have. Before there was even time for it to cross my mind that he might get into hot water with his father for having lost it while still brand new, I had taken it.

Yet far from this act getting me out of my troubles, I soon discovered that I had jumped out of the frying pan into the fire. When I put the wretched cap on it proved to be several sizes too large for me.

We will now digress for a moment to the subject of phrenology. It is often regarded by those who know little about either as comparable with palmistry, but in my view, as a guide to character the latter is infinitely superior.

During the long periods of boredom which occurred between flare-ups on the Western Front during the First World War I made a prolonged study of palmistry, and for some years afterwards practised it as an amateur with considerable success. To the occult side of it – as a means of foretelling a person's future – I will not refer here, as the proper place for that will be when I come to discuss such matters as a whole. Here I am concerned with it only as a guide to character, and the more one practises it the more convinced one becomes of its infallibility. From those who will take the trouble to learn the various mental attributes indicated by the shape of the hands and the lines on the palm and, where these tend to conflict, assess a careful balance, no secrets of personality can be concealed by those whose hands are submitted to them.

With phrenology, on the other hand, the shape of a head and the bumps on it can only serve as the roughest guide. Admittedly, head shapes do give certain indications. People with more skull above the ear hole to eye line than below it are of a higher mental capacity. Those who have narrow foreheads are rarely musical, those who have high ones usually benevolent, a big base to the skull indicates strong animal propensities, and so on. But to tell the finer shades of character by such means is impossible, let alone to discover such things as probable length of life, strength of imagination, commercial ability and the gift, or lack of it, to pick up foreign languages easily.

Above all, I regard as sheer nonsense the phrenologists' basic belief, that the measurement round the circumference of the skull at forehead level has a direct relation to the brain power contained within the head. In support of this I feel that without undue vanity I may cite my own case. I take only a six-and-a-quarter size in hats; the smallest usually kept in stock by hatters for a grown man. My intellectual make-up is poor in many ways, but few people would contest that my general knowledge, ability to plan, creative imagination, capacity to set my thoughts down clearly, and to reason logically, are considerably above the average.

Woods was a dull boy and, as I have heard nothing of him since I left Dulwich, I have no reason to suppose that later in life he distinguished himself in any way; whereas my name is known all over the world wherever books are read – only this morning I learnt that another foreign publisher had bought the rights to publish an edition of one of my novels, which will bring the languages into which my work has been translated up to twenty-nine – yet the head of this damn fellow Woods was a good two sizes larger than mine!

The sight of the new cap in my hand put an end to the nightmare of being questioned by my father each evening about why I had not yet bought one, but my old one was promptly thrown away by my mother, so I now had to wear my stolen plumage to go to school in.

Woods, on discovering that his cap had been stolen, naturally became angry, and as soon as he saw me in a brand new cap too large for me his suspicions were aroused. Fortunately, he had not had time to write his name in the lining, so no examination of the cap could prove it to be his, but after some sparring he accused me of the theft and threatened to take the matter to our form master unless I gave it up. The terrifying prospect of having to face my father without it overruled all other fears, so I hotly denied the theft and refused to hand the cap over. Yet I knew that if an investigation ensued, an inquiry at the school shop would disclose that I had not bought it, and so result in my conviction.

Such, then, was my frightful situation on the morning of a Wednesday in mid-October, 1909. And if a final straw were needed to weigh my spirits down to zero it was that, although Wednesday was a half-holiday, for some shortcoming in my work I had been awarded a punishment termed an 'extra lesson', for which I would be kept in school that afternoon.

After the mid-morning break on Wednesdays my class, with several others in the junior school, had their weekly singing lesson. Normally this was one of the few lessons I liked as, although I have never felt the least desire to sing solo. I have always enjoyed joining in choruses. But that day

my mind was too obsessed with the plight in which I had
landed myself for me even to think what I was singing.

Standing next to me in one of the back rows of the class
was my ox-like friend Springfield. Seventy-five per cent of
the scholars at Dulwich were day-boys, but there were four
Houses for boarders and Springfield was at one of them. He
was, as he had in recent weeks frequently bemoaned to me,
savagely bullied and so most unhappy there.

Now, it gradually penetrated my own grievously troubled
mind that, behind our music sheets and under cover of the
singing, he was pursuing the same theme, and further telling
me he could stand it no longer so had determined to run
away.

His words acted on me like a match to a Greek fire flare.
Here was a solution to all my problems. I could escape ex-
posure as a thief by Woods, break free from the loathsome
routine of Dulwich and rid myself for ever from the terror
my father inspired in me.

I asked Springfield when he meant to go. He had made no
plans and had most probably been only toying with the idea
as a result of gloomy wishful thinking. Having told him that
I would go with him, I at once took the lead and declared
that the sooner we went the better. We would leave within
the hour, during the lunch break.

I had a bicycle but he had not; so, in for a penny in for a
pound, it was decided that he should 'borrow' one from the
scores that were parked by day-boys in the bicycle sheds.
Without preparation of any kind, but spurred on by the zest
for freedom of two galley-slaves who had succeeded in breaking their chains, soon after one o'clock we were pedalling up
the hill towards the Crystal Palace.

Our ultimate objective had been promptly settled by me,
and it was Canada. To attempt such a journey destitute of
resources except for one shilling – Springfield's of course, I
was flat broke – and two thin mackintosh bicycling capes as
our only luggage, was certainly ambitious. But it must be
remembered that the courses of action open to a little boy of
twelve are strictly limited by his almost complete ignorance
of conditions outside his own small world.

My choice was based on the fact that apart from relatives

– to whom in the circumstances it was out of the question to turn – the only people from whom I could expect help were ex-school friends still at Skelsmergh. One of them, named King, had relatives in Canada, and Margate was a port. That few ships larger than coal-barges now used it had not registered with me. I planned to secure an introduction from King to his Canadian cousins and, with simple faith that our future in the new world would be secured by it, get Springfield and myself taken on as cabin boys in the first ship outward bound for Canada.

Crazy as this may seem, there was just a suggestion of sound reasoning in the plan. If King, instead of like ourselves being a boy of twelve, had been some years older and had a few pounds with which to finance us while we waited for a ship, and had Margate been Southampton, it might well have succeeded. How my life might have developed had it done so makes me positively shudder to think.

However, this was certainly an occasion on which 'ignorance was bliss'. Undeterred by the forebodings which greater knowledge of the world would have brought, we pedalled on through the afternoon and evening. Towards sundown we became hungry so raided an orchard, but the apples we stole were, unfortunately, cookers, so most unsatisfactory eating. As night came on, our healthy appetites unappeased and our spirits now somewhat damped, we sought a place to lie-up for the night. For this we chose a coppice a few hundred yards off the road. The only undergrowth in it being brambles there was nothing with which we could make up couches, so we endeavoured to settle down on the hard earth with no cover against the October cold except our mackintosh bicycling capes.

For some time we turned unhappily from side to side, with fading hopes of sleep. Suddenly the silence was shattered by a loud report. It was soon followed by others and the sound of small-shot rattling through the undergrowth nearby. It must have been a poacher making a midnight foray. Springing up, we seized our bicycles and capes and fled for our lives.

Close to the road there was a haystack that had already been cut into. Climbing to the top of it we settled ourselves

there, but it was by no means easy to pull out enough loose
hay from the tight-packed stack to make a satisfactory cover,
and by this time the chill of the October night was beginning
to get down to our bones.

Again we tried to get to sleep, but in vain. By that time my
midday castles-in-the-air had been shattered by grim reality.
Cold, hunger and the uncertainties of our future forced me
to formulate what some thirty odd years later, when I was a
member of the Joint Planning Staff of the War Cabinet, I
should have termed 'a reassessment of the situation'. The
conclusion I reached was that we had bitten off more than
we could chew so had better throw our hands in there and
then rather than suffer further discomfort by remaining
where we were for the rest of the night.

My oafish companion accepted my decision without protest and, loath as we were to return and face the music, we
climbed down from the haystack and set off towards London.
As neither of the bicycles we were riding was habitually
used at night neither of them had any oil in its lamps; so
after we had ridden a few miles the beam of a bulls-eye
lantern was suddenly flashed in our eyes and we were
challenged by a policeman on night patrol.

I confessed to him that we were runaways who now re-
pented our folly and wanted to go home; upon which he took
us to Bromley Police Station. I have at times since wondered how, during a whole afternoon and evening on push-
bikes, we had failed to penetrate much further into Kent.
But, having no map, it may be that during the afternoon we
wasted a lot of time taking a circuitous route through London's
outer suburbs, or perhaps we covered ten miles or more on
the way back before we met the policeman.

At the station the police – mostly bearded and bewhiskered
in those days – could not have been kinder. They gave us
thick meat sandwiches and mugs of strong, sweet tea. Hungry
as I was I had to refuse the former because there was cold
butter in them, but the steaming hot tea was most welcome.

The police got in touch with Springfield's father and mine.
His refused to turn out, but mine arrived in a hired car at
about five o'clock in the morning and took me home. To my
surprise the little he said to me expressed sorrow rather than

anger, and I was much more upset by my mother's tearful reproaches when I reached home.

Physically fatigued and emotionally exhausted, I slept most of the day, and was still in bed when my father got back from his day at the office. He then gave me the only beating I ever received from him, using the belt from his tennis flannels.

I made no pretence to heroics by biting the upper lip. On the contrary, I was already shrewd enough to calculate that the louder I yelled the more likely he was to believe that he had inflicted punishment enough upon me and stop. One result of my cries was that my mother, standing outside on the landing, added hers to them. Although I have since realised that her incurable meanness made her a far from perfect mother, there can be no doubt that in those days I was the apple of her eye, and she beat frantically upon the door while calling on my father to cease his brutal assault on her darling. But, anticipating an attempt by her to intervene, he had had the forethought to lock the door and, despite my shouts, the beating he gave me was a pretty severe one.

Next day, with the affair of the stolen cap once more hanging over me like a sword of Damocles, and the knowledge that I should certainly receive official punishment at school for having run away, I returned, filled with gloomy foreboding, to Dulwich.

My class master displayed no interest in my escapade but told me coldly that at midday I was to report to the Head in his study. He was at this time a Dr. Gilkes, a very tall, thin old man with a high forehead and grey beard.

Years later, after his death, someone wrote a biography about him, and reviews of it in the press extolled him as one of the great headmasters of his generation. He was unquestionably a fine classical scholar and his principal claim to fame is that he was in the forefront of the movement for revising the pronunciation of Latin – an innovation which resulted in additional toil, tears and grief to youngsters of my age who had been taught their little Latin at their prep. schools with the old pronunciation – and, for all I know, he may have been a brilliant organiser and administrator.

But one thing I do know. In the best sense he was very far

from being a 'great' headmaster; he was not even a passably good one. That is, if judged by what I believe to be the proper criterion which should be applied to all who are responsible for the teaching and training of the young. Surely their most important function is to develop the eagerness of their charges to learn by winning their admiration and affection. And particularly in the case of lazy, stubborn, apparently wicked, and in other ways difficult children, to talk to them gently so as to gain their confidence and induce them to overcome the reluctance natural in such children to disclose the mental kinks that make them as they are. To this should be added a constant scrutiny of the school curriculum and the sparing of no effort to make lessons more attractive and learning easier.

In all of the above Gilkes failed lamentably. With the boys he was most unpopular. A tall, grim, unapproachable figure, he was at times to be seen walking about the school grounds, a living symbol in our minds of harshness and punishment. Such of his masters under whom I sat were not so much unkind as disinterested. They gave us a quota of prep. to get through which was larger than we could easily manage, and if we made a poor showing in class next day indifferently inflicted minor punishments. I have no reason to believe that I was an exceptionally lazy, stupid or recalcitrant boy, but I do not remember ever receiving a word of encouragement from any of them. And, as far as we were aware, Gilkes's only interest in life was personally forcing the maximum number of his senior classical pupils through exams which would bring them scholarships, and kudos to the school. We know also, from Springfield's testimony, that bullying among the boarders had become real cruelty; yet Gilkes and his housemasters either knew so little of what went on in the school that they were ignorant of the matter, or too indifferent to the happiness of the younger boys to take measures to suppress it.

With regard to any endeavour to understand and reclaim to more promising ways his 'difficult' boys, my own experience speaks for itself. When I confronted him in his study he did not even ask why I had run away. His only words to me were, 'Take down your trousers; put your hands flat on the edge of that table, and bend over.' Then, although my bottom must obviously have been red and sore from the leathering given me the previous evening by my father, he gave it six swift cuts with a single thin, whip-like birch rod.

The pain made the tears start to my eyes, but this time I did not cry out. As I buttoned up my trousers he said, 'Since you defaulted at an extra lesson you will do it on Saturday and another next Wednesday.' On my murmuring, 'Yes, sir,' he turned away to his desk, indicating that the interview was over.

His treatment of Springfield was precisely the same, except that, not having cut an extra lesson, he was not given an additional one; but for having 'borrowed' a bicycle was ordered to report himself to the head-prefect for a second licking.

Lunch hour the following day, Saturday, was the first opportunity Springfield and I had to compare notes, and having collected some light provender we did so while eating it on the rough ground on the far side of the playing fields.

The college clock striking the quarter recalled to me that my afternoon must be passed in a stuffy classroom doing an extra lesson. Suddenly I was struck by an appalling thought: I had forgotten to bring the books required for it from my own classroom, and now it was too late to do so.

The main buildings of the college consisted of three large blocks. In the centre stood that containing Hall, in which the whole school gathered for prayers each morning, for speech day celebrations, etc., the buttery, the armoury of the O.T.C., and so on. At some distance from it, but both connected to it by cloisters, stood two symmetrical square blocks; that on one side housed the junior school, and that on the other the senior. Extra lessons were always held on the ground floor of the senior block in the sixth form classroom; my classroom was in the junior school and on half-holidays shortly after twelve-thirty the block was always locked up.

Worse, Gilkes of Dulwich, that 'great' headmaster, could think of no more pleasant or profitable way of spending his Saturday and Wednesday afternoons than in 'taking' these extra lessons. But the word 'taking' must not be taken here to imply that he taught anything to those sentenced to attend.

The subject was the same for all – his beloved Latin – but as the defaulters were drawn from classes on all levels no task in common could be set and individuals later questioned on it to the benefit of all. Each, according to his class, brought the work he was normally engaged upon and wrestled silently with a piece of extra homework set him by his own form-master. The only function performed by the eminent Dr. Gilkes was to sit on a dais scanning the class with his eagle eye, ready to blast any boy whose mind appeared for one moment to have wandered from his task.

How could I, or any twelve-year-old, have screwed up the courage to face this ogre and admit that I had forgotten to bring the books needed to play my part in his punishment lesson?

In vain I ran to the junior block and battered on its heavy door. The door was locked, the janitor gone and I had no idea where its key was kept. Springfield tried to comfort me with the suggestion that, as rarely less than a score and often over thirty boys attended each extra lesson, I might easily not be missed; then he persuaded me to come and watch with him a rugger match which was taking place on the home ground that afternoon between our first fifteen and that of St. Paul's.

I haven't an idea which side won and, as I afterwards push-biked up those beastly hills towards home, could not have cared less. I had temporarily evaded Woods, as for the past two days he had been absent from school with a bad cold, but the issue of the stolen cap had to be faced on his return, and on Monday I had little doubt that I would find myself in real hot water for having cut yet another extra lesson, this time, apparently, having defied old Gilkes's personal order.

It was still the family custom for us to have tea and dinner at Aspen House on Wednesdays and Saturdays, and to spend the day there from midday on alternate Sundays; so, it being a Saturday, I made my way there instead of going home.

After the events of the past few days I don't doubt that I found some solace in the benign presence of my beloved grandfather and the two aunts who delighted to spoil me, but they were naturally shocked by my having run away and distressed by the anxiety and grief I had caused my mother. In any case, this partial respite in a slightly less disapproving atmosphere than that which had for the past forty-eight hours pervaded my home, was only a temporary one. Soon after dinner I accompanied my mother back to Wootton Lodge.

My mind had been so full of my own troubles that it had not even occurred to me to wonder – although it was quite an exceptional occurrence – why my father had not been with us at Aspen House that evening. On reaching home my mother and I crossed the dining-room and went up the single flight of stairs in the south wing which led to the breakfast-room, where my father had been working on some papers.

As I reached the top of the stairs he advanced towards me, his face white, his round eyes hard as agates. He then did a thing he had never done before, and never did again. Lifting his fist he struck me in the face and knocked me down.

The blow did no more than slightly cut my lip and I was much more shocked than injured. The shock, in fact, was such that I do not recall what happened immediately after-wards. No doubt my mother carried me off, put me to bed and tended me. It was only later that I became aware that on my failing to turn up for my extra lesson, Gilkes had acted swiftly and decisively. He had written to my father that afternoon stating that he considered me to be a bad influence in the school, and required my immediate removal from it. Then sent his letter by special messenger.

I had been expelled from Dulwich.

In due course I learned that I had thus become one of a goodly company. Apparently it was Gilkes's habit to expel boys of strong individuality without a hearing when they had kicked over the traces. Yet despite this callous disruption of their school careers, a high proportion of them afterwards did far better in life than those whom he regarded with favour because under his stony eye they achieved brilliance in construing Latin.

Now, seventy years later, I am told that I stand high in the roll of honour of Old Alleynians – as ex-Dulwich boys are called. I have become famous so am claimed by Dulwich as one of her sons, and from time to time the college takes kudos in its magazine for having nurtured me.

What impudence! Let us be plain about the matter. During my two and a half terms there I learned next to nothing. My life was a misery and no master made the least attempt to better my lot. The lessons were dreary and the sports taught with brutality. The Head was an academician of the Victorian mould, who ruled by fear and cared nothing for the welfare or happiness of the seven hundred boys who had been confided to his charge.

To Dulwich College I owe nothing. The best day's work I ever did in my life was that which led to my being kicked out of it. It must however be borne in mind that I am writing about Dulwich College as it was very nearly seventy years ago, but friends who have boys there today tell me that it is an excellent school and that their sons are very happy at the college.

8

NUMBERS AND THE STARS

I HAVE mentioned in the last chapter that it was in my thirteenth year that disaster overtook me at Dulwich; so this seems the place to make a digression on numerology. The date of my birth was 8.1.1897, and the following gives some idea of how birth dates and other numbers appear to affect our lives.

The belief that everyone has lucky and unlucky numbers is as old as the earliest civilisations. In Chaldaea and Ancient Egypt the priests devoted much of their time to numerology and by it forecast the fate of men and nations.

It is not, of course, the numbers themselves which are credited with influencing people's lives, but the mystic power of the sun, moon and principal planets of our solar system.

Sceptics may maintain that it is nonsense to suggest that because at the moment of a person's birth a particular heavenly body happens to be in the ascendant his personality and fortune will be dominated by the characteristics attributed to it. But how little we yet really know about the boundless universe.

Go into your garden at night and you will see that the flowers have no colour; but the sun performs a wondrous magic upon them. Its invisible rays give each variety its different hue, through every colour in the spectrum. Scientists may now be able to explain why in daylight we see some as blue, others as red, pink, purple or yellow. They certainly could not have done so a hundred and fifty years ago.

Every few years science is now discovering new properties in the ether, and harnessing them for the benefit of mankind. Electricity was, I suppose, the first; yet the laws which govern it were still unknown a little over a hundred years ago. There followed the discovery of the X-ray, the infra-red ray, the ultra-violet ray, the cathode ray, and the stored-up power in uranium which we now know as nuclear energy. Know-

ledge of these invisible radiations has given us cheap light
and heat, telephones, wireless and television, the power to see
through solid substances and to plot the course of distant
fast-moving bodies in the air, on the sea and under the water;
while it is said that the power latent in magnetic fields may,
no great number of years hence, enable us to travel normally
at, or beyond, the speed of light.

It is generally accepted that the invisible rays so far discovered come from the sun, and there is some evidence to
show that the waxing and waning of the moon has an effect
on the growth of vegetation. In any case, it is absurd to infer
that science has already reached the end of the catalogue of
mysterious powers impinging on the earth from outer space.
On the contrary, it is far more probable that there are many
others which await discovery – or rediscovery.

I add 'rediscovery' because there is good reason to suppose
that, although the ancients failed to hit upon – or in some
cases such as gunpowder and the steam engine – to develop,
the inventions which have made the modern world, their
scientific knowledge was in some instances in advance of
ours. This applies particularly to a more exact understanding
than we have of the extraordinary capabilities of the human
mind – some of which we are now rediscovering through the
application of medical hypnosis. As astronomers, the Egypti-
ans were sufficiently advanced to base their calendar on the
helical rising of the star Sirius, which occurs at the same
day, time and place only once in every 1,460 years, and it
was the Hindu astronomers who discovered the procession
of the equinoxes, which occurs only once in 25,827 years; so
there may be much more truth in the astrological beliefs of
these ancient peoples than is commonly supposed.

Be that as it may, through experience accumulated over
many generations the priesthoods of India, Babylonia and
the Nile valley, all held the conviction that if a chart was
made of the Heavens at the hour of a birth the character
and future of the new-born babe could be read from it. This
casting of horoscopes has, of course, survived to the present
day; but to get a good one costs a lot of money owing to the
many hours of involved calculations entailed. Moreover the
possibilities of it proving accurate are dependent on the

ability of the horoscopist to decide on just how much weight should be given to the influence of each heavenly body, for its definite characteristics are modified and twisted into all sorts of tendencies, in accordance with the position of all the other bodies in relation to it.

Here, however, we are concerned only with numbers as symbols of the heavenly bodies, and the properties with which each has been associated through many thousands of years. I should add that one's birth date plays a major part in determining one's basic number, and this is always a single number. It is arrived at by, if necessary, adding the others together; i.e. $11 = 2$, $17 = 8$, $24 = 6$, $30 = 3$, $31 = 4$ $108 = 9$, $5674 = 22 = 4$, and so on.

No. 1 stands for the sun. People born on the 1st, 10th, 19th or 28th of any month have the following tendencies. They are creative, inventive and have strong personalities. They are ambitious and usually successful. They resent restraint and are inclined to be obstinate, but they are good at wielding authority and earn the respect of those associated with them. They should endeavour to carry out their most important plans on dates having their basic number; and this applies to all the other numbers.

No. 2 stands for the moon. People born on the 2nd, 11th, 20th and 29th have the following tendencies. They are gentle, romantic, artistic and have vivid imaginations, but they are not usually physically strong and often fail to carry out their ideas through lack of self-confidence. They are inclined to be over-sensitive and it is important that they should have cheerful surroundings, otherwise they easily become subject to depression.

No. 3 stands for Jupiter. People born on the 3rd, 12th, 21st and 30th have the following tendencies. They are lovers of order and discipline both in their work and in their homes. They are conscientious in carrying out orders but prefer to give the orders themselves. They are proud, dictatorial and pig-headed, so are inclined to make enemies.

No. 4 stands for Uranus. People born on the 4th, 13th, 22nd and 31st have the following tendencies. They are born rebels. They nearly always take an opposite view to the generally accepted one, and instinctively react against all rules and conventions. They are seldom successful in worldly matters, but this does not greatly worry them, as they are much more interested in social questions than in making money. They are highly strung, inclined to feel isolated and do not make friends easily.

No. 5 stands for Mercury. People born on the 5th, 14th and 23rd have the following tendencies. They are quick in thought and action, detest routine work and love every form of excitement. They are great gamblers and often hit upon ways of making money quickly. They are liable to nervous breakdowns; but they have wonderful powers of recovery.

No. 6 stands for Venus. People born on the 6th, 15th and 24th have the following tendencies. They possess more than the average magnetic attraction, so are much loved and often looked up to with devotion by those under them. They are inclined to be obstinate, but they become the willing slaves of people they love themselves. They like to see everyone about them happy, love beauty in all its forms, make lovely homes and are the art patrons of the world.

No. 7 stands for Neptune. People born on the 7th, 16th and 25th have the following tendencies. They have independent and rather restless natures. They love all forms of change; travel as much as they can. They frequently make good writers, painters and sculptors, the sea being their most favourable medium; and, on it as sailors, or trading across it as merchants, they are nearly always fortunate; but they are not particularly lucky in money matters.

No. 8 stands for Saturn. People born on the 8th, 17th and 26th have the following tendencies. They generally play some important role in life, but they are often misunderstood and suffer from a feeling of loneliness. They are inclined to be fanatical and sometimes appear cold and indifferent to the opinion of others, but are actually warm-hearted. They are nearly always great successes or great failures. They should beware of forming any intimate association with a person whose number is 4, and avoid as far as possible anything connected with that number, as the combination of the 8 and 4 almost always brings misfortune.

No. 9 stands for Mars. People born on the 9th, 18th and 27th have the following tendencies. They are born fighters and make excellent sailors, soldiers and airmen. They are often called on to surmount difficulties in their early years but courage and a strong will nearly always bring them success. They are inclined to be conceited, resent criticism and tend to quarrel with their family. They have such a craving for affection that they can easily be made fools of by the opposite sex.

We now turn to another factor which is of equal potency in determining a person's dominant number. That is the numerical value of their name. By a very ancient tradition each symbol – in our case the alphabet derived from the Phoenicians – has its equivalent number. The mystic key as passed down to us is as follows:

A, I, J, Q and Y all = 1
B, K and R all = 2
C, G, L and S all = 3
D, M, and T all = 4
E, H, N and X all = 5
U, V and W all = 6
O and Z both = 7
F and P both = 8

It will be noted that no letter is the equivalent of 9. That is because in occultism 9 stands for the nine-lettered name of God; so no single letter could be ascribed to it.

To illustrate the use of the key I will take my own names:

D = 4	Y = 1	W = 6
E = 5	E = 5	H = 5
N = 5	A = 1	E = 5
N = 5		A = 1
I = 1	T = 4	T = 4
S = 3	S = 3	L = 3
		E = 5
		Y = 1
23	14	30

Wheatley 30
—
53 = 8

Dennis = 23
Wheatley = 30
—
67 = 13
= 4

For the purpose of arriving at the numerical value of a person's name, the name by which they are *most generally known* must be taken – even if that be a pseudonym, or part of it, or only a nickname. In my case there can be no question about this being Dennis Wheatley with its numerical value of 8.

This, of course, greatly reinforces the 8 that I derive from my birth date, and that is even more strongly reinforced by the fact that it falls in the very centre of the period termed the House of Saturn (Positive) which runs from 21 December to 26 January, and is dominated by the 8.

In view of this is it not altogether surprising to find that my career is positively peppered with 8s of all kinds; straight dates, ages at which the most important events occurred, the additions of the final numerals of years – which are habitually taken without the century in such surveys – and the numerical values of the names of most of the people who have played a major part in my life.

I was born on 8.1.1897
    The day of the month.
    The period of year.   = Double 8

1st big change in life. January 1905.
    Sent to boarding school. Age 8,
    and period of year.   = Double 8
2nd big change in life. September 1914.
    Received a commission in the Royal
    Field Artillery. Age 17. Sailed for France
    on active service 8.8.1917.   =   Triple 8
3rd big change in life. January 1919.
    Entered family wine business at 26 South
    Audley Street. Number of shop and period
    of year.   = Double 8
4th big change in life. June 1923.
    Married at the age of 26.   = Double 8
5th big change in life. 26 May, 1926.
    My father died and I became sole
    proprietor of the business.   = Double 8
6th big change in life. August 8th and 8th
    month 1931. Married for the second time. = Double 8

Went to live in my new wife's flat at
    48 Queen's Gate, S.W.7.   = Partial 8
7th big change in life. Began to write.
    Age 35.   =   8
First book accepted for publication
    August 1932. The month.   =   8
First book published January 1933.
    Period of year.   =   8
Moved in 1935 to 8 St. John's Wood Park   = Double 8
After being bombed out in 1940 moved
    to a flat in Chatsworth Court, S.W.5.
    Numerical value.   =   8
8th big change in life. December 1941.
    Received commission in R.A.F. and became
    member of the Joint Planning Staff of the
    War Cabinet. Age 44. Period of year
    and age.   = Double 8
9th big change in life. 20 December 1944.
    Released from R.A.F. and returned to
    civil life. Period of year and year.   = Double 8
Bought Grove Place, Lymington (where I lived
    from June 1945 to September 1968) in
    January 1944.Period of year Saturn, and
    year.   = Double 8

There have, of course, been some other key dates in my life but none to compare in importance with the above. On only one, the occasion of my second marriage, was the 8th day of the month deliberately chosen, and it will be seen that over the others I could have had no control. Yet the 8 has figured in nearly every place in which I have lived or worked for any length of time, nearly every event of importance has occurred either in August (the 8th month) or between 21 December and 26 January (the astrological period dominated by the 8) and every decisive step in my career has been made at the ages of 8, 17, 26, 35 and 44, all 8s, or in the years in which the two final figures total 8.

In addition to the above, it seems something more than coincidence that names having the numerical value of 8 should have played such a great part in my life.

The numerical value of LAURIE, my cousin, and of GORDON ERIC GORDON-TOMBE, who between them did more than any other persons to form my character, are both 8s. And my best friend over a period of thirty years, JOE LINKS, has 8 letters in his name.

Four out of the six women whom I have loved best have had names adding up to 8, my second wife becoming an 8 by adding WHEATLEY to the name of JOAN.

For forty-two years Messrs. HUTCHINSON have published all my books; that name also reducing to an 8.

Finally, my first novel THE FORBIDDEN TERRITORY, which brought me success overnight and was reprinted seven times in seven weeks, has the numerical value of 8.

For anyone to be so dominated by one number is, obviously, an exception, as most people's birth dates and name values must be different. In consequence, their character will be a combination of the qualities of both numbers and a greater variety of days be moderately favourable. Here too, I should observe that while one cannot alter the first, one can the second.

In circumstances where the combination is an unfortunate one this may be advisable – particularly if the two numerals are 8 and 4. Most people have more than one Christian name, so by signing letters with it and asking their friends to call them by it, within a few months – according to numerological lore – they can attract to themselves more favourable radiations. Again, should a person with a birth number of 8 take a house the number of which is, or reduces to, 4, it is not compulsory to use the number. The house can be given a name having a value of 8, or that of wife, mother or other relative who will also be living in it.

All this may sound terribly far-fetched, but it derives some support from two experiences of my own.

Firstly, when on my father's death I became the owner of the family wine business, out of snobbism I decided to be known in future by the double-barrelled name of Yeats-Wheatley. If the reader turns back to the numerical value of my names, it will be seen that by using my whole name I combined with my birth number 8 the name value of 4. I succeeded in greatly increasing the turnover of the business but it was under-capitalised. 4 years later I was caught by the great slump of 1931 – which adds up to 4 – very nearly went bankrupt, and had to sell out to a combine.

Secondly, on marrying my second wife I went to live in her flat at 48 Queens Gate. Fortunately, although numerology played no part in the matter, she insisted on my dropping the Yeats because she considered that the use of a double name which was not inherited to be pretentious. Hence my first book was published as by Dennis Wheatley. But, parting with my wine business had left me without capital and with many debts; so during the years I lived at 48 I was at first in the unhappy position of having to let my wife support me, and later, still a prey to constant financial worries. It was not until we left this, for me, sinister combination and, in 1935, moved to 8 St. John's Wood Park, that I became once more comparatively affluent.

I must confess that, in view of the above, I have since taken some care to avoid as far as possible any permanent connection with the numeral 4. But do not let it be supposed that I have allowed numerology to affect my everyday life. If I have a free choice of days I do choose an 8 date for signing important documents, settling long-term plans or starting a new book; but such things happen only once or twice in a year. It is the height of folly for anyone to allow himself to become the slave of numerical systems for the purpose of gambling, or any form of belief which may cripple his normal activities. It may well be that on one's number days the stars do help one to secure a bonus but, as a general rule, I am sure that one can get further in this world by following the old adage: 'Never put off till tomorrow what you can do today.'

Readers may have noticed that 8 is very far from being a lucky number and wonder why, since it has appeared so consistently through my life, I should have been both happy and successful. Two factors have doubtless contributed to this.

The sun was then in my sign, Saturn; Venus, Mercury and Mars were all in the ascendant at the hour of my birth. The first two have given me the blessed ability to make friends of all classes with great ease; the last has caused war to twice advance my interests in a most striking manner. In September 1914 it was decidedly an exception for the son of a man who kept a retail shop to be given, at the age of seventeen, His Majesty's Commission. By lifting me while still in my teens into the company of a class higher than my own, the war broadened my horizons far more than a university education could have done. In the Second World War I had the exceptional good fortune to be specially commissioned in order that I might become a member of the Joint Planning Staff. Three years in the offices of the War Cabinet brought me into intimate contact with some of the finest brains in the three Services. This enabled me when already middle-aged to form a new circle of personal friends, many of whom later became admirals, generals and air-marshals and, several, commanders-in-chief.

The second factor is the astrological values attributed to the compound numbers of my names. To give the values of all the compound numbers would make this more than a reasonable digression. But Wheatley adds up to 30, which number indicates a capacity for logical deduction, and mental superiority over one's fellows; while Dennis – by which name I am known in my family, among all my friends and by scores of acquaintances – adds up to 23. This is perhaps the most fortunate of all numbers. It is known as the Royal Star of the Lion; it indicates help from superiors, protection from people in high places and success for one's plans.

Nevertheless, I am dominated by the 8, which means that I am one of the playthings of Fate. Only too often such people are suddenly hurled from success into disgrace and dire tribulation – often through some happening which is no fault of theirs. So far I have been wonderfully fortunate. I am grateful for my blessings, and can only pray that they will continue, for I am not yet out of the wood.

9

DISCIPLINE FOR DENNIS

On the morning following that fateful Saturday after I was expelled from Dulwich I was taken up to an empty six foot square attic with a sloping roof and locked in there. Throughout the day I was supplied only with prisoner's fare of dry bread and water and was denied all reading matter or other means of recreation; so I had many hours in which to contemplate my wickedness and the uncertainties of my future.

After dinner I was brought down to my father. He told me that in the afternoon he had been over to see Dr. Gilkes and pleaded with him to reconsider his decision to expel me, but the old man had proved adamant.

Apparently the contents of my desk had been gone through and certain papers found there had further blackened my case. They dated from the summer term, and so little did they really mean that I had already forgotten most of the nonsense I had written in them. But they concerned the Secret Society, since become dormant, of which I had been the self-appointed chief. Evidently I had let rip the imagination which was later to earn me the best part of a million pounds and, perhaps, proposed ways of inflicting death and destruction on the masters and ancient seat of learning which I had come to hate so bitterly. From what Gilkes told my father it seems that they led him to regard me as about as dangerous as a combination of Sinn Fein and Russian anarchists conspiring to blow up Buckingham Palace. How a grown man can possibly have come to such a conclusion from the ungrammatical scrawls of a boy of twelve passes my comprehension. However, he insisted that I was a thoroughly bad influence, and a danger to the well-being of the school; so must be removed.

My father then told me that, for him, what I had done

could not have come at a worse time as he was on the verge
of ruin. He had been speculating on the Stock Exchange,
been caught out by a slump, and both his own father and
W.Y.B. – presumably thinking that it served him right – had
refused to help him meet his liabilities. Hence, overwhelmed
by his own worries, he had lost control of himself and struck
me the previous night. He then burst into tears.

Naturally I was distressed and greatly embarrassed. I did
my best to express regret for the additional trouble I had
brought upon him and, as far as a boy of my age could,
comforted him. He then disclosed the reason why at times he
might have seemed unduly strict with me. It was owing to
his fear that unless some of my tendencies could be checked
I might turn out a wastrel and a thoroughly bad hat, because
in so many ways I took after my wicked Uncle Johnny. I
promised to do my best in future to be a good boy. He kissed
me and we parted with more friendly feelings towards one
another than had been the case for as long as I remembered.
But, alas, the barrier between us had been broken only by
this emotional crisis, and once normal conditions were res-
tored he could not bring himself to continue talking to me
with such frankness, so these happier relations did not endure
for long.

However, for me the worst was over, and next day I was
subject to a kindness that I shall ever remember with
gratitude. Our neighbour, Mrs. Sharp, arrived upon the
scene. Her son, Douglas, was not at Dulwich College. The
Sharps were not as well off as we were so he had been sent
to its less expensive associate, Alleyn's School, nearby. But we
had continued to be bosom chums, and the Sharps had
learnt of the mess in which I had landed myself.

Mrs. Sharp was a small, dynamic woman who still spoke
with the accent of Leicestershire which she had acquired in her
early years. She could afford only one servant, and at that
the type of teenage slave that was termed a 'skivvy'; but she
cheerfully worked her own fingers to the bone, cooking,
cleaning and making nearly all the clothes worn by her two
daughters and herself. Few people so circumstanced would
have been willing to burden themselves for more than the
odd night with a guest, but she pointed out to my mother

that after what had happened, if I were left to gloom about the house all day I should certainly get on my parents' nerves; then she insisted on carrying me off to stay until something had been settled about my future.

There followed a very happy fortnight. With the resilience of youth I soon forgot my troubles and entered heartily into being temporarily one of this family who, despite their limited means, got far more fun out of life than did mine. To have the constant companionship of my best friend week-ends, every evening and, above all, to share a room with him was a real joy. And kindly Mrs. Sharp did not even raise an objection when, with his elder sister, Dorothy, as our guest, we held there a feast of sardines, sweet biscuits and pineapple chunks.

Dorothy was then about sixteen, a pretty girl with a small Roman nose and dark curly hair. I was never in love with her, but sufficiently strongly attracted to screw up the courage to kiss her as she lay for a while after our feast, in the dark, between Douglas and myself on the big bed. She barely responded, perhaps thinking that to do so with a boy four years her junior would be a loss of face; on the other hand she gave no indication whatever that she objected. I mention the episode because, apart from in games at children's parties, such as postman's knock and kiss-in-the-ring, she was the first girl that I kissed.

On my return home I learned that the next step in my future had been settled. The Powers that controlled my Fate had decided that what I needed was discipline. The embryo bad man must be straitjacketed before it was too late, and dragooned into an orderly way of life; so that through prolonged set custom he would eventually be happy to tread between blinkers the path of an upright citizen and exemplary family man in the highest Victorian tradition. 'Discipline's the thing for him,' they said; and some friend of my father must have added, 'Why not send him to the *Worcester*?' This friend may well have been inspired by the printed instruction issued by the Honorary Committee of the ship, in para. 2 of which we find, 'The first lesson to be learned by a pupil on his joining the *Worcester* is "Obedience to Orders".'

The Incorporated Thames Nautical Training College
H.M.S. *Worcester* was a ship-of-the-line of the late Napoleonic
period, permanently anchored in the river off Greenhithe, a
Thames-side village that lies on the Kentish shore about
halfway between Dartford and Tilbury. It was a hybrid
foundation partially controlled by an official body – the
Elder Brethren of Trinity House – but financed by a number
of big shipping companies and administered by a board
nominated by their directors. Its function was to train
officers for the Merchant Navy, the pick of whom were
naturally taken by the shipping lines holding an interest in
the establishment. She had a sister ship, H.M.S. *Conway*,
anchored in the Mersey. From her were drawn most of the
officers for the Cunard and White Star lines – then separate
entities and both still using Liverpool as their home port.
The *Worcester* catered mainly for the P. & O., Union Castle,
Orient, Ellerman, Elder Dempster and Blue Funnel lines.
There were also six entries each year by which outstanding
pupils might receive commissions in the Royal Navy.

One prematurely dark afternoon in December my father
took me down to the ship for an acceptance interview with
her Captain. The old three-decker, her bulging sides
chequered black and white and her masts towering to the
skies, lay moored about half a mile from the solitary narrow
jetty running out from a cul-de-sac adjacent to the extreme
end of Greenhithe's long, depressing High Street. A water-
man hoisted a canvas ball to the top of a flagstaff on which
a watch was kept from the ship and, in response to this signal,
a boat was sent off for us.

A long landing platform ran for nearly the whole length
of the ship's landward side. From it two permanent gangways
led up to her decks, the forward one was in general use, the
after one reserved for the Captain, masters and visitors. We
were taken down to the main deck and through a narrow
passage aft to the Captain-Superintendent's office.

Captain David Wilson-Barker, R.N. (Retired) was a rather
frail-looking man – although I was soon to learn that there
was nothing frail about his temper. He had a brown pointed
beard and fiercely upturned moustaches similar to those
then worn by the Kaiser.

About the interview I recall only my father saying that
there was no vice in me – a statement he could make with a
clear conscience as, fortunately, my theft of Woods' cap had
remained undiscovered – but that I needed discipline; and
that as my grandfather's heir I should one day inherit a
quarter of a million pounds.

Evidently, however, he was not altogether tactful about
his reasons for wishing me to join the *Worcester*, as the Captain
took him up somewhat sharply to the effect that the *Worcester*
was not a penal establishment, but the equivalent of a good
public school. The other matter was news to me, and marvellous news at that. A quarter of a million in 1909, with the
enormously greater purchasing power of money in those
days, no super tax and income tax only a shilling in the
pound, was worth at least four million by present standards.
No wonder I fail to remember the rest of the conversation;
my mind was already far away building castles in Spain.
But I forgot to allow for my father's tendency to fool himself
innocently about the value of his possessions, actual or
potential. In this instance he considerably exaggerated the
amount of W.Y.B.'s fortune, and, anyway, my mother was
to have the enjoyment of it before, in the event, I shared the
remnants with my sister. Even then, the latter received the
lion's share and I, at the age of 60, only a few thousand
pounds. All the same, it was a pleasant thought to carry with
me through my boyhood; that, providing I did not blot my
copybook too badly, one day I'd be rich enough to live like
a fighting cock.

A few weeks later at Da Silva's, the nautical outfitters near
London Bridge, I was measured for my uniforms and provided with a number of garments strange to me; then, towards the end of January, 1910, I began a new chapter of my
life as a *Worcester* cadet.

Although for educational purposes it resembled any other
school, in that it had civilian masters and classes in which
all the usual subjects were taught, in almost every other
respect it was entirely different. The hours of the day clanged
out on the ship's bell, and we referred to them not by the
clock, but by the number of strikes. The shrilling of bosun's
pipes assembled the ship's company at the run for prayers or

divisions, or the duty watch for lowering or hauling up boats. There were no servants at all, other than cooks, so we had to both wait upon ourselves and clean the ship. There was no matron, so we had to do our own mending, and we slept not in beds but in hammocks.

Moreover, in addition to the usual subjects, nautical ones were taught – navigation, trigonometry, astronomy, meteorology, magnetism and chart drawing – the time devoted to these increasing as one worked one's way up the school. No doubt for this reason the three lowest classes were known as First, Second and Remove English, and the senior ones Third, Second and First Nautical. An hour or two each day was also devoted to practical seamanship – sailing, signalling, splicing ropes and learning to tie a variety of knots, etc., for which classes the civilian masters were replaced by ex-naval petty officers known as instructors. Finally, half an hour each morning was taken up by sweeping, washing paintwork and cleaning brass, and the whole of Saturday morning to scrubbing decks.

As a result of this multiplicity of subjects and numerous chores, no room could be found in the curriculum for Latin and – a grave mistake I've always thought in the case of boys training for a profession which would necessitate their spending the greater part of their lives in travel – only one hour a week was devoted to French. Yet, taken as a whole, the great variety provided by our weekly programme was an admirable antidote to getting bored with lessons, and I have no reason at all to suppose that our standards in English, history, geography and scripture were lower than the average at public schools, while in maths our seniors could have left the sixth form at Dulwich standing at the post.

The fact that we lived in a ship instead of in buildings also made a profound difference, for there were neither classrooms nor dormitories in the ordinary sense.

Immediately under the poop lay the Captain's private quarters, where he lived with his wife – a dark and, to us, somewhat myserious French lady. In a centre V under the fo'c's'le lay the main ship's galley, and on the outer sides of passages flanking it were the instructors' cabins.

The open upper deck, between poop and fo'c's'le, was

where we took our exercise, slewing, as walking with linked
arms two or three abreast round and round the main-mast
was called.

Beneath the poop lay a warren consisting of the masters'
cabins, galley and mess; beneath the fo'c's'le, the cadets'
mess. Between them the spacious area of the main deck was
a scene of constant activity. We assembled at its after end for
morning prayers and Sunday services, also for the daily in-
spection – termed 'divisions'. During school hours we sat on
benches there in six classes without separating partitions, and
evenings and weekends it served as a great common-room in
which we read, wrote our letters, played indoor games or
just sat about in groups talking.

The lower deck from stem to stern – except for the forward
end which was our washroom – was one great dormitory,
lined at the sides with the long rows of our sea-chests, opposite which each of us slung his hammock at night.

Below that came the tier deck. It was only just above the
water-line and had a wide entrance on to the landing-stage.
Part of it had been partitioned off as our bathroom, and contained some dozen old-fashioned baths each about as large
as a Roman sarcophagus. It was in use every evening, but
each of us had a bath only once a week. This was not felt to
be a hardship, as the majority of us, myself included, came
from homes in which a once-weekly bath was then customary.
The remainder of the tier deck was given over to boats that
were being repaired, sails, ropes and other tackle. It was also
the usual rendezvous for our fights, because it was nearly always deserted and well away from the main and upper decks,
where instructors were always on duty during our hours of
recreation.

The greater part of the hold of the ship was one square, lofty
chamber with a stage at one end and several stepped-up tiers
on either side, which could be used as seats. Normally it was
the gymnasium, but it was also used at times for concerts.
The hold also contained the furnaces, of which more anon.

In accordance with naval tradition the Captain kept himself very much aloof and rarely appeared except on his
official duties; but the Chief Officer, Mr. May, was much in
evidence. He was an elderly Lieutenant R.N.R., white-

haired, taciturn but kindly. The chief instructor, known as
the 'Gunner', was another taciturn type, but far from popular.
He and his half-dozen mates were all ex-petty officers of the
Royal Navy.

On the scholastic side the lowest form, the First English,
was taken by a Mr. Elwell; a simple and not unkindly man.
The Second English was an unhappy class, as it had Mr.
Brewer, a tyrant whose favourite way of demonstrating his
displeasure at work ill-done was to hold a boy on tiptoe by
the short hair just above his ear, and anyone who cares to
try this on themselves will promptly realise how exceedingly
painful it can be. The English Remove fared little better
as it was taught by Mr. Orme, the Head. He was the only
master who had university honours, and it was said that he
regarded the others with contempt, also that he had become
embittered because he thought he deserved a better post. In
any case, he was severe, cynical, and devastatingly sarcastic,
held those of whom he disapproved up to ridicule, and took
it out of everyone with the whiplash of his tongue. To the
relief of all concerned, after my fourth term he left to become
the headmaster of Reigate Grammar School.

The Third Nautical sat under the ship's chaplain, Mr.
Purdy, a fat, bald man who was far from popular and made
free use of his gunter – a three-foot rule which all the masters
used as a pointer to their blackboards and to inflict casual
punishment during class.

Mr. Jock Witney took the Second Nautical. He was the
youngest master, strict but good humoured, and the most
popular, with the exception of Mr. Beatty, who took the
First Nautical and, to our delight, was made headmaster on
Orme leaving.

Mr. Beatty was the very best kind of master. He was
highly intelligent, had a most pleasant sense of humour, took
great pains to make perfectly clear all that he was trying to
teach us, and displayed a real personal interest in every boy
in his class. We loved him and worked willingly for him; and
it is not too much to say of my rather patchy education that
I learnt more from him during my final year, when I was in
his form, than from all the other masters that I sat under
between the ages of eleven and sixteen.

E

Apart from the discipline inculcated by the ship's routine of bells, bosun's pipes and the gunters of the masters, there was also that arising from time-honoured customs among the boys themselves; and they had, I think, created a more rigid hierarchy than is usual in public schools.

There were no personal fags, but all boys in their first year were known by the unattractive term 'new-shits', and all seniors had the right to 'fag' the nearest new-shit to hand to go and find someone, carry a message, fetch their book or perform any other small service. New-shits, too, had to wear their caps straight on their heads, and stitch up their trouser pockets; they were not allowed to wear the bottoms of their trousers turned up, or have on their belts more than one Turks-head for each term they had been in the ship.

For their second year boys ranked as 'old hands'. They could then no longer be fagged, but had not yet the right to fag others. However, to be an 'old hand' made such a tremendous difference to life that, for once, one did not regret a holiday – that which preceded this step-up – coming to an end; and for the first weeks of the term all the fourth termers could be spotted on sight, because they strutted about with their caps on the very backs of their heads and both hands stuffed deep into the pockets of their trousers. Such bullying as took place – and it was not considerable – was done almost entirely by these new little cocks-of-the-walk, some of whom, not altogether unnaturally, felt the impulse to get their own back on the newcomers for the hard time they had had themselves during their first year.

The sixth termers – as all who had been in the ship for two years or longer were called – were the élite. They had the right to fag any new-shit and to wear as many Turks-heads on their belts as they liked. They were rarely bullies, considering such conduct beneath them; instead, many of them took much younger boys under their special protection; a practice that I shall refer to later.

Nearly all the sixth termers were 'badge boys', although one could be granted this distinction any time after one became an 'old hand'. This was frequently the case with boys who did not join the ship until they were about fifteen; so went straight into English Remove, thus becoming the con-

temporaries of the majority who had taken a year or more
to work their way up there. Theoretically the Badge was an
award for good conduct; but, in fact, unless a boy's record
was particularly bad he received it automatically as a mark
that he was competent to act as a sub-prefect and take charge
of a boat's crew or shoulder other small responsibilities. The
Badge was a small gold anchor with a silver rope twisted
round it, and was worn low down on the right hand sleeve
of one's jacket or jumper.

The cadets were divided into two watches – port and
starboard – and each watch again into a number of 'tops' –
fo'c's'le, fore, main, mizzen, etc. Each division consisted of
about fifteen boys under a cadet petty officer – who filled the
role of a prefect – and was responsible for the turnout and
behaviour of the members of his 'top'. On the arms of their
jackets these Petty Officers wore a single gold ring, and above
it a triangle in the centre of which was the anchor badge.
They had a small common-room of their own, in which they
were permitted to administer lickings to juniors who had been
reported to them for refusing to fag, or impudence to seniors.
They were selected for their prowess in the activities of the
ship as an example to others and were headed by a Chief
Cadet Captain, who usually received the King's Gold Medal
for the best all-round cadet at the end of the year.

Perhaps I was just not that sort of boy. Anyhow, although
I remained in the *Worcester* several terms longer than the
normal training course, I was never made a P.O. But nothing
short of crass stupidity could prevent my becoming in due
course one of an even more select community known as 'The
Upper Twelve' – the equivalent of 'Pop' at Eton – and during
my last four terms no prefect ever had the audacity to order
me about; so my life was a very pleasant one.

Yet let no one suppose that in 1910–13 the *Worcester* was
not far short of Hell for her youngest cadets. They were subject
to far greater discomfort than they would have met with at
most schools, expected to get a quick grasp of many matters
and customs which were as strange to them as those of
Eskimos or African Pygmies, called on to expose themselves
in any weather as boat crews, could rarely settle to letter-
writing or a book for a quarter of an hour without being

'fagged' to go on some errand; and, above all, the food we were given would today have been rejected by the inmates of a prison or a workhouse.

I have said that bullying was not considerable, but there was one custom the anticipation of which played upon first termers' nerves for some six weeks, probably to a greater degree than anything short of the severest bullying would have done. This was new-shits' singing; an initiation that took place in the evening of the Saturday nearest to half-term, and was held down in the gym.

The prefects sat in a semi-circle on the stage. To left and right on the stepped-up wooden tiers sat the rest of the ship's company, except for the new-shits and sixth termers. The former, in a white-faced group of about twenty strong, stood cowering at the foot of the broad ladder that led down to the gym. In front of them the large padded mats used for gym had been laid out end to end leading up to the stage. Forming a lane, on either side of the mats, lay the sixth termers. Each held in his hand a short piece of rope the end of which had been spliced into a weighty knot.

A deafening chorus, sung by all but the victims, and seeming almost to rock the ship, was repeated over and over again. It ran:

> *Hi! Hi! Up she rises. Hi! Hi! Up she rises.*
> *What shall we do with a drunken sailor?*
> *What shall we do with a drunken sailor?*
> *Hoist him up with a running bowline*
> *Earlie in the morning.*
>
> *Hi! Hi! Up she rises. Hi! Hi! Up she rises.*
> *What shall we do with a drunken sailor?*
> *Put him in a boat until he's sober*
> *Earlie in the morning.*
>
> *Hi! Hi! Up she rises. Hi! Hi! Up she rises.*
> *What shall we do with a drunken sailor?*
> *Shave his chin with a rusty razor*
> *Earlie in the morning.*

And so on, while the prefects beat time with their gunters,

and the sixth termers also did so in practice strokes with their ropes' ends on the mats.

Into this surge of deafening sound and excited sadism one of the new-shits either stepped, or was pushed, forward. As he reached the edge of the first mat he was supposed to throw himself down upon it, if not he was pulled down. From there up to the stage he had to wriggle forward on his stomach while the sixth termers belaboured his bottom with their ropes' ends, some of them often delaying his progress by holding him back by the heels so that others had a better opportunity to get a good whack at him.

Eventually he reached the low stage, was allowed to clamber up on to it. He then had to stand on a three-legged stool from which, without accompaniment, he was expected to entertain the company with a song.

Few victims ever reached the stage without having been reduced to a blubbering jelly, yet, somehow, most of them got out a few quavering bars. After the degree of courage displayed had been assessed, the Cadet Captain, by means of a string attached to a loose leg of the stool, pulled the leg out, precipitating the almost inarticulate singer back on to the near end of the line of mats.

Then, strangely reminiscent of the Roman emperors deciding the fate of a gladiator in the circus, the main body of the boys occupying the ringside seats gave their verdict. If it was some unfortunate little boy who lacked the stamina to support this ordeal and had made a poor showing, they would shout at him. 'Crawl! Crawl!' which meant that he had to take a second beating, running the gauntlet on his stomach back again along the mats. If a boy blessed with more courage had, in spite of tears, put up a good show they would cry 'Walk! Walk!' and the sixth termers laughing and calling congratulations to him allowed him to walk back untouched.

However, an element of rough justice also played a part in these verdicts. If, during his first half-term a boy had proved a willing fag and shown the makings of a good chap, he was certain to get off much more lightly than one who had been surly or cheeky. In fact it was at times deliberately used as a means of taking down a peg biggish boys who had joined the ship when a year or so older than the average first termer, and shown resentment at the restrictions imposed on new-shits.

I am not by nature a pugnacious type, and for most of my life have avoided trouble, like the chameleon, by assuming as quickly as possible the colour of my background. In consequence, while I was not especially popular, I had made no enemies; so I had nothing to fear on that score. Moreover, I had had the sense to choose a song of the period that was particularly suitable.

The first two lines of its chorus ran:

All the nice girls love a sailor. All the nice girls love a tar,
For there's something about a sailor. Well, you know what
sailors are . . .

After I had got out the first line or two everyone joined in this rousing chorus. The boys may not have been very tuneful, but they certainly made up for this by the volume which they enthusiastically put into their singing. Thumbs up was the verdict on my effort; so the loose leg was not pulled out of the stool and I walked back to recieve the congratulations of my small friends on having got off lightly.

One hardship endured by boys in the *Worcester* to a much greater degree than their contemporaries at schools on land was the cold and wet. To have only ice-cold water to wash in every morning was common to all schools in those days, but we had no windproof classrooms or dormitories; so, although the main and lower decks were both fitted with hot water pipes, in winter the cold was often sufficiently severe for us to need rugs and mittens; while up in the heads, at the extremity of the fo'c's'le, the bitter blast coming up the chutes was so biting that it almost froze one's bottom.

The big twelve-oared barges, in which we went ashore on Wednesday and Saturday afternoons to our playing fields, were moored near the ship; but the Captain's gig, the second gig, the jolly-boat, and at certain seasons the long whalers in which we rowed races, had to be lowered each morning and hoisted up to their davits every evening. Their weight was such that a whole watch was required to haul on the ropes; so on alternate days, at the shrilling of the bosun's pipes, half the ship's company – all those whose hammocks were slung on either the starboard or port side – had, several times, to leave whatever they were doing and hasten to the upper deck. However hard it was raining the job had to be done, and as each boat took about ten minutes to lower or hoist, that was quite long enough for us to be half soaked and shivering before we were free to go below again.

Far worse, at times, were our turns as 'duty crew'. Their job for the day was to row the Captain, masters and any visitors to and fro as required between the ship and shore, and in the jolly-boat to bring off the posts and ship's provisions. In summer it was a thing to look forward to, for it meant a day free from lessons; but in bad weather in winter it could be Hell. With a cross sea running and a howling gale it was gruelling work for four boys to propel the heavy jolly-boat the half mile to the jetty, and to have to fetch off a belated master in darkness and driving icy rain or snow was a horrible ordeal. We seemed to tug at the oars interminably without making any progress, and I have known the job take well over an hour, with only one brief respite at the jetty for the waiting passenger to jump down into the heaving boat.

Yet the worst thing of all about the *Worcester* was the quality of the food. It was disgraceful. For breakfast, coarse porridge, bread, margarine, and the cheapest possible marmalade; for midday dinner, meat so bad that at times it actually stank, followed most days by suet puddings in which there were globules of solid fat as large as currants; for tea, bread, margarine and nondescript, unpalatable jam; for supper, a mug of watery cocoa with spots of oil floating on top, and iron-hard ships' biscuits.

The only fish we ever had was plain boiled cod without egg sauce to help it down; the only fruit, stewed prunes and old, stringy rhubarb; the only pastry a flat apple tart the crust of which was straight flour and water, and so hard that it needed sharp stabbing with a fork to break it in pieces; the only vegetables were cabbage, carrots and turnips. We never saw an egg, a rasher of bacon, a fried potato or one roasted in its jacket; or toast or brown bread – let alone a piece of cake.

No doubt this was harder on me than on most of the boys, because many of them were the sons of ill-paid merchant sea-captains so came from comparatively poor homes in which the food may have been good, but pretty certainly was very plain. Whereas my mother, having brought me up to share her own liking for such things as omelettes, kidneys, sweet-breads, chicken livers, roes or sardines on toast, soufflés, fish *au gratin* and so on, had, to some extent, made simple food lack attraction for me.

Even so, I do not recall having disliked the ordinary boarding school fare that I had been given for four years at Margate, whereas that in the *Worcester* actively repelled me; so it must have been of a very low standard indeed. In fact, I am certain that much of it today would have been con-demned as unfit for human consumption.

However, I should here admit frankly that all my life I have been exceptionally difficult about food, as there are a number of things, among them onions, vinegar, mustard, capers, pickles, boiled milk, margarine and butter, that I cannot swallow without their making me sick, and many others that I dislike so much that I would rather go hungry than eat them.

Such marked dislikes are highly inconvenient for, although rather than appear impolite as a guest I will gamely push down a beef-steak or chop, mutton, spinach, carrots, old boiled potatoes, bitter marmalade and dry Martini cocktails, that cannot be done with things to which I am actually allergic such as cold butter.

At children's parties I suffered acute embarrassment through having to refuse bread and butter and instead, pre-sumably owing to greed, awkwardly make it clear that I would eat only cake. When older, at weddings and buffet suppers, it deprived me of the things I liked best, such as *foie gras* and smoked salmon, because they were spread on buttered toasts. At picnics, too, I often had to make do with biscuits and fruit – except when I was with people who knew of my allergies and provided a special package of sandwiches

marked 'D.W.'; as even a smear of butter in a ham sandwich was enough to make me vomit.

I have many times endeavoured to conquer this unfortunate reaction but have never succeeded; and I think it is the
slimy taste of butter and margarine which upsets me; for,
happily, hot butter has no adverse effect upon me at all. In
fact, I enjoy hot buttered toast, tea cake or crumpets. Skate
is to my mind an excellent fish provided it is served with
plenty of black-butter sauce, and salmon, new potatoes,
asparagus and globe artichokes, all of which I love, would
not taste half so good without melted butter.

The best beef dripping was always put aside for me and it
is a curious commentary on my mother's character that when
I was away from home she never sent me so much as a packet
of biscuits, yet every fortnight or so she would send me a pot
of dripping. Such parcels, easily recognisable from their
shape, were hardly calculated to make a hungry schoolboy's
fingers tremble with eagerness to discover their contents;
yet she had so trained me to think her marvellous in every
way that it was not until years later that I realised how
parsimonious she was, and how much happier she could have
made my school days by the occasional expenditure of a few
shillings.

Mention of the shape of these parcels reminds me that they
were ordinary one-pound jam jars wrapped only in a single
sheet of brown paper, and I never remember one arriving
broken. Who, in this present age of mechanisation and
cynically careless labour would care to trust anything so
fragile to the post unprotected by several layers of packing?
But in those days employees in all despatch departments
regarded other people's property as entrusted to them and so
to be handled with care. It is a sad commentary that few
now do so – presumably because they have little to fear
from losing their jobs.

Both my wives have most generously pandered to my likes
and dislikes; but both were of the opinion that these were the
result of being badly brought up, and that if a child is made
to finish everything that is put before him he will soon get
over any tendency to dislike certain dishes. Many people
also maintain that only rich children who are spoiled when

young grow up faddy, and that those of the poor never do so because hunger drives them to eat anything they can get.

But I regard such theories as highly questionable and against them would cite the case of my grandfather Wheatley. His parents were far from rich and had they spoilt him it is hardly likely that he would have run away from home at the age of twelve. Yet he had a life-long allergy connected with hens' eggs. Not only could he not eat one, he could not even eat a piece of cake that had been made with them. Fortunately, as a poulterer, duck, turkey and goose eggs were always readily available to him, all of which he liked; and on his retirement to Westgate he kept flocks of these birds to ensure himself a constant supply.

Reverting to the *Worcester*, how I managed to survive there I can now hardly think. Monday was salt-beef day, and the saltpetre disguised the tang of the meat; so that was all right. So, too, were the overdone outside cuts on joints of beef or the knuckle of mutton – when I could manage to get them. Sometimes I was lucky enough to get sufficient gravy from under the joint to soak a slice of bread in; that was a great treat. Otherwise I made do by cutting the eyes out of the big boiled potatoes and mashing them while still hot with a little margarine, and large helpings of duff, out of which I first prised the revolting little lumps of solid fat. About every tenth day, however, either I or one of my companions had little time to eat anything at all, as it came to our turn to be messman; which meant that every time anyone at one's table shouted for more bread, spuds, marge or water, one had to jump up and fetch it.

Yet, despite the many hardships of being a *Worcester* cadet, it had very considerable compensations. I acquired there a smattering of many subjects not taught in ordinary schools; to row, sail and cox a boat, about the weather and the stars, to draw charts and diagrams to scale accurately, to recognise certain flags and to signal by semaphore and morse, to tie knots swiftly which would not come undone, to recognise various types of ship at a distance, the principles of navigation, how to shoot the sun with a sextant, much nautical lore; and many of these odd bits of knowledge have come in useful since I became an author.

Further, although my nature is such that throughout my life I have spared no pains to protect myself to the utmost degree possible from every form of discomfort, my years in the *Worcester* engendered in me a hard core of stoicism and resilience, which enabled me to confront hard times – such as those frequently unavoidable while serving in two world wars – philosophically and even with cheerfulness.

But there was also a much more immediate benefit, which we began to enjoy in the holiday succeeding our very first term. We were no longer as other boys, but set apart, our uniforms as cadets making us appear older than our contemporaries and much superior to them.

Ordinarily, while in the ship, except for Captain's divisions on Sundays, and church parade, we wore coarse blue cloth trousers and blue serge jumpers. The latter took the form of very roomy open-necked shirts which, when the bottom was tucked into our trousers top, stood out in loose bulges all round the body. It was an admirable garment, and the salvation of new-shits, who were not allowed to use their trouser pockets, as inside the jumper where it bulged out from the waistline, all sorts of oddments could be carried without risk of loss, and things much too big to go into pockets, such as books, were habitually carried about in our jumpers by all of us.

During holidays, however, we wore uniforms and caps with gold badges that made us look like miniature naval officers. Better still, for dances and parties we had our mess-kit; tight-fitting bumfreezers and white waistcoats with gold buttons. Given approximate equality in address, looks and physique, how could boys in Norfolk jackets, or black relieved only by the school symbol of an Eton collar, hope to compete with us for the interest of girls eager to ensnare with their youthful charms a beau who would do them credit?

The song said, 'All the nice girls love a sailor.' While a *Worcester* cadet I was loved a little by several very pretty ones. Owing to my ardent nature I loved even more of them quite a lot.

10

A NEW HOME

WHEN, in April, 1910, I started my first holiday from the *Worcester*, I went on the directions I had been given to a strange house that was to be my home for the next four years.

Whether either of my grandfathers had relented and come to my father's rescue, or he had managed to weather his financial crisis on his own, I do not know; but he had not had to become a bankrupt. Nevertheless, his unlucky speculations on the Stock Exchange had resulted in his having to sell Wootton Lodge and move to a much smaller house. This was No. 1 Becmead Avenue, a modern semi-detached only a stone's throw from Streatham High Street, in a road that led down to Tooting Bec Common.

It was a cut above 10 Raleigh Gardens, particularly since, with the coming of motor cars, Brixton was now rapidly going down in the social scale, and better class people were tending to move further away from Central London; but that was all that could be said for it.

After Wootton, with its spacious rooms and big garden, it was a sad come-down. There were no stables, potting sheds, chicken-run, old summer house, shrubberies, and other delights which had hitherto been such a joy to me during my holidays.

Curiously enough, while I can recall every nook and corner of Wootton I have not the faintest memory of the interior of Friars Croft, as the new house was named. I can see its short front garden, with the bay windows on its ground and first floors but no more. Yet the house must have been of a fair size, as in addition to a living-in cook and housemaid we continued to keep a nurse for my young sister, Muriel, then aged six.

However, the move did bring me one new and enduring

blessing; a girl-friend of my own age. Her name was Hilda Gosling and she lived next door. Her mother was always most kind to me and her father, a manufacturer of men's ready-made clothes, was a very jolly and friendly man. In this case by 'girl-friend' I mean to convey something much more profound than the generally accepted use of the expression; although it is difficult to describe our exact relationship.

I certainly became her permanent stand-by cavalier, and at times we indulged in mildly amorous kissing, but neither of us was ever actually in love with the other. She was an only child, and as my sister was seven years younger than myself, so large a gap put it out of the question for her to be a suitable companion. In effect, therefore, I was also an only child, and Hilda, being only a few months younger than myself, stepped into the role of a sister to me.

She was a very fat girl – an affliction she did not succeed in overcoming until well on in her teens – with a squarish face, good eyes and brown hair which she wore in two long plaits. Her great assets were her vitality and a grand sense of humour. She was also much more intelligent than the average girl – later she went to Girton, and after her marriage became a very successful business woman, both assisting her husband, who was a print-seller, and running a book-shop of her own.

During the holidays we were much in each other's houses and frequently went for walks together on Tooting Bec Common, so we soon reached a degree of intimacy in which we had no secrets from one another. As a result I inevitably picked up quite a bit about the interests, aspirations and psychology of the normal teenage girl, for Hilda talked freely to me about her friends as well as herself; and as I naturally reciprocated she gained an equally valuable insight into the average boy's point of view.

As we were not in love we were never jealous of one another, and through her I met most of the respectable girls with whom for brief periods I carried on youthful flirtations. These rarely lasted longer than a single holiday and consisted mainly of snatched kisses when sitting out at dances, followed by letters delivered in secret and, perhaps, a few clandestine meetings.

That last sentence may appear strange to modern eyes, but in those days well-brought-up girls under eighteen were not usually allowed to receive letters from their youthful admirers, but most people's maidservants were only too happy to accept a small tip for undertaking the romantic mission of smuggling a love-letter to their young mistresses.

I am by nature a hoarder and put all sorts of oddments aside with the idea that sometime or other they will come in useful and, although my family have frequently complained of this habit, it is surprising how often I have been able to produce from an attic just the thing for the job. From about the age of fourteen, too, I began to keep any letters of interest that I received, dance programmes, bills and other documents. As time went on these increased until a dozen or more deed-boxes and trunks lay in the vaults of my bank, crammed with papers covering every important aspect of my life.

When I decided to start writing my memoirs, I had a few of these boxes out and went through some of the earliest collections. They have brought back to me many faces and episodes long since forgotten, and are proving most valuable in giving the right dates for various events. No one, I think, can be wholly accurate in recalling happenings long past during a very full life, but this mass of papers will enable me to do so in the main.

If I do make some mis-statements they will be in connection with public events that I have not checked because I believe my memory of them is correct. As an author I have found that such few slips as do creep into my books are nearly always on that account. For example, in one novel I stated that the principal character had been educated at Ringwood Grammar School in Dorset. Had I had the least doubt about the county I should have looked it up, but I didn't, and Ringwood was then in Hampshire. The Bournemouth papers leapt upon me and devoted their reviews to this unfortunate slip, which had no bearing whatever on the story. But if one checked every reference to every subject no book would ever get written, and should some errors about time or place be found in this account of my life it must not be assumed that the vast majority are not accurate, and all reasonable care has been taken to make them so.

Among the earliest of my hoarded papers are letters from girls whom I knew in my *Worcester* days, and after almost seventy years it has given me much amusement to read them again. Their primness would amaze young people of today. In that era no boy called a girl by her Christian name to begin with. In fact, to do so almost amounted to a declaration of love, and one had to screw up one's courage to speak to her for the first time, as Renée, Agnes or Peggy, fearing that one might well be rebuffed for taking such a liberty.

These series of letters nearly all start 'Dear Mr Wheatley', then go on to 'Dear Dennis', 'Dearest', and finally 'Darling', with a row of hastily scrawled kisses at the end. But this gradual progression had a thrill all of its own; and the fact that these calf-love affairs had to be carried on in secrecy added enormously to the kick one got out of them.

These short-lived romances with Hilda's prettiest friends did not constitute my only early associations with the opposite sex. There was a completely different category of young girls whose acquaintance I made by less orthodox means. They were the daughters of local shopkeepers, and suchlike, who were not hedged about with the same restrictions as those of a higher class. Usually in couples, they paraded Streatham High Street in the evenings and were not averse to being picked up.

Picking up was then a very usual activity, and probably still is. Douglas Sharp and I engaged in it frequently, but the results were mostly disappointing. On occasions when we 'got off' with a couple of pretty ones we took them down to Tooting Bec Common and spent an hour or so on a seat flirting with them; but generally they proved giggly and tongue-tied and there were comparatively few cases in which we made appointments to meet them again.

One exception was an extraordinarily pretty girl named Irene de Lacy who, as a dentist's daughter, came from a good home and was not allowed out alone. But one afternoon when I was on my own strolling in The Rookery – the public gardens adjoining Streatham Common – I sat down on a bench on which she was also sitting with an elderly nurse in charge of a pram with a baby, and I got into conversation with them. After that I used to meet them frequent-

ly, as the old nurse evidently enjoyed playing the role of the
nurse in *Romeo and Juliet*, and raised no objection to Irene
and me going off for a stroll together. But as neither of us was
in a position to tell our parents that I had virtually picked
her up, neither of us ever went to one another's homes, until
much later when we had met socially.

Another exception was a girl whose Christian name I
never even got to know, yet who dominated my thoughts for
several months. On Sunday afternoons the upper slope of
Streatham Common resembled Hyde Park Corner, in that
Socialists, religious cranks and other soap-box orators set up
their stands, each attracting little crowds of from a handful
to a hundred or more people. One Sunday in August, 1910,
Douglas and I spotted two pretty girls on the edge of one of
these crowds. Both were wearing large, floppy straw hats, the
one decorated with poppies and the other with cornflowers.
The girl with the cornflower hat had masses of golden hair,
enormous blue eyes and a milk and roses complexion. I fell
for her at once, and to distinguish her from her sister we afterwards referred to her as 'Blue Hat'.

With some difficulty we succeeded in picking them up and
later walked nearly home with them, but they proved extremely shy and tongue-tied. As we approached the point at
which Streatham High Road merges into Norbury one of
them said, 'Please leave us now, we live just here and will
get into trouble if we are seen with you.'

That naturally ended the first episode. We met them again
on the two following Sundays, but got little further than
learning that they were sisters and their name Davies. By
then the sight of this beautiful but silly face had entirely be-
witched me. From Sunday to Sunday I could scarcely think
of anything else, and in the hope that I might catch a glimpse
of her I made several expeditions to the vicinity of her home,
but without success. It was a corner building consisting of two
floors of living accommodation over a small garage. The fact
that her father was probably a greasy mechanic who earned
his living servicing cheap cars and motor bicycles made not
the least difference to me. For the first time in my life I was in
love.

But at the age of thirteen few youngsters are consulted

Cousin Laurie

Wicked Uncle Johnny

Wootton Lodge, my home from 1904 to 1910
(Top) *Front view*
(Above) *Back view: croquet on the lawn*

(Top) *Springfield, Westgate, Grandpa Wheatley's house*
(Above) *Aspen House, Grandpa Baker's house*

In mess kit

H.M.S. Worcester *as dressed ship*

about plans made for them by their parents. For several years after we left Wootton – probably on account of my father's losses – they abandoned their custom of taking a holiday abroad. This year they had decided to go to Ventnor, in the Isle of Wight; and, willy-nilly, I had temporarily to abandon my pursuit of the lovely Blue Hat to accompany them.

In the wagonettes, since replaced by motor-coaches, we visited the beauty spots of the island; Shanklin Chine, Carisbrooke Castle, Osborne, and Alum Bay with its remarkable strata of different coloured sands. It was then a local industry to fill glass moulds shaped like small lighthouses with the coloured sands, and with such skill that the sands formed a picture of the nearby Needles rocks. Hundreds of children kept such souvenirs on their nursery mantelpieces, and I still have two that I use as paperweights; but the making of them is now one of our lost arts and present-day souvenirs of Alum Bay are by comparison pathetic, being no more than small glass phials filled with the sand in layers.

Apart from these excursions neither my parents nor myself derived much pleasure from this holiday. Before the First World War the resort in Great Britain most popular with the Germans was the Isle of Wight, and a big percentage of the staffs of the best hotels were also Germans. At the one where we stayed we heard hardly a word of English spoken and were the only British visitors, with the result that my parents made no new acquaintances and I had no one to play with.

From this it must not be assumed that as a nation we then had any special antipathy to the German race. On both sides our Royal Family were the direct descendants of Germans who had for long occupied the British throne. For centuries the Germans had been our allies in most of our wars against our hereditary enemies, the French, and we looked upon them as a musical, home-loving people at whom we poked mild fun on account of their insatiable greed for sausages and beer.

As Germany had few colonies and *Lebensraum* was already becoming a problem, many thousands of them emigrated every year, particularly to the United States and Great

Britain – there then being no restrictions upon people of any nation making a home and earning their living in another. In Britain, except in country towns, the majority of waiters were Germans; also a great number were barbers. Their government also financed them with loans at low interest to set up small businesses, solely on the security of their having learnt a trade and their honesty having been vouched for by responsible relatives. They retained their own nationality and usually returned to their own country on retirement, but they made industrious and law-abiding citizens and, as such, were welcomed by us.

The fact that the ambitions of the Kaiser and his *Junker* generals were becoming a menace to the peace of Europe had not yet penetrated the consciousness of the British masses. Unlike the Germans, very few French people ever came to England for a holiday, or settled here. The Entente Cordiale was then barely five years old and although attempts had been made to popularise it – such as a vast statue twenty feet high of King Edward shaking hands with President Poincaré, made out of solid butter, which I recall seeing at some trade exhibition – we still looked on the French with suspicion and as a race of dirty 'frog-eaters'.

With Anglo-American goodwill, an open door in every country and their immense capacity for hard work, had the Germans maintained their policy of peaceful penetration for another twenty or thirty years, there can be little doubt that they would have secured financial control of all the South American republics, captured the lion's share of Europe's commerce and become, without firing a shot, the richest and most powerful nation this side of the Atlantic. That they should instead have twice brought ruin on themselves, caused incalculable misery to countless other people all over the world, and created a state of things in which the survival of Christian civilisation is still precarious, is the greatest tragedy that has befallen mankind since the Goths and Vandals brought about the Dark Ages by the destruction of the Roman Empire.

During our holiday in the Isle of Wight my thoughts were naturally never far from Blue Hat and plans for developing my so far slender acquaintance with her. Immediately on our return in September, I went along to Norbury hoping to catch a glimpse of my divinity. My distress and despair can be imagined on finding the garage empty and the windows of the rooms above it curtainless.

I had been living only for the time when I should see her again. That she and her family should have moved during my absence was a most terrible blow. Yet one of my few virtues is that I have never given up without a fight the pursuit of any aim I have undertaken. In my still illiterate scrawl I wrote to the house agent whose board now advertised the premises to let, asking for the address of the late tenant.

I received a courteous reply saying that they could not help me, but giving the address of the landlord. I wrote to him with the same request, but again drew a blank. It seems probable that the proprietor of the little garage had got into financial difficulties and made a 'moonlight flit'. Anyway, I never saw the beautiful but dumb little creature again, and for many months I was inconsolable.

What happened to her, I wonder? Did her loveliness gain for her the glittering life of a West End chorus girl, with champagne suppers, bouquets of roses and perhaps a rich husband? Was she white-slaved – a fate which befell more than a few girls of her type and class in those days? Did she die while still young and beautiful, as the result of some accident or disease, or in middle age as the victim of the blitz in Hitler's war? More probably she married some mediocrity and is still alive, old, grey and wrinkled, her breathtaking beauty now only a memory of the past.

So far in this chapter I may have given the impression that my mind had become entirely preoccupied with girls, and that I spent the greater part of my holidays from the *Worcester* with Douglas Sharp trying to pick them up in the street.

This was by no means the case. We rarely went out with that object in view, although the tendency to do so naturally increased as we grew older. Very often we took a tram for several miles before starting our walk, and then explored other districts; Herne Hill, Clapham, Thornton Heath, Norwood, Wandsworth, sometimes going as far as Croydon, Mitcham or Purley. It was only on occasions when we happened to see two pretty girls, who were apparently out just for a stroll, that we indulged in this sport. And sport is the right word for it, as it was a type of hunting which called for a measure of skill and address to be successful. I should add, too, that the 'kill' was always painless, for we were still too young to have any immoral designs on the hunted.

Moreover, many of my days were spent with my mother, and as far as general knowledge is concerned she made a very considerable contribution to my education. Not only did she always take me with her when she went up to London to shop in the West End, but also on many special expeditions, to the British and South Kensington Museums, St. Paul's, Westminster Abbey, the National Gallery, the Wallace Collection and the Tower. I was devoted to her and she to me, so we spent many happy afternoons either choosing her hats or sightseeing.

There were, too, our regular afternoons and evenings spent at Aspen House. Now that we had no garden of our own my Grandpa Baker's was a greater joy than ever. My friendship with my adored cousin Laurie continued, my Aunt Nell and Aunt Betsy made a great fuss of me, and by this time I was becoming old enough to take an interest in the great collection of *objets d'art* with which my grandfather had filled his house.

For another summer holiday we went to the Hydro at Llandudno, and that I thoroughly enjoyed, as the Hydro provided a much greater range of entertainments for its guests than was common in large hotels. There was dancing, a concert, or a conjuror, or a lecture with lantern slides every night, tennis and croquet whenever we cared to play, and a gymkhana every Saturday afternoon. In addition to sea-bathing there was an indoor swimming pool and strange excitements such as needle baths.

In 1911 we went to the Grand at Lowestoft. It was perched up on a cliff at the southern extremity of the town. As had been the case at Llandudno there were a number of young people of my own age, so I had a jolly time.

That summer was memorable for three things. Its wonderful weather, which produced one of the finest vintages of the century, the floods in the eastern counties that followed the long, hot spell, and the Agadir crisis.

This last filled my mother and me with considerable anxiety, as my father had gone to Germany on a business trip. Some time previously, through the German wine-shippers Messrs. Julius Kayser & Co., he had acquired the sole agency for Great Britain of a sparkling mineral water called Moselaris. It had an attractive label of a waterfall descending from among pine trees and rocks, and was put up in a then new type of bottle with a hinged china stopper, so that when only part of the contents of the bottle had been used, the fizziness of the remainder could be retained.

At that time our firm had not the resources, or reputation to have become a serious competitor to such old-established wine-merchants as Justerini's, Berry Brothers or Block, Grey and Block, and the greater part of our business consisted of trade in mineral waters and beers, which the others did not stock.

We were the principal West End agents for Schweppes and Bulmers, and supplied hundreds of Mayfair, Belgravia and Bayswater mansions with Malvern water. In those days no 'person of quality' would have dreamt of drinking water from a tap; although in fact many of them did, and were mildly victimised because they could not tell the difference. Their butlers used to fill up the Malvern bottles with tap water, and periodically ask my father to add an extra six dozen to the bill, then give them the money; a practice he had to acquiesce in from fear of losing their goodwill and with it a valuable account covering many other items.

It was, too, the era in which the fashionable doctors' favourite remedy for aristocratic ills was to send their patients to foreign spas for a course of the waters, and often they ordered a continuance of the treatment in London, so we stocked several score of Continental medicinal waters, and shipped consignments of Vichy, Contrexeville and Evian by the hundred cases.

In consequence, the firm was in a strong position to launch on the market a sparkling table water which it was hoped would rival Apollinaris and Perrier. Since my father's principal interest in life was his business and he had plenty of drive, this new venture soon began to prosper, and in the summer of 1911 he had gone to Germany to negotiate with

Herr Kayser means of extending it. But my father was not a really lucky man. By August, 1914, the hard work he had put in had resulted in Moselaris ousting its rivals from the tables of a great part of the nobility and being stocked by most of the leading hotels and restaurants in London, from whence a demand for it was rapidly spreading through the Provinces. Then the outbreak of war cut off supplies. By the time we were able to trade with Germany again over five years had elapsed, so to launch it anew would have meant our starting again from scratch, and our wine business had by then so greatly increased that it did not appear worth it.

The venture, too, ended with a bitter pill. In 1920 we were suddenly faced with a bill from the Reparations Commission of £240, that being the value of the last consignment of Moselaris sent, which was lying in barges in the Thames at the outbreak of hostilities. As it had not been paid for, my father had to cough up, and, of course, the money from the sale of the water had long since been absorbed into the profits of the business.

While we were at Lowestoft and he was in Germany the Agadir crisis blew up, the Kaiser having officiously despatched a warship, the *Panther*, to that port in Morocco, with a threat to intervene in an affair that was no concern of his. Overnight the chancellories of Europe became in a dither, and the newspapers ran scare headlines stating that war between France and Germany was imminent, with the probable involvement of Britain.

To everyone's relief the crisis was resolved, but it had a far-reaching effect on the British public. For the first time they began to realise that Germany, with the powerful new fleet she was building, was really becoming a menace. They suddenly betrayed a truculence which was well expressed by the jingle:

> We've got the ships, we've got the men, we've got
> the money too,
> We don't want to fight, but by jingo if we do!

But we hadn't got the ships – at least not an adequate number of up-to-date ones – and the populace's agitation enabled the ever-vigilant Winston Churchill, then First Lord of the

Admiralty, and Admiral Earl Mountbatten's father, Prince Louis of Battenberg, then First Sea Lord, to secure Parliamentary acceptance of their programme for building a new battle fleet of Dreadnoughts; while Field Marshal Lord Roberts, beloved by the public as 'Bobs', stumped the country raising volunteers for Lord Haldane's new creation, the welding of the out-dated militia system into the later invaluable Territorial Army.

By the time my father got back from Germany great rains had flooded large areas of the eastern counties, and when he came down to join us at Lowestoft the water inland from the town was so deep that the train could go through it only at a walking pace, the floors of the carriages being actually awash. A few days later when we returned to London the floods had gone down considerably, but it still appeared as though the train was slowly ploughing its way through an inland sea. For miles around, the scene was one of terrible devastation, with parts of hayricks, hen coops, gates and dead cattle floating on the sullen water.

The following year we again went to Lowestoft, but to the Royal, which was on the front and much nearer the harbour; as, owing to erosion by the sea, the Grand up on the cliff had been condemned as no longer safe for occupation. As I have come upon a menu among my papers I am able to give it as an indication of the extraordinarily high standard of living before it was so drastically reduced by two world wars. Here is a typical dinner at that first class, but not de luxe, hotel:

CONSOMMÉ ROYAL PRINTANIÈRE
FILET DE SOLE À LA COLBERT
COMPÔTE DE PIGEONS À LA PROVENÇALE

QUARTIER D'AGNEAU RÔTI
ÉPINARDS, TOMATES ET POMMES PURÉE
GROUSE RÔTI, CRESSON, POMMES CHIPS
GELÉE AU CITRON
GLACE À LA VANILLE
MACARONI AU GRATIN
DESSERT

One did not have to eat every course but the majority of

people did; and, if my memory serves me, the cost to guests not living *en pension* of the whole nine courses was only five shillings.

During this holiday I met with a disconcerting experience. A fattish, prematurely bald man staying in the hotel got into conversation with me. He proved a friendly person with a fund of amusing stories, and in the course of a few days I went for several strolls with him during which he bought me ices and sweets. He then invited me up to his bedroom to see his collection of tie-pins. When I had admired them he led me to the open window to watch the people walking on the front. As I leant out of it he got behind me, pressed himself against me and put his hand round to my front. I can then have known very little about homosexuals but, instinctively, I broke away and got out of the room as quickly as I could.

I was much too frightened of my father to mention this episode to him but, evidently fearing that I might do so, my erstwhile friend left the hotel next day. Fortunately, I am evidently not a type that readily attracts such attentions, for I have never again been approached by anyone in that way.

Another incident caused me much more concern, and for long hung heavily upon my conscience. Every day I went about with a number of other youngsters staying in the hotel, to the beach, the pier, the harbour, and to concert parties. One evening it was decided that we should all go to a concert, the entrance fee to which was a shilling, and I had already spent every penny of my pocket money. I was ashamed to admit to the others that I had no money, and could not screw up the courage to ask my father for an advance; so I borrowed the shilling from my young sister's nurse. I meant to repay her before going back to the *Worcester*, but bills I had run up the previous term at the local tuck shops in Greenhithe had to be met, and would leave me so little to start the new term with that I never did. Nanny Fisher had been with us a long time. I loved her dearly and she loved me; so I am sure she never grudged me the shilling; but I was aware that the low wages of servants made their shillings precious, and for months afterwards felt terribly guilty at having abused her kindness.

Probably my reluctance to admit to the others that I could

not produce a shilling was mainly due to the presence among them of a girl named Gwen Shepard. She was not particularly pretty, but good fun, and the only girl among us several boys, all of whom competed for her attention. Afterwards, in London, she invited me to her home in Tufnell Park, but I have never been really attracted to any girl or woman who lacked beauty and, there no longer being the spur of competition, after that one visit I let our friendship lapse.

In addition to these holidays at the seaside, I went several times to stay for a week or so in the country with a friend of my father's. This was Mr. William Wiles, the owner of a high-class fruiterer's and florist's just off the Edgware Road, with a very fine Mayfair connection. In fact, so fine that it enabled Mr. Wiles to buy a pleasant property in Wiltshire called Hungerford Manor.

For him this was the perfect background, as he was a big, ruddy-faced man who was by nature, and looked every inch, a country squire. Willy Wiles was a great character and, owing to his bluff, jovial manner, he achieved, for a tradesman, the almost impossible feat of being treated as a friend by many members of the aristocracy. Not only did he hunt and shoot with them when he was in Wiltshire, he and his wife received badges every year for the Royal Enclosure at Ascot. In view of the social barriers then so rigidly adhered to, for anyone not in Debrett to enjoy a permanent place on this most exclusive list was little short of fantastic. Yet in his grey topper, full stock and grey cut-away coat, he looked as fine a man as any Lord with broad acres.

Beneath his bonhomie he was an extremely shrewd business man; he was said habitually to underpay his employees and to be a very harsh landlord to the tenants of the slum properties in which he invested his savings; but to me he was always most kind. It was with him at Hungerford that I learned to shoot – although he was justifiably peeved one day when, through ignorance, I brought down a treasured golden pheasant. Owing to him, too, I had my first experience of riding in a private motor car. His first resembled a pony cart; passengers entered it at the back by a set of let-down steps, then sat facing one another behind the driver's seat. Later he had a Mercedes, which was like a high carriage on a spidery chassis with thin wheels, but it was capable of doing sixty miles an hour on the flat. And perched up in the open on a high chassis, such a speed was little short of terrifying to the majority of us who were habitually used to the slow clop-clop of a horse.

Somewhere about 1912 my father initiated another venture with Willy Wiles as his principal partner. One of the leading caterers for society weddings, ball suppers, etc., was Kingston, Miller and Co. The shining light of the firm was an unctuous little man named Thomas Kingston. He was then about forty, married, with two children, and quarrelling bitterly with his father because, although he did all the work, the old man refused to pay him a salary that was more than a pittance. On his pouring out his tale of woe to my father and Wiles, it was decided that a new firm to be called the Mayfair Catering Company should be formed, of which Tom Kingston, having severed his relations with his old firm, should become Managing Director.

Having put up several hundred pounds apiece themselves, my father and Wiles then made the round of the big houses that they served, proposing to the stewards and butlers in them that they should take shares in the company, and by securing the business of their masters for it, help to ensure a big dividend on their own holdings. The idea of investing in a company which they were in a position to help prosper immediately appealed to scores of upper servants, and th readily raided their savings to acquire shares.

The amount required was soon fully subscribed but, shortly afterwards, my father had another most unlucky break. *John Bull*, Horatio Bottomley's often scurrilous rag that with, or without, good grounds made a speciality of unmasking new flotations that might possibly contain an element of fraud, printed an article on the Mayfair Catering Company entitled 'High Finance Below Stairs'.

In it were listed against each block of shares taken up – Mr. Glass, butler to Lady Glitter. Monsieur Casserole, chef to the Duke of Downshire, and so on. About the project there was nothing remotely fraudulent, but it might well be suggested that shareholders would be tempted to secure for the company catering engagements which their masters or mistresses could have had carried out equally well at less cost. The article properly put the cat among the pigeons, and my poor father, as the Chairman of the company, had to bear the brunt of the storm.

A few old-fashioned autocrats sacked their servants on the spot for having the impertinence to ape their betters by becoming shareholders in a private enterprise, but the majority conceded their right to invest their money as they saw fit, and promised to give the new company their business providing its quotations were competitive with those of others. So the storm blew over and, in due course, the Mayfair became a thriving concern which, I believe, is still flourishing today.

Yet, sad to relate, in the early twenties little Tom Kingston, having an insatiable greed for power, ungratefully entered on an underhand intrigue to oust my father and Wiles from the Board. I, too, had by that time been made a director, and despite my indignant urging that they should stand firm, they were so disgusted that they both resigned and, of course, I also had to.

Another venture backed by my father was a patent medicine called Solspar, which it was claimed would cure a wide variety of ills. But the great chemical combines were not going to let any new panacea get a hold in their preserves, and swiftly used their power and money to force it off the market.

Poor father, he was certainly a trier, and deserved better luck; but at least his efforts in his own business were not wasted, for he succeeded in building up a fine connection as a wine-merchant, which included the Dukes of Portland and Westminster, the Rothschilds, the Joel brothers, and scores of other titled people and millionaires; thus forming a basis which later enabled me to become the wine-merchant to over a score of kings and princes.

Since he worked so hard he was understandably averse to entertaining at home or going out in the evening. Moreover, he was not a man who made friends easily and had no real intimates, so we rarely had dinner parties and never anyone to stay in the house.

But although he grumbled at having to get into a black tie

and dinner jacket, he enjoyed an occasional theatre once he
got to it, and among the plays he took my mother and myself
to see I particularly remember Lewis Waller in *The Three
Musketeers* and *Monsieur Beaucaire*, H. B. Irving in *The Lyons
Mail*, Fred Terry in *The Scarlet Pimpernel*, Tree as Cardinal
Wolsey in *Henry VIII*, Matheson Lang in *The Wandering Jew*;
Romance, *Drake*, and *Romeo and Juliet*.

Before the First World War we went several times to see
the wonderful conjurors, Maskelyne and Devant, and to the
Anglo-French Exhibition at the White City. The Court of
Honour at the latter, with its white Indian temples, cascades
flowing into a big balustraded lake and chains of fairy lamps
at night, was a dream of delight and I think unsurpassed by
anything of the kind I have seen since.

It was later reproduced for the second act of *Our Miss
Gibbs* in which the enchanting Gertie Millar, afterwards
Countess of Dudley, appeared. Among its members were
'Yip-i-addy-i-ay', 'I'm such a silly when the moon comes
out', 'When country cousins come up to town', and half a
dozen other delightful tunes. The play was one of the many
bright Gaiety shows, the music of which is still popular, that
we were taken to see by dear old W.Y.B., and were followed
by champagne suppers at Gow's, Gatti's or Romano's, then
the best restaurants in the Strand.

The White City exhibition had been preceded a few years
earlier by one in the old gardens at Earls Court before they
were built over; but it was not to be compared with its
successor, and was memorable only for two features. It had
a great ramp down which passengers careered in flat-
bottomed boats to a water-splash, and it was there that I,
and innumerable other people, saw for the first time, wildly
flickering on a little screen, a motion picture – the forerunner
of the vast cinema industry. A few years later it had been
developed to a point at which the luxurious Cinema House
was opened in Oxford Street. Also in Oxford Street was a
show that consisted only of a double row of seats arranged
like those in a long bus, and the travelogues, which were the
only films shown, gave one the impression of being in the cab
of a train speeding through strange country.

There were also annual exhibitions, such as that of the

bakers at the Agricultural Hall, Islington, from which my
mother and I always returned laden with samples; and
Olympia with its Naval and Military Tournament and
Buffalo Bill's Wild West Show. In the latter, real Red
Indians, shooting off guns and giving blood-curdling war-
whoops, attacked a stage-coach, or a frontiersman's cabin,
and were driven off only just in time by Colonel 'Bill' Cody
and his cowboys.

In that pre-cinema age such spectacles were the most
popular form of entertainment. Among the most outstanding
were two plays, *The Hope*, and *The Whip*, at Drury Lane, in
the last act of which the revolving stage became a race course
with jockeys galloping real horses on it. At the Hippodrome
there were shows in which the whole of the stalls and pit were
turned into a tank-like arena, into which thousands of gallons
of water cascaded down from a rocky waterfall built high on
the stage, sweeping men, women and boats along with it.
Pageants were also most popular and held all over the
country. One year the pageant of London was put on in the
grounds of the Crystal Palace, with vast crowds of players
and several different episodes for every day of the week.
One of the last of these great spectacles was *The Miracle* at
Olympia, in which the breathtakingly beautiful Lady Diana
Manners played the part of the Madonna.

At Olympia, too, there was the Christmas Fun Fair. It was
run by the husband of one of my mother's greatest friends,
a Mr. Rose; so we received 'most favoured nation' treatment.
First a slap-up lunch, then, a striking figure in his frock coat
and glossy topper, he used to take us round himself. What a
day out it was for me; as many rides as I liked on every form
of whirligig, free entry to every side-show that took my fancy,
and after unlimited cream cakes for tea a huge box of choco-
lates to take home.

Sad to say, this gay and generous 'courtesy' uncle died
while still in his prime. He was told that he had a heart condition which necessitated his giving up all the things he enjoyed and leading a very quiet life. Having put his affairs in
order he went down to the Metropole Hotel, at Brighton,
gathered his friends together and gave a practically non-stop
party, dining, dancing and knocking back bumpers of cham-

pagne, till at the end of the week he was carried off by the expected heart attack. My father thought it most reprehensible, but I thought he had shown sound sense and that it was a fine way to die.

It was the Christmas holidays that I enjoyed best, for in addition to the fun of helping to decorate the house with holly, mistletoe and paper chains, and the presents, and hoping to get one of the golden half-sovereigns from the Christmas pudding, it meant a succession of jolly parties which, now that I was in my teens and had passed out of the phase of watching conjurors or progressive games, were young people's dances.

To learn dancing I had been sent to a Miss Trail who, in those days when many wealthy families lived in South London, ran a highly exclusive academy. Her star pupil in my time, and a good friend of mine, was Ruby Miller, who afterwards became a famous musical comedy star. She was a very pretty and vivacious red-head, and years later I met her again at a party given by a friend of mine at the Berkeley, who had had the amusing idea that, without telling the girls, all his male guests should bring red-heads as their partners.

I fear I did no special credit to Miss Trail, but she taught me the secret of fast waltzing, which is to get the knee of the right leg well up under the knee of the left – and vice versa when reversing – with each turn. She also taught me to polka, barn-dance, one-step and two-step. The two former were still danced but on their way out, while the new American ragtime, which had just begun to come over, was making the latter two increasingly popular.

In addition to private dances, there were regular subscription dances at the St. Leonard's and Madeira Halls in Streatham, and I often went to these, generally with Hilda Gosling as my partner. The most popular tunes we danced to were from *The Chocolate Soldier, The Girl in the Taxi, The Quaker Girl, Gipsy Love, The Merry Widow, The Count of Luxembourg*; and the new hits from America, 'The Bunny Hug', 'Everybody's Doing It', 'Waiting for the Robert E. Lee', and 'Alexander's Ragtime Band'.

From the foregoing account the reader will now have gathered a fair idea of my activities during the holidays while

I was in the chrysalis stage – no longer a little boy but by no means yet a man – but for all this time two-thirds of each year was spent by me on board the *Worcester*; so I must now catch up on that other aspect of my youth which, unlike my year at Dulwich, did much to make me the man that I later became.

II

'IT TAKES ALL SORTS....'

AMONG the papers that I began to hoard in my teens I find a notebook. It contains the names of many of my contemporaries in the *Worcester* with from one to six hundred words about each. In most cases only their ages, physical and mental characteristics, nicknames and peculiarities are recorded, but in some, episodes have been set down which bring out my own character at that time and my reactions to various types of boy; so I feel a few of these justify another major digression.

Unfortunately none of my best friends receive even a mention – presumably because I knew them so well that I did not think I would ever need an aide-mémoire to recall them; but this chapter would be incomplete if I left them out altogether and failed to give some account of our activities.

My closest friend was J. H. Beardsworth, a smallish, clever, amusing lad with finely cut features, whose father was the vicar of Harbury, near Leamington Spa. Next came Harry Ayres, a red-headed boy who lived with his aunt, Ruby M. Ayres, the celebrated writer of romantic fiction. One holiday I went over to spend the day with them at Watford, so met this lady who numbered her readers in millions, little thinking that half a century later the sales of books that I was to write myself would far outnumber hers. The third was Harry Robson, another red-headed youth of rather heavy build who was frequently afflicted with a rash of pimples.

With my mind dominated by Alexandre Dumas I welded this little fraternity into a juvenile 'Three Musketeers' pledged to their motto 'All for One and One for All', reserving, of course, the part of d'Artagnan for myself.

In the *Worcester* a fanatic participation in ball-games was not insisted upon; so although at times we played soccer and cricket, those of us who were not particularly keen were not often pressed into elevens. Instead, on Wednesday and Saturday afternoons, having accompanied the others ashore and past Ingress Abbey – an old Jacobean mansion which, now that the ship is no more, is the present H.M.S. *Worcester* – to the playing fields, we were left free to ramble about the dykes and marshes in their vicinity. In secluded spots we held secret conclaves – about what I cannot think – but I recall that we decked ourselves out in scarlet orders fringed with silver braid, had secret signs of recognition, and wrote down our deliberations in invisible ink.

We also owned a variety of lethal weapons, including obsolete French bayonets as long as short swords. These we had bought from Messrs. Gamages, who in those days issued to all schools a wonderful cloth-bound illustrated catalogue several hundred pages thick, over many items in which we used to gloat with longing. However, the bayonets were a mixed joy, as each term when we rejoined the ship we could get them aboard undetected only by concealing them down a trouser leg, which make walking far from easy.

Arms had a special fascination for me, and a readily accepted excuse for not playing games was to join the Rifle Club, which I did with alacrity, becoming for the fantastically low subscription of seven new pence a term quite a passable shot. In 1912, too, I bought my first sword cane, a thin, square Japanese blade ending in a deadly point, and sheathed in a crook-handled cherrywood stock. I have the bill for it still and it cost only 50 new pence. Later I acquired a beautiful Wilkinson blade in a fine silver-mounted Malacca, and that I always took abroad, finding it quite a comfort to carry whenever I ventured into dubious night haunts. My last I bought as late as the Second World War when, owing to the black-out, robbery with violence at night in the West End became quite a common occurrence. It was in the form of a swagger-stick but, instead of being covered with brown leather, I had it covered in pale blue to match my R.A.F. uniform. I also gave a duplicate of it – with a loop at the end so that it could be carried over the wrist – to my beautiful young step-daughter, Diana, who often had to come home on her own after working late at night in the offices of the

F

Secret Operations Executive. These innocent looking swag-ger-sticks contained slender poignards only about ten inches long, but one swift jab with such a weapon, aimed upwards to pierce beneath the chin, would promptly have settled any man's business.

I had been taught the rudiments of boxing at Skelsmergh and continued to box a little while in the *Worcester*; but I was never a great enthusiast, doubtless because I am a physical coward and saw no point in exposing my face to possible injury simply for fun. Moreover, I was never a very strong boy and below the average height for my age – when fully grown I stopped at five feet eight and a half. It was this that led to my buying a book on ju-jitsu and, although we never became very proficient, my friends and I spent quite a lot of our time during our secret meetings on shore practising the holds illustrated.

Another of our occupations on half-holidays, during the autumn term, was searching for mushrooms, as, if one could take a dirty handkerchief full of them to the Captain's galley, one was rewarded with a good slice of cake.

Two other friends of mine are worth recalling owing to the excitement we derived from following romances in their families. One, 'Squeaker' Stephens, was the nephew of Mr. Harry Pélissier, whose name was then a household word owing to the great popularity of his pierrot troupe, Pélissier's *Follies*, which every year did a long West End season. He was thirty-eight and, having fallen in love with the youngest of his pierrettes, a girl of only sixteen, wished to marry her. As she was the beautiful and talented Fay Compton, who later became famous as a star, his passion for her was not surprising; but there was much opposition to the match on account of the disparity in their ages. In those days for a man of his age to marry a young girl was thought by many people to be indecent. Her parents refused their consent, and his friends feared that if he went through with it he might lose much of his popularity with the public. But they had the courage to defy opinion and, I believe, the marriage was a happy one.

The other case was that of my friend Dewsbury's sister, and the objection to the match precisely similar, for she was only nineteen, while her lover, although a well-off, jolly and most amusing man, was fat, bald and over forty. His name was Silas Boreham, he was an estate agent and, it so happened, a friend of my father's, who travelled up with him in the train every morning to Victoria. As the girl made her young brother her confidant, pouring out her hopes and fears to him in a series of frequent letters, we all followed their romance with intense interest. Miss Dewsbury's father threatened to horse-whip Boreham if he saw him in the neighbourhood of the house again, but clandestinely he managed to keep in touch with her and plan an elopement. One night he got a garden ladder up to her bedroom window and carried her off. In this case, as I later went with my parents on several occasions to visit them, I can say definitely that the marriage proved a very happy one.

Now for the pen-portraits in my notebook. I wrote them immediately after leaving, so they refer to contemporaries of mine who were then senior cadets but, of course, most of them had been my companions for two or more years and come up the ship with me. These notes may amuse the erudite but prove an encouragement to young people with literary ambitions who as yet still find difficulty in expressing themselves correctly, as they show my own fantastic lack of punctuation and even the lack of capitals after full-stops, when writing at the age of sixteen. The explanations in brackets have been added by me now.

'R. C. Paget upper twelve known as Boiley Bottom from suffering from that complaint, he was about 5 ft 6 17 years old what you would call greasy I suppose this was on account of his being very fat and round and generally perspiring he had rather bulgey brown eyes not much hair, he played the piano a little and sang rather good comic songs. I always thought Paget a good PO who knew his job until a wet half-holiday we were ordered out for boat pulling then it was my misfortune to get into the B barge with a crowd of kids the only big chaps besides myself there being Taylor, Paget tak-ing the helm and Squeaker Stevens with a game leg sitting in the stern as a passenger, there was a very strong up tide and up wind we went up stream easy enough for about three quarters of an hour then I said to Paget arnt you going to turn back now, he gave oars (the order to stop rowing) but he thought because the whalers much lighter boats had gone further and could get back easier we had to also in the huge B barge which it was very hard to pull against the stream, he let the thing drift and drift till we were about three miles up the river, then I took the law into my own hands calling him a damned fool with no more sense than a new-shit and gave the order Back Starboard up Port and turned the boat round but it had already drifted so far it was the devil of a job in mid-stream, tide and wind against us Taylor and I being the only big chaps who could pull in the whole crew the other ten being all new chaps who could not pull or small chaps who had no weight. Squeaker took the tiller and got her as near in shore as he could without danger then we pulled like blazes it was four solid hours pull back. I was just about dead when we did get there it was simply awful you dared not leave off or you drifted back and you couldn't swop oars as there was no one to take your place, the sweat rolled off me although the rain was coming down full tilt and it was a cold March day we were all stripped naked to our waists, after that I always considered Paget a fool who did not know his work.'

'E. F. Avery better known as Ivery from Sarthend the appelation he earned as a new cadet upon being asked his name and where he lived. he also derived great fame on his first day as when meeting another boy at a small junction where they were changing trains and finding the other was also a new cadet he said Be moi pal, the other gentleman cadet apparently not liking this mode of address declined the offer and when he had been some weeks aboard revealed the incident. I had little or no acquaintance with him as I was always above his term and set, he was about 5 ft 6 dark hair and little side whiskers like a butcher or a grocer by his ears he had black piercing eyes. He was very much disliked and curried favour with everyone. Mr. May, the Chief Officer once told me that he would believe Avery before any boy in the ship, Beatty praised him for his work in school, but although he flattered the Skipper and Beatty by his questions he did

not disdain in the same hour to sit talking with the lowest
galley-fug [male scullery hand] when you come to think of
it everyone has something to give the Skipper PO ships and
the galley hand toast pickles and suchlike. for these reasons
he was bullied so started boxing and used to with Squeaker
in the tier (lowest deck) I used to sometimes when I went
down for a round with Squeaker, he improved greatly and
he sparred pretty equally with me but he had that nervous
shakey way of going to work if I had liked I could of killed
him at leasure in a fight. Squeaker often remarked to me,
he's not a bad chap Dennis old man and if he does suck up
it is only his nature you know, so I was never rotten to him
and used to let him in his cringing way call me Old Dennis,
sometimes he came to me for advice which I gave him in that
cold direct way never spareing him the truth, he was never
a chap whom I counted among my friends, he was about 16½.'

'Robert Goldreich in the upper twelve better known as
Jew Boy, physically typical of that race. Robert was quite a
wit and used to keep us all amused he always used to call me
Mr. Wheatley sir and everyone was Mr. to him he was
always extremely polite to anyone who was anyone always
used long words and could argue a cube round, he was a
great stamp collector but would do you when swapping if
he possibly could, once he was swapping with Robson and
he accidentally swept some stamps off the desk onto the deck
then carefully put his foot on some he wanted then picked
up the rest and calmly apologised as the clumsiest devil un-
hung – he always demeaned himself – Robson however saw
the dodge and he said Oh Goldreich I think one blew under
your foot and removed the object and discovered three nice
stamps below it. Goldreich however was not the least dismayed said Oh Mr. Robson sir how can I ever express how
sorry I am that the clodhoping supporters of this unfortunate
body should have dirtied these most beautiful and interesting specimens of yours, however I wouldn't have you loose
by my clumsiness I will give you a shilling for these three
although I have somewhat spoilt the faces I thank you Mr.
Robson sir. the latter gentleman however seeing that the
specimens were not spoilt as Goldreich had taken care not

to put his foot heavily upon them and the fact of the three
being worth about 1/9 he declined the offer with due thanks.
another time Jew Boy went ashore in charge of a boat – he
was PO of Fosc'l Port – and he took a visitor ashore who
tipped him 10/– for the crew, instead of giving the rest 2/–
each our friend said wait here I will go and get some scorf
with it and later returned with bags of biscuits cakes chocolate ect which he carefully divided among the crew, now he
said that he had spent the 10/– but we afterwards found that
he had spent only 5/– and pocketed the other 5/– not bad eh
6/– out of 10/– the crew were only new youths and did not
dare to question a PO it only came out because although Jew
Boy took the boat in it should have been Robson's boat as
he was on duty but could not be found so when the boat came
back Robson demanded at least one sixth of the cash, jew boy
however palmed him off with scorf but I being hungry held
that he should have had more and so by an investigation the
thing came to light, Goldreich and I however were always
good pals enough until towards the end of my last term
when the Jew made some overtures of friendship to Dieseldorff (my jam) and left with a flea in his ear, then to be
revenged he wrote a lot of most insulting poetry about
Dieseldorff and me and showed it to my friends, my friends
told me and said they had laughed because Goldreich was
rather held in awe, he was about 5 ft 7 with the strength of
an ox and boxed well, however I who am angry only on very
rare occasions was very wroth and after much deliberation
with my friends who would have persuaded me from it I
went to the brawny jew and demanded an explanation
challenging him to fight me in the tier (lowest deck) for the
insults he had done my friend and me, feeling that having
learned to fight well I could at least give as good as I got.
however after an hours talk in which I continually held to
my point and he first told me to run and play as I bored him
then scorned me as a fool then laughed at me for challenging
him then threatened at last he climbed down and said in his
usual humble language that he made me his promise not to
molest or bully Dieseldorff after I had left the ship but
claimed the right to make verses about who he liked, the
wily jew came out of it with his honour unscarred but so did

I and without having to fight and needless to say he gave me no further trouble. he was 18.'

'V. A. Ramage this was a fairly small chap about 5 ft 6 dark oily hair black eyes rather a Brickey [common] he was nicknamed Schooner Bows because he had a nose that obstinately refused to point anywhere than to the sky, he was as mean as you can make 'em and would make a pot of paste last a fortnight, he never joined in any scorfs but was a friend of the Skipper's hence in his fifth term he was made Carpenter's mate and a badge boy which he never deserved at all but his people knew the Skipper and that was everything. one Saturday afternoon Hobson [a friend of mine who had left the previous term] came down and seeing Ramage I pointed him out and said What do you think of our new carpenter's mate, perhaps my tone was a little scornfull but one cant help that with such a creature. Hobson said What that thing, is the old man mad or what. I laughed and walked on then to my surprise I heard a voice mocking mine behind me say. Oh don't you know I'm Dennis Wheatley. I am the Gun hand what [I cleaned the brass on our 4.7 which was regarded as a privileged chore] I ought to be a PO only I'm not, the old mans mad or I should be, then a roar of laughter from Ramages two cronies Hunt and Cunningham, the former a dirty fat little sod and said to be the son of a barmaid and the latter a dark sly little knave fit companions for their master. I went up to Ramage bowed smiled and said I should have much pleasure in giving the Honourable gentleman a walk in the tier when I got back on board [my conduct was, of course, straight out of Dumas]. When I got back on board I did not deign to fight him he was smaller than I and it would have sullied my reputation to have smashed him up, so I walked up to him took him by the back of the neck and shook him as a terrier shakes a rat boxing his ears at the same time with my other hand, then throwing him on the deck I told him I hoped that would teach him manners in future and that if he had been favoured by the old man that was no reason why he should cheek his superiors. I let him off lightly as after the affair Hobson and I had gone to the tuck shop also Beardsworth had proved a

generous host, as he always was for that matter, and I felt
good tempered.'

'A. G. Everest about 5 ft 6 dark curly hair and dark eyes
rather projecting teeth from which he was known as Sabre-
tooth, a clever chap and very fine athlete won eight prizes in
the last sports, he was hated by Squeaker Stephens who was
constantly drawing caricatures of him as a walrus. he was
PO Afterguard Port only a fifth termer but extremely good.
he never did me any harm until one day after Scrub-decks
when I had done the Gun but they were still scrubbing the
upper deck I came down and started to shave [this would
have been on a Saturday and by then I should have been
shaving about once a week]. He happened to be on watch on
the lower deck to keep chaps from coming down and skulking,
and he walked up and said Now then Wheatley get back on
deck up you go now, with all the dignity of his new PO ship.
I nearly had a fit and asked him what he ment, he said I had
better clear out or else he would give me a licking in the
POs cabin. I asked in biteing sarcasm whether he did not
know only having been in the ship five terms that it was a
Focs'lmans priviledge to come down below when he liked.
He said he didn't care a damn about Focs'lmen then I burst
out you damned miserable little worm blown up with pom-
posity do you know that I have been here twice as long as you
do you know I am your senior in school your senior in sec-
tions [practical seamanship] the senior Badge Cadet of the
ship with a POs priviledges and you tell me to clear out, do
you know that I had the pleasure of beating you up the matt
and was already a Badge Boy when you came here as a
Newshit and that all your senior POs treat me as an equal
and a friend, another word from you you pompous little beast
and I'll chuck you down the hatch. Then the silly fool
seemed to realise that although he was a PO I really was his
senior and said 'Oh I'm sorry' and went off. I of course told
all the other POs and he got well paid out for meddling with
me by their witicisms at his expense.'

Re-reading these notes gives me quite a different view of
myself when in the *Worcester* to that which over many years

I had come to hold. They make it clear that the majority of the senior boys in the ship were much bigger than myself and considerably older – in some cases as much as two years, which is a lot in one's teens. It is just possible that this may account for my never having been made a P.O., in spite of my having been longer in the ship than any other boy and become one of the upper twelve. But the fact that I took no interest in games must have counted against me, and I still have a deep-rooted feeling that, although no one could actually pin anything on to me, I was regarded by the Captain and Instructors with vague suspicion or, anyhow, as not the clean-limbed wide-eyed master's joy who can be counted on to set a good example to the younger boys.

That I was a snob is obvious, but what schoolboy is not? And although all the boys who came to the *Worcester* were supposed to be 'sons of gentlemen' – and a considerable number were – that had to be taken as an extremely elastic term to fill the bill. It was, in fact, a pretty savage jungle in which a boy could not hope for a very happy time unless he was able to keep his end up in one way or another. After the first year the increased prestige automatically attached to every additional term contributed a lot to that, but it is evident that one had always to be ready to back one's claim to immunity from aggression by either a sharp tongue or one's fists.

That I, with my dread of being hurt, should have been so bellicose now surprises me. As far as my challenge to the amusing but dangerous Jew is concerned, I am fully convinced that I should never have made it had I not feared that I should lose face with my friends if I failed to do so. And face is everything. Evidently, although not feared by the older and stronger boys, I had built up a position for myself that no one cared lightly to challenge and, although I make no claim to have been particularly popular, I was fortunate in having acquired a lot of goodwill and many friends.

I had to fight all out only once. My opponent was a boy named Mack. He was the son of the captain of a merchant-man and came from Glasgow, so his background was one of neither opulence nor culture. His head was as round as a cannon ball, he wore his hair close-cropped like a convict and he had the small dark eyes of a mischievous monkey. He was about my size but much stronger and filled with diabolic energy. Not a moment of his time was given to reading, stamp collecting or any other quiet pursuit; he delighted only in violent horseplay. His favourite pastime was to creep up behind someone who was reading, snatch his book or magazine and make off with it which meant chasing him half round the ship to get it back. He had other tricks all calculated to ruin one's leisure and I was one of the people this horrid little tough singled out to torment.

For a time I put up with it because I was much too frightened of him to do anything else; but one day the murderous hatred that his persecution had aroused in me got the better of my caution and when, as usual, he taunted me with being too much of a coward to fight him, I took up his challenge.

With a number of other boys who had been spectators of the scene we went down to the tier deck. I felt certain that I had let myself in for a nasty licking and could only hope that I might get in a lucky blow or two before he knocked me down. Instinctively, instead of attacking him, I stood warily on guard waiting for his opening move.

When it came it was most unorthodox. Lowering his bullet head to the level of my stomach he charged me, wildly flailing his clenched fists. I was too full of cold rage to panic at this onslaught. Instead I side-stepped and dealt him a smashing uppercut in the face. He staggered back but with hardly a second's pause came at me again. Again I got home with an uppercut. His stupidity was only equalled by his endurance. For the best part of ten minutes he hurled himself at me time after time, and every time he did so I smashed my fist up into his face. One of the instructors then happened to come on the scene and stopped the fight. Both Mack's eyes were blacked, his button nose streaming with blood, his lips swollen and cut; except for the skin off my knuckles I was untouched. There could be no question about who was the victor and the news ran round the ship like wildfire.

The fight occurred early in my second year, and was for me an extraordinarily lucky break. Quite undeservedly it earned me a lasting reputation as a very dangerous antagonist and for the remainder of my time in the *Worcester* I never had to fight again.

12

HIGH JINKS, THE CAT
BURGLAR AND GREEK LOVE

THE summer term of 1911 was particularly memorable
because during it there took place the coronation of King
George V.

In order that we might see it with our families we were all
given special leave. One of my father's business friends was
Lord Rothschild's steward, a Mr. Shephard, and he had been
given permission to invite a number of guests to the Rothschild
mansion, 148 Piccadilly (demolished in 1960), which looked
out on Hyde Park Corner. My father, mother and I were
given seats in a stand that had been erected over the short
semi-circular drive-way in front of the house and there can
have been few better places in London to watch the procession, as it came down the slope of Piccadilly, passed within
a few yards of us, made a U-bend round the great triangle
on to which our stand faced, then passed under the great
arch and along Constitution Hill on its way back to Buckingham Palace.

We had been fortunate in receiving a similar invitation at
the time of King Edward's funeral, and from the Rothschild
stand I had seen most of the Crowned Heads of Europe,
including those of the German states and the minor princi-
palities – there were then well over a score of them – and it
was intriguing to see in the flesh such men as Kaiser Wilhelm,
Alfonso of Spain, and others who then controlled the destiny
of millions, as they walked in a somewhat uneven group behind the flag-draped coffin and the groom who led the late
King's charger. But for all its solemn pageantry the procession did not compare for splendour with that of the coronation, and I doubt if any such magnificent spectacle has taken
place since.

In the great open space in front of our stand there was

drawn up a mounted battery of Royal Horse Artillery resplendent in their Hussar-like uniforms of blue, yellow and gold, and grouped round the Duke of Wellington's statue one of the bands of the Brigade of Guards in black, gold and scarlet, which entertained us with gay music.

The procession itself was seemingly endless, for it was the heyday of the Empire and contingents of fighting men had been sent from every corner of the globe, thus providing an immense variety of brilliant costumes.

Most splendid of all, following the Royal Coach, on horseback or in other gilded coaches and state landaus came the innumerable foreign royalties. It is against protocol for Crowned Heads to appear in the train of an uncrowned King, but they had sent their heirs apparent to represent them, and in those days each German state still had its own royal family; so after the mile-long march past of Mounties, Bengal Lancers, Maori warriors, befeathered Redskins and Zulu impi, there came another half mile of Princes, Princesses and grand dukes interspersed with Indian rajahs, Arabian sheiks, African potentates and Asiatic dignitaries.

In one open landau there was a lovely little golden-haired German princess of about my own age. I caught her eye and waved to her. Perhaps her fancy was caught by my uniform. If my day had needed making, she would have made it, for she waved back and blew me a kiss. I often recalled her gesture with delight long after I had returned to the daily grind in the ship.

Old examination papers and their results show my educational progress there. Each spring term we were given a General Knowledge paper; it was the same for everyone irrespective of form and the maximum marks for it 250. In 1911 I got 50, in 1912, 96, and in 1913 (my last term) 122, which can hardly be said to be spectacular.

I find, too, that at the end of the autumn term, 1911, I was, scholastically, exactly halfway up the ship, as I was in the Third Nautical, but bottom boy. Doubtless that fact did much to overcloud the earlier part of my Christmas holidays, for I must have watched every post with dread until my report turned up. My reports, alas, were never more than barely passable, so to face my father when one came to hand was always an ordeal, and being bottom of my form could not have been easy to laugh off.

However, I had the big consolation that on returning to the *Worcester* in January, 1912, I became a sixth termer, so had graduated to all the privileges, including being entitled to fag the first year boys. By then, too, I had a group of old friends and we had agreed to meet at London Bridge to go down on an early train. Our object in rejoining ship an hour or two before we had to was due to an idea of mine inspired by my life-long urge to secure a maximum of comfort. New hammock mattresses were provided only for the new boys – approximately fifteen per cent per term – and after two or more years' use the stuffing in these mattresses became hard and lumpy. By arriving before the new boys we were able to make off with their new mattresses, replacing them with our worn and knobbly ones. Henceforth we continued this admirable aid to sound sleep at the beginning of every term.

The summer of 1912, my last in the ship, was again memorable as during it there occurred the jubilee of H.M.S. *Worcester*.

As a jubilee treat we were taken to London in a body to see the Naval and Military Tournament and, among other celebrations, Admiral Count Togo paid an official visit to the ship.

It was only some forty years earlier that an 'enlightened' Mikado had resolved to westernise Japan. Having decided that Britain had the best navy in the world and Germany the best army, he had selected a number of promising boys from the families of the nobility and sent them to be trained as sailors by us or as soldiers by the Germans. These little Japs worked hard, spurred on, it was said, by the knowledge that the Son of Heaven had decreed that should any of them fail to pass well up in their exams, on their return to Japan their heads were to be cut off.

The results of this policy became apparent in the almost clockwork victories of the Japanese over the Russians on both land and sea in the 1904–05 war. Togo had been trained in the *Worcester* and we had good reason to be proud of him, since he was, and I think still is, the only admiral who ever sank or compelled to surrender an entire fleet of steam-powered, steel-armoured warships.

At the time of the Russo-Japanese war I had been just old enough to understand some of the intriguing diagrams of ships, mines, guns, forts and trench systems that appeared in the *Illustrated London News* and to talk about them. The British people were strongly pro-Japanese, and sentimental ditties such as 'Only a little Jappie soldier' were very popular. But, even at that tender age, I could never be persuaded that we were right to back an Asiatic race against a European one. Even so, that did not prevent my joining heartily a few years later in the rousing welcome we gave Admiral Count Togo.

The summer term also meant Sports Day, Boat Race Day and, on our breaking up, our annual prize-giving. Running and jumping held for me no more interest than ball-games, and although I was a passable 'oar' I was nowhere near hefty enough to be selected for any of the senior crews. However, my light weight coupled with my long experience got me a place as cox, and as a cox I was pretty good. To bring a heavy whaler moving on a fast tide sharply round so that she comes smoothly to rest alongside a landing-stage needs considerable skill, and I never failed to get a kick out of doing it.

The fact that our school was a ship enabled Prize Day in the *Worcester* to be made a more colourful gala than was the case at ordinary public schools. A big paddle steamer of the *Margate Belle* type was hired for the occasion and the committee and the boys' parents and friends went aboard her at London Bridge at about ten o'clock in the morning. On their way down river they were given lunch then, soon after the steamer was sighted from the *Worcester*, the order was piped 'Man Ship'.

This drill consisted of some eighty to a hundred cadets swarming up the rigging of the three masts and distributing themselves along their yards. We actually stood on the yards, about five feet apart and with our hands just touching those of our neighbours. Our only support was a thin wire which ran behind us at hand level, temporarily attached to the outer yard stay and the mast. It could not be leant upon but was just enough to enable us to keep our balance. We were dressed in our mess-kit, so on a sunny day these lofty ranks of white waistcoats and cap covers, gilt buttons and badges, together with flags and pennants fluttering from stem to stern of the old wooden-walled battleship made a brave show.

On my last Prize Day I had the dubious privilege of being one of the two cadets picked to take the outermost station on the main-top-gallant yard – the highest in the ship. It must have been nearly a hundred feet above the deck, and the fact that safety nets were spread about twelve feet up to catch us if we fell did not greatly lessen the ordeal. For as long as I can remember I have had a fear of heights, and nothing would now induce me to go nearer than a yard to any sheer drop unprotected by a parapet; so how I got through this performance I cannot imagine. I suppose the feel of the thin wire gave me a degree of confidence and, for the rest, I was compelled to it by the Dumas-induced determination never to lose face.

After about ten minutes the steamer drew alongside; we were then allowed to clamber down to greet our visitors, and duly formed up on the upper deck for the prize-giving. In the matter of prizes *Worcester* boys were more fortunate than most as, in addition to the normal number of form prizes, there were others for seamanship and many special prizes given by donors interested in the ship. H.M. the King gave a gold medal for the year's best all-round cadet. Other prizes were given by the Elder Brethren of Trinity House, the Royal Geographical Society, the Royal Meteorological Society, the numerous shipping companies who drew most of their officers from the *Worcester*, and many private people of eminence in the shipping world. Many of them were valuable sextants, telescopes and other nautical instruments.

The prize for English Composition was given by the Chairman of the Honorary Committee, the Earl Brassy, and I recall him seated on the dais as a little round-faced old man. Such was the gulf before the First World War between the aristocracy and the class from which we *Worcester* boys came that I would never have believed it had the archangel Gabriel himself then whispered in my ear that one of his grand-daughters was one day to become my step-daughter – still less that one of my step-sons was to marry a Princess.

The back-scratching speeches and prize-giving over, we cadets went down to change into shore clothes while our parents made the round of the ship. We then accompanied them on board the steamer for a gala tea while she carried us up the Thames to London Bridge and our eight weeks' summer holiday.

The only prize I ever won was for scripture. This must not be taken as an indication that I had got over my antipathy to organised religion brought about by the long sermons of my Margate days. Far from it; rather than surrender some of my precious leisure to preparation for confirmation I succeeded in wriggling out of it, and I have never been confirmed.

My success in scripture was due solely to a method I had devised for counteracting the results of my lack of attention in class during most of the term and ensuring myself a place fairly well up in the form when it came to taking end of term exams.

At maths, of which a great part of our studies to become proficient navigators consisted, I was never more than fair, and maths papers were always hazardous. The brightest pupils could make slips in a few involved calculations and so come out in an exam much lower than they deserved. But other subjects were free from such unlucky pitfalls – particularly scripture, history and geography.

My practice was to get the night-watchman to call me at five o'clock in the morning during the fortnight preceding the exams, I then went up to the main deck and, swathed in rugs, read over again and again until I knew them by heart, the Gospel, period in history and geographical data we had been given to learn that term. The result was invariably very high marks in all three subjects, which brought up my average to a respectable place when the marks of all the exams were lumped together for place in form.

In front of me now I have the examination papers for the end of my last term and they make me wonder just how much we really get out of advanced education. There is hardly a question in them that I could answer today, although I was then in a fair way to mastering the mysteries of such subjects as magnetism, spherical trigonometry and theory of navigation. For me now even the algebra paper might just as well be written in Sanskrit and, perhaps strangest of all, most of the English paper foxes me completely. I note question 3 of it, which reads:

What do you know of the following characters: Will Wimble, Sir Andrew Freeport, Will Honeycombe, Dick Minem?

I have not the faintest idea who any of these people were, and could not care less. Yet, remarkable to relate, I came second in this examination.

In the First Nautical that term there were twenty-five boys. Unfortunately for me so much time had to be given to mathematical subjects that we no longer took history, but my old pal scripture got me a second place and I was top of the ship for chart drawing – a thing I have always loved and since found invaluable for making maps and plans. Dictation pulled me down as I am a congenitally bad speller and usually, if a mark was knocked off for each mistake I got a nought. But in the combined results from all subjects I came tenth out of twenty-five.

On leaving I received a First Class Certificate, both scholastic and for seamanship, which meant, in theory, that I was capable of passing the Master Mariner's Examination, and, in practice, that if I chose to go to sea I could sit for my Second Officer's 'ticket' after serving only three years as an apprentice, instead of four.

Now, as it has emerged from these old papers that I was at least a year younger than the majority of my classmates, I am inclined to think that I must have been quite a bit brighter than I have for long supposed. In fact it seems that had I really concentrated on my work I might even have carried off a number of prizes, and so achieved better relations with my anxious papa; but that, for many years, was not to be.

My frequent lapses into inattention during classes were due to day-dreaming about exciting stories that I was reading. In addition to devouring every Dumas that I could get hold of, I read most of Stanley Weyman, Baroness Orczy, Rider Haggard, William le Queux, E. Phillips Oppenheim and Conan Doyle; but, although the *Worcester* had quite a good library of fiction, we were allowed to change our books only once a week, so a great part of our reading consisted of short stories in magazines. In those pre-cinema days there was a great field for such magazines; *The Strand, The Red, The Royal, The Windsor, The Story Teller, Pearson's* and many more all flourished, and we used to swap copies round until they were in tatters.

The fiction library, as distinct from the reference library, consisted of some shelves of books in the Captain's office and at the same time as we changed them we drew from him our pocket-money. Apart from this weekly occasion we rarely came into contact with the 'old man' and, even then, we were far too scared of him to linger in his presence longer than was absolutely necessary.

It was this that made our day each term as Mate of the Deck a mixed joy. In effect, this was to serve as Officer of the Watch, and the duty was taken in turn by all cadets in the Nautical classes. At seven-forty-five, dressed in his best shore-going clothes, the Mate took up his position on the quarter-deck, telescope under arm. He was free from all lessons and fatigues, and had only to keep an eye on signals from the shore for a boat, receive visitors, and strike the hours on the ship's bell. Also he ate his meals alone and enjoyed special food.

But there was a snag to it. At nine o'clock the 'old man' arrived on deck. Beneath his critical eye the Mate had to read the thermometer and barometer, judge the force and direction of the wind, assess the amount of cloud in the sky and give its technical description, etc.; then enter all these items in the Log. Few ever succeeded in getting more than a grunt of approval out of him and for a fractional error he was likely to tear the unfortunate Mate's head off.

In the evening the Mate dined with him and his French wife in private. That was another ordeal for, although I never knew him at such times to be anything but courteous, and his wife was a kindly woman, he was far from forthcoming and he ordinarily inspired such fear in us that we were terrified of saying something silly or making some social gaffe.

Over twenty years later, after I had spoken as a guest of honour at a Foyle Literary Lunch and was making my way through the crowd to leave, a little old bearded man came up to me. For a moment, as he was in civilian clothes, I did not recognise him; but it was Captain Wilson-Barker. In an almost apologetic tone he recalled himself to me and congratulated me on my success. We talked for some time and I found him gentle, intelligent and charming. What a minor tragedy it was that, unlike our headmaster Mr. Beatty whom we loved, such a naturally pleasant person as the 'old man' proved to be, should, while our Captain, have earned our dislike by showing himself only as a harsh disciplinarian.

I have mentioned that once a week we drew our pocket-money from him. Each of us had a pay book in which was entered the sum deposited by our parents at the beginning of the term and the amount of our withdrawals each week. I see from my last term's pay book my father had sent twelve shillings – evidently on the basis of one shilling per week – but by the seventh week I had drawn the lot; so clearly I was still plagued by the same old devil of expenditure exceeding income.

In part at least that was due to sheer hunger. My parents started me off each term with a supply of tuck, but that was soon gone and I never remember them sending me a further ration; although at half-term I always received a big plum cake from old Aunt Betsy. Also, just before half-term I always wrote a letter to W.Y.B. and this never failed to bring back a reply from that generous man with a postal order for five shillings. He also always gave me five shillings to start the term with; and on the few occasions when my parents came down to see me my father was good for another 2/6d. But about 125 new pence in all, plus the initial tuck and half-term cake, can be said to be my total resources in cash and kind for a twelve week term.

On half-holidays when we went ashore, the wife of a baker just off the hard always had ready a big pan of hot sausages to be stuffed into slit crisp new rolls. As we never otherwise saw a sausage from term's end to term's end they were a temptation almost impossible to resist. Further along the village street there was a bearded grocer named Rawlings, who could be persuaded to let one have Bourbon biscuits, potted paste and sardines on tick, and would even let his bill stand over till the beginning of the next term – another pit-fall for the weak-minded. Worst menace to solvency of all, for half an hour each evening the ship's tuck shop opened to offer a fine selection of marzipan bars, Devona toffee, My Queens and other Clarnico specialities.

Perhaps I was abnormally greedy, or it may be that owing to the repugnance with which most of the food given us filled me, I was seriously undernourished. I only know that I suffered a perpetual craving for these delights.

To my shame I recall one aspect of this obsession. With me in the *Worcester* there was a boy named Geoffrey Hobson who lived on Tulse Hill and whose parents were friends of my parents. Later I had a brief affair with his very pretty sister; but Geoffrey was not a popular boy. He was nick-named 'flycatcher' because, poor chap, his adenoids never having been removed, always went about with his mouth wide open, and he had a most violent temper – inherited no doubt from his father who, he told me, had once chased him round the garden with a brick.

However, his father was in Sheffield steel, so well off, and Geoffrey was always well supplied with tuck – particularly an inexhaustible store of Petit Beurre biscuits. I never counted Geoffrey as an intimate friend yet, knowing that every morning during the break he would come down to his sea-chest to get himself some biscuits, I used deliberately to hang about in the vicinity. He knew why I was there and, with a contemptuous smile, would throw me one. I never had the courage to refuse it. More, how much it meant to me can be judged from the fact that I never gobbled it up, but nibbled the little points off one by one, then the corners, and so on, slowly to the last morsel.

Hunger, too, drove me to become a cat-burglar. Naturally, the masters fed much better than the cadets, and with some pluck plus considerable skill their supplies could be pillaged. Every afternoon a score of hampers containing bread were brought to the landing stage, then carried up to the various galleys. The majority held only white loaves for the cadets but in those for the masters there were also brown ones. By careful timing it was possible to pull one of the masters' baskets into the semi-darkness of the tier deck, swiftly undo the straps, snatch a brown loaf and thrust it into the ample bulge of one's jumper. Those stolen Hovis loaves tasted better to me then than *pâté de foie gras en croûte* does now.

But my more daring exploits were at night. The night-watchman made his rounds of the ship at set hours. I kept awake until midnight. When he had passed I knew that a quarter of an hour later he would be back in his cabin and that I would have a clear run of the ship until just before two o'clock. Getting out of my hammock I put on only a dressing-gown and socks, then set out on my foray.

Sometimes I invaded the masters' quarters, stealing stealthily down the passage past the cabins in which they were sleeping, I raided their galley for cake, eggs, bacon, fruit or left-over portions of pudding. At other times I did a tricky gymnast's act of climbing down through the skylight of the cadets' galley to get handfuls of currants, apples or, if nothing better offered, potatoes. The eggs, bacon and potatoes I took down to the furnace in the bowels of the ship and roasted on hot ashes.

It was a nerve-racking business, as to be caught would have meant expulsion, but I never took anything but a carefully calculated risk, learned to take warning from the slightest unusual sound, and to move in my stockinged feet up and down normally creaking ladders as silently as a ghost.

On these expeditions I never took a companion. Like the Secret Service characters in my books, Gregory Sallust and Roger Brook, I preferred to play the lone wolf, so that if I was caught it could only be through my own carelessness or ill-luck, not owing to the bungling of someone else. And I never was caught.

Although my father was not over-generous in the matter of pocket-money and much too busy to send me tuck, he took a very liberal view about my future. Instead of coercing me into accepting his own wishes, in the autumn of 1912 he offered me three choices. (1) I could, if I liked, make the sea my career. (2) I could see something of the world by serving a three-year apprenticeship at sea, then leave it to go into his business. (3) I could spend a year each in France, Germany and Portugal learning how wine was made, then join him in South Audley Street.

I did not hesitate for one moment. In those days after many years at sea few captains in the Mercantile Marine could hope to earn a salary of more than £600 per annum; most of their lives were spent away from home and, during foul weather, often in great discomfort. On the other hand, a West End wine-merchant could expect to make a much higher income in incomparably more pleasant circumstances. And if one was going to be a wine-merchant it would have been the height of folly to spend three years roughing it as an apprentice at sea while one might have been learning one's trade.

My choice, of course, coincided with my father's hopes and he lost no time in taking a first step towards my metamorphosis. This was to have me bound as an apprentice to a liveryman of the Vintners Company.

The Worshipful Company of Vintners is one of the Great Twelve. As a guild the Vintners have existed for over 800 years and for many centuries they ruled and regulated the whole of the wine trade of England. In the middle ages their wealth and power were immense and many of their Masters, as Lord Mayors of London, wielded an influence as great as that of the greatest nobles.

An outstanding example was Sir Henry Picard. In the reign of King Edward III the Government's resources had fallen to such a low ebb that it was unable to prevent pirates in the North Sea interfering seriously with the shipment of Rhenish wines from Germany. Therefore Sir Henry fitted out his own fleet and swept the seas clear of these marauders. Such, too, was his prestige that one night in 1363 he entertained to dinner in Vintners Hall the Kings of England, Scotland, France, Denmark and Cyprus. It is to honour this unique event, which has never been equalled by any other company or institution, that when we drink the health of the Company we cry afterwards, 'With Five'.

The Hall, too, is unique in that its court room is the oldest room still occupied by a City Company in the City of London. By a merciful dispensation Vintners Hall is one of the very few of the beautiful buildings that escaped the great fire and also Hitler's bombs. Its rooms are filled with many find paintings and historic treasures, and the great hall provides a splendid setting for the banquets still held there.

A port shipper named Robert Grey agreed to take me as his apprentice, and on 8 January, 1913, my sixteenth birthday, I appeared before the court of the Company to be bound to him. My father and I were informed with mild merriment that from then onwards until I was twenty-one my master, Mr. Grey, was solely responsible for me. He would feed, clothe and lodge me at his expense, in return for which I must work for him and obey him in every particular; and that I might not marry or go abroad without his consent. Further, that within the City limits I could no longer be arrested by the police, only by the Lord Mayor's bailiff.

This, of course, was in accordance with the ancient indenture that I had signed; but in practice these were no longer observed and, in fact, I don't think I even saw Mr. Grey again until after I was invalided home from the war in France and, when convalescent, received into the Livery of the Company on 11 July, 1918.

Towards the end of January, 1913, I went back to the *Worcester* for my last term, and to take up a new line of study. My father, I gathered later, had a poor idea of French morals and feared that I might succumb to the wiles of some pretty mademoiselle; so he had decided that my first year abroad should be spent in Germany. To prepare me for that he wished me to start learning German. It then transpired that no master in the *Worcester* was capable of teaching me that language, so it was arranged that twice a week I should go to Dartford in the evenings and receive private tuition there. Dartford was about three miles up river from Greenhithe, and I much enjoyed these solitary trips in the dark of the winter evenings, although I learned little German. To get there I was provided with the train fare, but sometimes I walked there and back so that I could spend the money on tuck. This resulted in my both knowing the Dartford railway station and the quickest way to reach it by road from Greenhithe. The possession of this information enabled me, towards the end of the term, to undertake a daring adventure.

In the last chapter I mentioned jamoirs, or jams, as small boys who had a special friend among the big boys were called, and it will have been evident from my note about

Jew Boy Goldreich that I had a jam named Dieseldorff. He
was British-born but of German extraction, about thirteen
years old and one of the most beautiful little boys I have
ever seen. His hair was flaxen and curly, his eyes blue, his
features clear-cut, his complexion milk and roses, and his
body well made. But he suffered from an infliction not un-
common among boys of his age; at times, during sleep, he
could not prevent himself from wetting his mattress. On this
account he was subjected to the jibes usual in such cases and,
during my last year, I took him under my protection. The
result was that I fell in love with him.

However, there are many types of love and I wish to make
myself as clear as possible. We older boys were on the verge
of manhood. During the holidays most of us had romantic
affairs with girls of our age but each term, for a three months'
spell – which is a long time when in one's teens – we hardly
even saw a member of the opposite sex. It was not therefore
surprising that we should sublimate our urges into tender
feelings for one or other of the more attractive among the
younger boys.

I do not seek to deny the physical element in this. It was
common practice to take one's jam to some dark corner of
the ship in the evening and there kiss and cuddle him. But
matters rarely went further. During my four years in the
Worcester no boy was expelled for immorality, and I never
heard even a rumour that one of the older boys was practising sodomy. Having a jam was a form of homosexuality but
hardly more so than the well-known phenomenon in girls'
schools, wherein young girls get what is termed a 'crush' on
the games mistress, or some popular older girl who has shown
a special interest in them.

The relationship is, I think, best defined by the term Greek
Love; for, with the possible exception of the Spartans, the
ancient Greeks were not abnormal with regard to women,
but at the same time enjoyed the companionship of young
boys, and assumed towards them the role of a more than
usually affectionate and understanding uncle.

However that may be, I devoted much of my leisure to
Ralph Dieseldorff, scaring off those who would have bullied
him, helping him with his lessons, warning him against pit-

falls and generally giving him the benefit of my experience;
for all of which, as he was an intelligent and friendly little
chap, he showed his gratitude. It will therefore be readily
appreciated what a blow it was to me when, towards the end
of my last term, he fell ill, was transferred to the sick bay and,
on further examination, invalided home to his people.

A London doctor diagnosed appendicitis, which was then
regarded as a far more serious matter than it is today. Indeed
it was only a few years since King Edward VII had been
among the first to have undergone the new operation for the
removal of the appendix. Ralph's mother wrote to me in
great distress to let me know that she had decided to take the
risk of having him operated on, and that Sir Alfred Fripp,
the famous surgeon who had operated on King Edward, was
going to do the job in Guy's Hospital on April 1st.

My concern for my little friend was so great that I decided
to take 'French leave' and go up to London to visit him in
hospital on the Saturday following the operation. To do so
without being caught presented a pretty' problem, as it
needed very careful timing, and was complicated by the fact
that I dared not take a train from Greenhithe, because on
half-holiday afternoons masters often went up to London by
the only train which would enable me to get back to the ship
early enough for no one to realise that I had not spent the
afternoon on the playing fields.

It was here that my knowledge of Dartford came in. I
knew exactly how to get to the station there without stopping
to ask, and if I ran most of the three miles I could hope to
reach it just in time to catch the train there. But there still
remained the snag that if a master was in the train he would
almost certainly spot a cadet in uniform if one was waiting
on the platform as the train came in. As a precaution against
that I bought a cheap tweed cap and managed to borrow a
brown mackintosh.

On the Saturday, carrying the cap and mack in a small
brown paper parcel, I went ashore with the others. After
leaving them, ostensibly to buy tuck at Rawlings's, I walked
quickly out of the far end of the town, then broke into a run.
Fortunately the road to Dartford was little used, so about
halfway along it I was able to do my quick-change act out

of sight of anyone. Wrapping my naval cap and dark blue mackintosh in the piece of brown paper, I hid them behind a hedge and hurried on. I arrived at the station breathless but with several minutes to spare. As the train came in I kept my back to it, apparently looking at a bookstall; then turned and dashed for the nearest empty third-class compartment.

When it reached London Bridge, from fear that I might yet run into a master, I remained in it until all the other passengers had left the platform, and only then made my way to the street. That Ralph should happen to be in Guy's – which is within a stone's throw of London Bridge station – was a lucky break for me. Ten minutes later I was sitting at the bedside of my friend.

His mother had already let me know that the operation had been successful and, although he was still suffering a certain amount of pain, he was well over the worst, and delighted to see me. I was with him for about half an hour. That left me just time to give myself a glorious treat – a poached egg on toast at a Lyons teashop – then I returned to the station.

The train was in but I dared not take a seat in it. On Saturdays there were no lessons in the morning; so sometimes masters went up to London in the morning, lunched there and returned to Greenhithe by an afternoon train. I could only lurk watchfully behind a corner of one of the buildings on the platform until all the passengers had taken their places. My terror can be imagined when, believe it or not, I saw a short bearded figure in a homburg and an Inverness cape coming towards me; of all people it was Captain Wilson-Barker.

My heart stopped beating. As I hastily turned my face away and prayed for deliverance I momentarily forgot that I was wearing a cheap tweed cap and a dirty old brown mackintosh. It was those that saved me. He passed within a yard of me without even giving me a glance. A few minutes later the guard blew his whistle and I dived into a compartment that had only two elderly women in it. Still hardly able to believe my escape I travelled back to Dartford in the same train as the 'old man'.

But I was not yet out of the wood. I had spent just over an hour in London, and the slow trains, to which there were no alternatives, took over forty minutes each way. My shipmates would return from the playing fields at about five o'clock and if I were not at the causeway in time to go off to the ship with them I would be in serious trouble. The margin was terribly narrow.

There was, too, the awful possibility that someone had found my brown paper parcel and made off with its contents. The thought haunted me as I pounded along the road to Greenhithe, my lungs almost bursting. To my immense relief the parcel was still where I had left it behind the hedge. Ripping it open I changed caps and mackintoshes and ran on.

I have always believed that some fine old Pagan god, who does not believe in humility but does believe in audacity, gives his special protection to those who challenge Fate for not altogether selfish motives. He didn't let me down. I reached the far end of Greenhithe in time to mingle with the chaps returning from the playing fields and, except for a few of my special friends, no one ever knew that I had been to London.

About a fortnight later I said goodbye to my kind headmaster, Mr. Beatty, and all my other friends in the *Worcester*. Although I could not now tell a cosine from a tangent I learnt a wonderful variety of useful things there and, in spite of the bad food, I still look back on my last two years in the old ship as very happy ones. I was sixteen and three months; and my schooldays were over.

13

IMPERIAL GERMANY 1913

ALTHOUGH I have made a life-long habit of hoarding all letters and papers that I thought might later hold the least interest for me, I have never kept a diary. For nine days out of every ten my mind has been much too fully occupied with the work or pleasure of the moment for me to give time to jotting down the trivial events of every day existence.

Yet, probably at the urging of my mother, I evidently intended to keep one during my stay in Germany, as I find a diary for 1913 among my hoarded junk. Alas, my good resolution petered out after exactly one week. But, for what it is worth, the first of the seven entries reads:

Friday, May 9th. Left home 7.45. Left Charing Cross 9 o'c. Seen off by Grandpa [Wheatley] and Aunt Ettie at Dover. One-and-a-half hours wait at Ostend. Left Ostend at 4.5. First bottle of hock on train. Arrived Cologne 12 o'c., went to Metropole Hotel. Walked down High Street, had lemonade at Bear shop [presumably a café], turned in about 1 o'clock.

How inadequate those brief sentences are to describe the excitements of that day when I first left home for a foreign country! My father took me over and, as the busiest time of his year – the London season – was just getting under way, had chosen the Whitsun weekend to make the trip. Although normally an earnest and somewhat taciturn man, he liked travelling and we were both good sailors, so we enjoyed our journey.

At Ostend I had my first big thrill. It was to see the Pullman coaches of the long Orient Express pull out. They carried the magic words, VIENNA, BUDAPEST, BELGRADE, SOFIA, CONSTANTINOPLE. What such a sight meant to a youngster whose mind had been steeped in stories of international intrigue can easily be imagined.

My second thrill was at Herbesthal, then the frontier. As we all left the train to be herded into a waiting-room where our baggage was to be examined, I saw my first German officer. There he stood, stiff as a ramrod, a monocle screwed into his eye, wearing a long field-grey cloak, shiny jackboots and a spiked helmet, on the front of which was splayed a big gilt eagle.

To may amazement my father informed me that this resplendent and supercilious-looking being was the station master. He then explained that the German railways were under military control and that all important stations were kept in immediate readiness against a sudden threat of war. He added that in Germany officials of all kinds wielded much greater authority than they did with us, and that there even an ordinary policeman should be addressed as 'Sir'.

As I was only sixteen, except for visits to theatres I had rarely been in central London after dark; so the main street of Cologne at midnight, brightly lit, still thronged with strolling people and with gay music issuing from the cafés delighted me.

Our hotel was on the Domplatz and trams ran round the whole square. Later in life I might have been kept awake owing to the din made even in the small hours by their bells, but then their strange, rather musical note pleasantly rang out for me the end of that long, fascinating day.

The same sound was the first I heard next morning. Jumping out of bed I ran to the window to see opposite me the twin spires of the cathedral soaring up into the summer sky. Already an insatiable sight-seer I bolted my breakfast to go the sooner across the road into the cool depths of the vast edifice and admire its beauties.

It had been arranged that I should begin my study of the wine-maker's art under Herr Julius Kayser, the owner of the firm of that name which has its headquarters at Traben-Trarbach on the Moselle. We were to meet Herr Kayser in Cologne; but he was in Berlin on a business trip and his return was delayed for a day, so my father and I had to fill in the Saturday on our own. We took the electric train to Bonn and spent most of it in that then sleepy university town. In the evening, as neither of us understood German well enough to appreciate a theatre, we went to Schumann's Circus, and there I saw one quite extraordinary turn.

A tall, thin Russian named Rogniski came into the ring. On either side of him a table was placed. On one an attendant set a number of glasses and two huge jugs containing respectively water and beer. On the other were set two big glass bowls in which six goldfish and six medium sized frogs were swimming.

Rogniski began his performance by drinking tumbler after tumbler of water and beer until he had emptied both jugs. This alone was a remarkable feat, as most people find it physically impossible to drink more than three or four tumblers of liquid in as many minutes, and Rogniski swallowed a dozen with only a short pause between each. It could not have been a trick, for no conjuror, however skilful, when standing in the middle of a circus ring, could pour *liquid* from a jug into a glass, hold it up to his mouth and by sleight of hand make it disappear into his pocket.

Rogniski then scooped one of the goldfish out of the bowl. Tilting back his head, he held the wriggling fish up between finger and thumb, by its tail, several inches above his open mouth, He let it drop into his mouth, his throat appeared distended for a moment, then he swallowed it. This procedure he repeated with all the goldfish and all the frogs until both bowls were empty. After a few minutes his Adam's apple began violently to oscillate, he regurgitated and spat up a goldfish. Catching it in his hand he popped it back in its bowl where it swam merrily round no worse for its adventure, as in turn did its companions and all the frogs when he had brought them up one after another.

At times when I have told this story listeners have expressed polite doubts about my powers of observation, so I was particularly pleased some years later to come upon a newspaper article by Mr. Mills (of Olympia fame) who had seen the performance in Brussels. The article states that Rogniski could also swallow several banknotes – encased in small rubber capsules – and bring them up in any order called for; and that he performed this still more fantastic feat under the closest supervision.

On Sunday morning I went to High Mass in the cathedral.

Apart from my visit there the previous day, it was the first time I had ever been inside a Catholic church. In the Britain of that era the prejudice against Roman Catholics was incomparably greater than it is now. My grandfather, W.Y.B., was no Protestant bigot; he went to church only on social occasions and in most matters was a most tolerant man; yet I had heard him declare that he would never allow a Catholic or a Jew inside his house, and his attitude was regarded as quite a normal one.

I naturally shared this middle-class prejudice in which I had been brought up, and regarded both Catholics and Jews almost in the light of untouchables until, in my middle twenties, I married one of the former and came to know several of the latter whose fine qualities made me later proud to count them among my friends. So I went to Mass that morning just as I had gone to the circus the previous evening – simply to witness an interesting spectacle.

It impressed me enormously; the hundreds of candles, the melodious chanting, the beautifully timed movements of the many priests in their gorgeous vestments, the acolytes with their swinging censers and the heady smell of the incense. I decided there and then that if one wished to worship in public that was the way to do it, but the idea of becoming a convert never entered my head. There were so many more exciting things to do on Sunday mornings than go to church.

Herr Kayser arrived from Berlin that morning. He was in his middle forties, a true Rhinelander, dark-haired, fresh-complexioned, a little above middle height, stoutly built, a typical master-man used to being obeyed without argument, but an enjoyer of life, good humoured and with a kindly disposition.

We left at once for Koblenz but broke our journey at Königswinter, the first beauty-spot on the Rhine where the great river leaves its flat lower reaches with their many factories. There we lunched at the Grand Hotel Mittem, and what a lunch it was for a greedy ex-schoolboy! Afterwards we went up the Drachenfels Mountain, which lies behind the town. Like Königswinter it has since become the haunt of thousands of trippers, and now has a vast glass-walled hotel-restaurant on its top, but then the restaurant was only a little place with a wood-fenced terrace.

Sitting at a table there, while admiring the magnificent view, I participated in my first peach *Bowle*. It is a simply-made but heavenly drink. One bottle of still hock or moselle and one bottle of sparkling, with two or three peaches pricked all over with a fork put to soak in the wine. Since then I have made it hundreds of times to the delight of many friends.

By evening we arrived at Koblenz, where the Moselle flows into the Rhine. That Whit Sunday saw the opening of what is still its finest hotel, then named the Bellevue, a handsome building overlooking the river. We found the great entrance hall packed with people as the opening of the hotel had been pressed forward to coincide with an event of major importance. Starting next day, on the plateau behind the city, there was to take place Germany's first great flying meeting under the auspices of no less a person than the Kaiser's brother, Prince Henry of Prussia.

He was staying at the palace, but was to attend a banquet at the hotel that evening, so a great part of the crowd there was composed of the scores of officers who were to dine with him. They were all wearing their dress uniforms and decorations. Every arm was represented; the Prussian Guard in their white and gold, cavalry, artillery and infantry in pale blue and pearl grey, *Jäger* in green, and the Imperial Navy in dark blue and gold. Moving up and down the great staircase they presented a scene more colourful and impressive than the finale of any musical comedy show dressed regardless of expense.

Although accommodation in the hotel must have been at a premium, Herr Kayser had secured rooms for us there. After a wash and brush-up we had another sumptuous meal in the restaurant, and so ended another happy day.

On Whit Monday morning Herr Kayser's two eldest sons, Juli (short for Julius) and Oscar, joined us at the hotel. They were only two years and one year older than myself; both fine, handsome chaps wearing the bright-coloured caps of students. Juli spoke quite good English and Oscar's standard was about as good as my German, which was not up to much

but enough for us to get along on. Like all young Germans
of that day and class they treated their father with the deference that a subaltern would have accorded a very senior
officer; but I soon found that they were full of fun and they
could not have given me a kinder welcome.

We then all went up to the plateau where the three-day
Flying Meeting was to be held, to watch the arrival of the
machines, most of which for the past week or more had been
making their way by short hops – the utmost of which they
were capable – from all over Germany and several other
neighbouring countries.

It was less than four years since Blériot had achieved the
epoch-making feat of flying the Channel, so aeronautics
were still in their infancy. My mother had taken me to see
Blériot's machine when Gordon Selfridge, with his flair for
advertising, had hired it to exhibit in the basement of his
then only partially-built, store; and I doubt if I had ever
seen another. Trenchard, who was later to weld the R.A.F.
into a force that saved the free world, was busy with his co-
pioneers experimenting down at Farnborough, but in Britain
aeroplanes were still only very rarely seen and so things to
goggle at. The amazement of my father and myself can
therefore be imagined when on that Whit Monday we saw
between forty and fifty of these revolutionary craft land within half a mile of us in the space of a few hours.

They were, of course, mostly single seaters constructed of
bamboo and canvas, with no metal in them except for their
small, spluttering engines and fuel tanks of very limited
capacity. Their pilots, with legs dangling, sat in canvas-
bottomed seats like garden chairs, but at least these precarious perches had one advantage; if a machine crashed and
caught fire on landing the occupant had a sporting chance
of jumping the few feet to the ground and so getting clear.

In spite of H. G. Wells' prophetic novel, *The War in the Air*,
no one in the big crowd that had assembled to watch the
antics of these flimsy structures could possibly have dreamed
that in their lifetimes great fleets of aircraft would lay many
of Europe's finest cities in ruins. Even the great majority of
Army officers still poured scorn on the idea that the aeroplane
might prove a valuable weapon in war, and the few more

G

imaginative exceptions did not dare to claim for it more than a possibly useful means of reconnaissance.

Those officers who attended the meeting no doubt put far more faith in the Zeppelins, no fewer than seven of which were floating overhead. Long, cigar-shaped and rigged on their steel frameworks, these German airships seemed to me, too, much more potent as weapons of war, and far in advance of the flabby dirigibles that were then being built by other nations.

Not being mechanically minded, the differences in engine power of the various flying machines, as given in the programme, had little interest for me. On the other hand, I was fascinated by the scene in the nearby royal enclosure. As on the previous evening, I again had a ringside view of the élite of the far-famed German Army. With swords slung, spurs jingling, monocles glinting and eagle-crested helmets flashing, the officers strutted back and forth as proudly as any pride of peacocks. They were a race apart, immune from arrest by the police, they could be tried only by their own courts of honour and, if found guilty of a disgraceful act, they were simply given a pistol with which to shoot themselves. The civilian population had been conditioned to regard them with abject veneration. Ladies, as well as men, when approaching one of them in a street, stepped off the pavement into the gutter to give them ample room to pass, which they accepted as their right and did not acknowledge even by the flicker of an eyelid. Awed and admiring, I watched them greet one another with a graceful salute, a click of the heels and a sharp bow from the waist. It was years later before I realised that very few of them had any brains at all in their shaven or close-cropped heads.

That evening there was a great fireworks display. After dinner we all went out on to the broad first-floor terrace of the hotel. Across the Rhine the ancient fortress of Ehrenbreitstein was outlined by hundreds of electric lights, making a perfect permanent back-drop for the rockets and showers of golden rain sent up from barges moored in the middle of the river.

The terrace was crowded and the Kaysers were greeted by numerous acquaintances, among them a couple named

Emert, who had their daughter with them. Herr Emert was a bulky, rather silent man. Frau Emert was small, ugly but extremely vivacious. The daughter, whose name was Pia, I had to look at twice to believe my eyes.

My three days in Germany had already convinced me that the average German *Backfisch* – as their flappers were called from the big bow half way down their backs at the end of a single plait – was anything but attractive. Most of them were much too fat, with stumpy legs, pudding faces, piggy eyes and straight hair that, although fair, lacked golden lustre. By contrast Pia was something to wonder at. She had a slim figure, an oval face, finely chiselled features with a slightly Roman nose, a head crowned by truly golden curls, a smiling mouth and big blue eyes. Added to all this she was one of the very few really well-dressed German girls I had so far seen *and* spoke fluent English.

I fell, almost literally, at her small, neat feet, and remained glued to her for the remainder of the evening. She was just on twenty, so some years older than myself, but she did not seem to mind that, perhaps because I was a foreigner and a new conquest. Anyhow, we found lots to laugh about together while watching the fireworks and knocking back ample rations of *Sekt* as Kupferberg Gold and other German sparkling wines were termed.

Next morning, with my father and the Kaysers, I left Koblenz, eager to see Traben-Trarbach, which was to be my home for many months to come, but sadly regretting that my acquaintance with the gay and lovely Pia Emert had been so short and that in a little river town the odds were a thousand to one against my finding a girl who could hold a candle to her.

The middle and upper reaches of the Moselle, between Cochem and Trier, form one of the great beauty-spots of Europe. There are as many ruined castles crowning their vine-clad hills as there are on those of the Rhine. The river corkscrews round these steep carefully terraced slopes in bends that in places actually become loops so that it runs for a few miles in the opposite direction to its course; thus exposing an ever-changing vista to anyone following the waterway. The townships and villages strung out along it are very old;

their only industry is wine-making so, unlike those on the Rhine, they are unmarred by factories or new buildings, and much more picturesque. Again unlike the Rhine, the outer banks of many of the bends on the Moselle consist of lush water-meadows in which cattle graze, or orchards of apple, plum or cherry, the blossom of which gives them an additional loveliness in spring. Yet, even in 1946, this beautiful valley remained uninvaded by the tourist.

The reasons for this are several. The valley leads nowhere except to Trier, and that ancient city, once the western capital of the Roman World, is too far off the beaten track to induce a visit from travellers who can afford only a few weeks' holiday in the Rhineland. Even those who decide to make the trip, mostly being unaware of the beauty of the valley, are put off from following its incredibly twisting course because from Koblenz that would entail a run of well over two hundred miles. Instead, they go by the seventy miles of fine autobahn which carries them direct through the pleasant forests of the Hunsrück. Again it is this question of distance that protects the valley from motor-coaches. In summer thousands of trippers take the excursion up river as far as Cochem, to see one of the loveliest of all the fairy-tale German castles there, but it is only after Cochem that the middle Moselle begins, and for coaches to go further, then return to Koblenz, would make too long a run. Even the railway denies travellers a sight of the Moselle's beauties, for the main line leaves the river near Cochem, at Bullay junction, and from there to continue up the valley one must change on to the little *Klingelbahn* that chugs at thirty miles an hour along the river bank.

It was in this toy train that we arrived in Traben which, with its sister town of Trarbach on the opposite side of the river, lies almost exactly halfway between Koblenz and Trier. Traben consists of little more than a single street running along the flat inner curve of the river. Behind it a gentle slope planted with vineyards rises to a considerable height on which there is a broad plateau. The foundations of a big fortress built by Vauban, King Louis XIV's great military engineer can still be seen on it, and it was there too that during the revolutionary wars General Jourdan formed a vast camp as winter quarters for his army in 1794–95. Trarbach also consists of little more than a single street, but that runs inland, the town occupying the mouth of a valley on either side of which rise steep wooded heights, one of which is crowned by a ruined castle.

In those days no one in Traben-Trarbach owned a car and the twin towns were too small to require a service of buses, so our luggage was trundled on a hand-cart and we walked with Herr Kayser down to his house. All those of any size looked out over the river and, like most of them, his had a pleasant vine-covered terrace raised some feet above the tow-path. Almost opposite it, on the Trarbach bank, stood his offices and cellars. They were the only modern building to be seen, but in no way spoilt the outlook, as they had been built like a long, low two-storeyed fort with battlements and a small tower.

At the house we met Herr Kayser's other two children, Lenchen, an ugly, dark-haired girl of about thirteen to whom, on account of her acid manner and sharp tongue, I never took, and Kurt, a boy of about ten.

After lunch we crossed the river by Herr Kayser's private punt. This revealed the only weakness I ever discovered in my new master. Although a handsome stone bridge connected the two towns he rarely used it, and if he did he asked whoever was with him to take his arm, because he suffered from a fear that one day he might throw himself from it into the river.

In Trarbach we went to a tall stone-fronted eighteenth-century house in the main street. It was owned by Herr Julius's cousin, Herr Fritz Kayser, and it was there I was to live; because, Herr Julius having four children, there was not room for me in his house.

Herr Fritz proved to be a far from likable personality. That he was a hunchback was his misfortune, but he had a mean and carping disposition, and when he showed his yellow teeth in a servile grin while nodding his bearded head up and down and washing his hands with invisible soap he reminded me of Uriah Heep. His wife, on the other hand, was charming. She was only twenty-one, so less than half his age, with dark hair, dark eyes, a rich complexion, and would have been quite lovely but for one thing – she was, for her years, the fattest woman I have ever seen.

It certainly was a case of beauty and the beast without any redeeming feature, as I learnt from her in due course. She came from Stuttgart and her father had died leaving her mother, herself and several younger sisters desperately badly off; so her mother had forced her, at the age of seventeen, to accept hunchback Fritz's proposal of marriage simply to get her out of the house and have one fewer mouth to feed.

Herr Fritz spoke no English, but she spoke it fluently and was in other ways much better educated than he, as well as being quite a talented musician; so if only she had been allowed to wait a year or two there can be little doubt but that her good looks and other assets would have brought her a choice of several suitors.

As it was, not only had she been exiled from the gay city of her youth to this little backwoods town, she had not even the compensation of having made a rich marriage. Herr Fritz was the poor relation of the Kayser family and to make ends meet they had to take in three lodgers, of which I was to be one. Added to which he had already given her three children in four years and, divorce or separation then being almost unheard of among the German middle classes, the poor girl was now condemned for life to *Kinder, Kirche, Küche* with a husband that she feared and hated.

It was the thought of just this kind of tragedy which always made me seethe with rage when people spoke in praise of the high morality of family life maintained during the Victorian era. Only too often parents abused the obedience they exacted from their children for their own selfish ends. How these sanctimonious hypocrites can have worshipped regularly at church and held daily prayers in their homes to a God regarded as the embodiment of love, yet at the same time, without the least scruple, forced their offspring into loveless marriages, or worse, compelled their daughters to refuse offers so that they might be retained for life at home in the role of sterile upper servants, utterly passes my comprehension. It was this, coupled with the appalling conditions imposed for gain upon the poorer classes which, to my mind, makes the upper- and middle-class Victorians – both in

Britain and on the Continent – the most sanctimonious and truly immoral generations of which we have any record.

After *Kaffeetrinken* – the German substitute for afternoon tea – with the Fritz Kaysers we recrossed the river and saw my father off at the railway station. I felt no qualms on his leaving me, because nearly everyone I had so far met spoke some English and had displayed the greatest friendliness towards me, which made me feel confident that I should soon settle down and enjoy my new life. Having waved him away I hurried back to my new home to unpack in the pleasant bedroom I had been given on the top floor of the house. That evening I wrote a letter to my mother, whom I still adored, and so to bed.

Next morning I was called at six, had my first breakfast at half-past and by ten to seven was on my way to work. And work in Germany is regarded as a full-time occupation. Even today the Germans regard British labour's demand for a forty-hour week with amazement and contempt; and it is quite certain that, had the German people lacked the guts to put their backs into the job, they could not possibly have performed the economic miracle which, after the terrible devastation their country suffered during Hitler's war, has so swiftly recovered for them a state of prosperity and plenty.

In 1913 offices and works opened at seven and closed at six on weekdays, Saturdays included. Most offices also opened for a few hours on Sunday mornings so that executives could keep up to the minute with their correspondence. However, I was let off lightly, it having been arranged that I should work mornings only and be free in the afternoons either to take physical recreation or – in accordance with my father's instructions – study to improve my German. In the event, as he had no check on what I did, this boiled down to my amusing myself in any way I felt inclined.

The fortress-like Julius Kayser *Weinhandlung* consisted of three levels. The lowest was a lofty cellar, very small compared with such vast cellarage as that of Deinhard's at Koblenz or Sichel's in Mainz but, even so, containing several hundred casks and a number of great concrete vats in which thousands of gallons of the cheaper wines could be blended. The river side of the upper floor was a great open area in which the labelling, capsuling and packing of the wines took place, while behind it lay the general offices. Above this was only the flat roof, which had been turned into a rose garden and, in its middle, the squat tower of two floors containing the tasting room and, above it, Herr Kayser's private office.

Like a god on Olympus he rarely emerged from this charming penthouse to give his orders to us lesser mortals who laboured below; and for a good part of the year he was away in the big German cities, the Scandinavian countries and Britain, marketing his wines; so except on Sundays, when I had a standing invitation to lunch at his house, I rarely saw him.

My immediate chief was the *Kellermeister*, a real old-fashioned, hefty sergeant-major type, with a fierce up-turned grey moustache modelled on that of Kaiser Wilhelm. However, his bark was worse than his bite and he always treated me very decently. The cellar staff consisted of six or eight brawny fellows, including a jolly and hugely fat man named Johann. They ragged me a little now and then but I soon became good friends with all of them and during my nine months in the cellars I could not have had a more pleasant crowd to work with.

Between 8.45 and 9.15 we had a break, during which I took the short walk home and back for my second and more substantial breakfast. At 12 o'clock they knocked off for their dinner hour and I finished work for the day. What I was given to do on that first morning I do not remember, but a line in the penultimate entry in my diary reads, 'work frightfully heavy'. However, they were probably trying me out as in the last entry, made the following day, I recorded, 'work not so tiring'.

Anyhow, my labours on that first morning cannot really have been very exhausting, as I was sufficiently recovered by the afternoon to climb the best part of a thousand feet up the steep mountain to see the fine view from the old castle on its top; and that evening to stay up till well after midnight at a very jolly party.

Herr Kayser was a widower and his children were mothered by his mother-in-law, an elderly widow named Frau Hausmann. She was very well-off and did not live in his house but in her own, which was one of the finest on the river bank of Traben, and it was there I had been invited to dine.

Juli and Oscar were present and I was surprised to learn that although their own home was only a few hundred yards away they also had rooms in their grandmother's house where, after dining with her, they sometimes slept. Frau Hausmann spoke no English but before we sat down to dinner she made a little speech to me in German and handed me a silver napkin ring. Her words were translated to me as follows.

'Now that you have come to live in Traben-Trarbach in the care of Herr Julius I wish you to think of yourself as another of my grandsons. This napkin ring is a symbol that there will always be a place for you for breakfast, lunch or dinner at my table and a bed for you in my house.'

What could conceivably have been kinder to a young foreigner just arrived in a strange land? When thinking of the German people one must set against the brutalities later perpetrated by the Prussians and the Nazis such acts of true generosity and thoughtfulness, of which I was to experience many in the next few months.

Juli and Oscar had brought with them several of their fellow students from the *Gymnasium* – a sort of high-class grammar school with emphasis on the classics – where they were studying and which was situated in the wooded valley behind Trarbach. When dinner was over Frau Hausmann left us and for the first time I participated in a 'wine-drinking' evening.

Bottle after bottle of moselle was consumed and as they were emptied each dead man was added to a row lying down in the middle of the table. Meanwhile we joked, laughed and sang at the top of our voices. I contributed 'What shall we do with a drunken sailor' and 'Alexander's Ragtime Band'.

The latter was an enormous success. Ragtime was then a comparatively new import from the United States into Britain and still totally unknown in the remoter parts of Germany; so it may be said that I brought ragtime to the valley of the Moselle. Innumerable times in the months that followed my friends made me stand on tables in *Weinstuben* and *Biergärten* and sing for them 'Alexander's Ragtime Band'

and 'Waiting for the Robert E. Lee' while they joined lustily in the chorus. I returned the compliment to a small extent by bringing back to my friends in England that delightful ditty, *'Püppchen, du bist mein Augenstern'*.

As the evening progressed I had to drink the *Brüderschaft* with each of the others in turn. This consisted of linking right arms while holding full glasses then drinking down their contents – not an easy feat unless it is well-timed and both drinkers raise glasses and put heads back simultaneously. Another custom into which I was initiated was a type of challenge-toast. One of them would suddenly cry, *'Herr Den!'* (as they called me) *'Auf den Nagel!'* I then had to drink up whatever was in my glass, tip it up and rap its rim on my left thumbnail to show that it was quite empty. Anyone could do this to anyone they chose as often as they liked and the challenge always had to be accepted. As the toaster nearly always picked a moment when the toasted's glass had just been refilled, responding to these courtesies meant consuming several bottles of wine in an evening.

Being unused to quantities of wine I was soon quite drunk, but none of them thought the worse of me for that, and within a couple of hours they were all drunk too. In the Germany of that day it was customary for young men of good family to get as drunk as the proverbial Lord, and to boast of their wine-bibbing exploits; indeed, frequent participation in these Bacchanalian carousals was considered an indication of a proper manly spirit, and no self-respecting girl would have had anything to do with a chap who did not take part in them.

Fortunately I had a pretty good head and although my speech became slurred and my legs wobbly I never actually passed out, as at times did some of my companions. I was also fortunate in that I found no difficulty in following the Roman custom, which many of them practised. Not everyone can vomit almost at will, but a touch of my index finger on my uvula has always been enough to empty my stomach. When engaged in these drinking bouts I used to leave the company for this purpose two or three times in the course of an evening, have a quick wash and return feeling as fresh as a daisy.

Soon I formed the habit after these parties of inducing a final throw-up the very last thing before going to bed, and I am sure this greatly contributed to my rarely feeling any pain and grief when I woke in the morning. The adoption of this sensible Roman custom also served me well later, when as a young officer I took part in the terrific binges that were customary on guest nights during the 1914–18 war; particularly as after dining we would knock back round after round of spirits and liqueurs, which were far more liable to result in a thick head than the quantities of good clean *Moselwein* that I imbibed with my friends in Germany.

After many centuries, evenings devoted to heavy drinking by parties of men have now gone out of fashion and, unless some revolutionary change occurs in the present relation of the sexes, they are unlikely to return. They were doomed from the moment in the first quarter of this century when women attained a dominant voice in ordering our social life. Unfortunately it seems that women are congenitally incapable of really enjoying dining and wining at a gathering consisting only of members of their own sex; and, having obtained equality, they are no longer prepared to remain at home while their men go to stag parties – other than formal banquets from which they can be expected to return early and sober.

Young people, of course, occasionally go out on the spree but, again owing to the new demand of the female sex to be treated as equals, only in mixed parties, and that is an entirely different matter. Even if a young man enjoys seeing his girl knock back vodka for vodka with him, and does not particularly mind if she is involuntarily sick in the taxi on the way home because he is pretty tight himself, such nights on the tiles are no substitutes for the wonderful sense of camaraderie arising out of a company of men with similar interests holding a long session round a big table for the enjoyment of wine and song. To my mind it was one of the great pleasures of life and that future generations should be deprived of it owing to the demand for equality in all things, which is the parrot cry of the modern age, is greatly to be regretted.

Reverting, after this slight digression, to Traben-Trarbach, my second day as a part-time cellarman held a most pleasant surprise for me. My two fellow-lodgers at Fritz Kayser's both enjoyed the prefix to their names of Herr Doktor, because they were masters at the Trarbach *Gymnasium*. One was a rather dour little man who for a time gave me private tuition in German: a most unsatisfactory chore for the poor devil since I found that nearly everyone spoke a little English, and I was far too busy amusing myself to give even a thought out of tuition hours to German grammar – the other was a real stage-type German, fat, shaven-headed and with rolls of flesh bulging out at the back of his neck, but a jolly fellow.

It was the latter who, after *Kaffeetrinken*, took me to the tennis club and had me made a member. The club was situated about a mile outside Trarbach up in the valley and adjacent to a small *Kurhaus* at which during the summer months a few people stayed for a rest-cure. The club consisted only of two courts and a little pavilion, but it was delightfully situated among the woods with a mountain stream tumbling musically over rocks nearby, and I was to spend many pleasant evenings there.

On this occasion there were about a dozen people present including two jolly but not very pretty girls, all of whom made me welcome. In those days, although I was not very good at tennis, I greatly enjoyed it, and as the standard of play there was not very high I managed to pass muster in my first set.

I then sat out a set, and while I was watching the others play, two hands suddenly emerged from behind me, then were clapped over my eyes.

'I give you three guesses who it is,' said a voice in English.

Completely puzzled, I could not even make one, and admitted it. The hands were removed and I swung round in my chair. To my amazement and delight I found myself staring into the laughing face of the girl I had met in Koblenz – the beautiful, blue-eyed, golden-haired and altogether adorable Pia Emert.

'What in the world are you doing here?' I gasped.

Her lovely eyebrows lifted in surprise. 'But didn't you know? I was only in Koblenz with my people over Whitsun for a few days' holiday. I live in Traben and got back yesterday.'

I had already conceived a great admiration for Juli, and I felt that with him as my mentor and friend, and with the gay and glamorous Pia to love, my stay in Germany could not fail to be a happy one. And indeed, it proved one of the happiest years of my life.

14

HAPPY DAYS

THE basic reason for my having such a happy time while living in Germany is not far to seek. It was not because I was so kindly received, had comfortable quarters and ample leisure, made many friends among young men of my own age and enjoyed the frequent companionship of a lovely girl. I have been similarly blessed for the greater part of my life. It was not even because I had just put my schooldays behind me and for the first time was more or less my own master. It was because this was the only period between my going to boarding school and nearly forty years later, when my income as an author began to exceed £10,000 a year, that I had enough money for all reasonable requirements.

When I produce my budget that statement will appear farcical. The wage of Herr Kayser's cellarmen was twenty-four marks (then worth 120 new pence) a week. How they managed to live and maintain families on such a sum passes comprehension; yet the fact remains that they did, and were strong, healthy, contented and cheerful. As I worked only half days and was an unskilled hand I was paid six marks a week.

To this must be added twenty marks that my father left with me, ten marks sent to me by W.Y.B., and a further twenty marks given me by my father when he came out with my mother to visit me in September. My board, lodging and washing with Frau Kayser were, of course, paid for by my father direct. But from the above it will be seen that my cash receipts during my nine months' stay totalled only £14.40.

The explanation lies in the self-sufficiency of the small isolated community of which I had become a member. Almost the whole of Traben-Trarbach's population of five thousand were either engaged in wine-making or dependent

on it. Some twelve families owned the vineyards round about
Traben and many others in districts up and down the
Moselle; they also owned the *Weinhandlungen* that made and
later shipped the wines to all parts of the world. The remainder of the population were their employees in vineyards,
cellars and offices – apart from a tiny minority of local
government employees and people who either owned or
served in not more than twenty shops.

In consequence, while these owner families made no pretence of being an aristocracy, they did form a definite élite.
In the course of centuries they had all intermarried, so to be
received by one meant acceptance by them all and, automatically, an invitation to such social occasions as weddings,
christenings, birthdays and all other parties they might
give.

In addition there were the clubs of which they were all
members. The tennis club, the boating club, the swimming
club and the casino. The latter was not, as its name suggests,
a gambling club, but a pleasant old house on the Trarbach
bank used for social purposes, dances, receptions, concerts
and amateur theatricals. The subscription to each was only
a few marks and I was at once made a member of them all.

The result was that I enjoyed an extraordinarily full social
life without having to pay a penny for it. All the families kept
good tables with an abundance of food and wine, a week rarely
passed without one or more parties and between times there
were picnics on the river and wine-drinking evenings with
my student friends. I was not tempted to buy any books
because no English books were available, and even if I had
sent for some I should have had little time to read them. My
only other outlay was on cigarettes and sweets, and these
were so cheap that my requirements came well within my
means. Apart from that the only times I put my hand in my
pocket was on Sundays.

The German Sunday was a revelation to me. Pre-1914
England was still only gradually emerging from the gloom of
the Victorian Sunday. In stricter households, such as that in
which my second wife was brought up, no recreations were
permitted, not even reading, except religious books. Even in
my own middle class to play a game of cards or tennis was

unthinkable, and to have held a sing-song or dance would have been taken as a clear indication that one had sold oneself to the Devil.

That is part of the price we paid, and to some extent – the restriction on the opening of public houses for example – are still paying, for having once allowed ourselves to be dominated by the Puritans. It was they who first demanded the forbidding of Sunday games. King Charles I refused to pass the Bill, replying, 'I will not sanction it; for if the common people be deprived on Sundays of their games what times would they have left in which to recreate themselves?' The kindly King lost his head, the Puritans got their way and their spiritual descendants have ever since derived sadistic pleasure from forcing their unfortunate contemporaries to don some form of hair-shirt on the one day in the week that they don't have to work.

But on the Continent there was no gloomy Lord's Day Observance Society fighting with myopic, tenacious bigotry to prevent people from enjoying harmless pleasures on Sundays. And I do not think the Germans were any less religious than the British. A high proportion of Rhinelanders are Roman Catholics and along the Moselle villages mainly populated by Catholics alternate with ones having Lutheran majorities. In Traben-Trarbach the proportion was about fifty-fifty, and the two denominations had long since settled down to ignore the difference in their faiths in their everyday lives, so that although I knew the Kaysers to be Protestants, and that fat Johann was a Catholic – because he wore a little gold crucifix at the neck of his cellarman's smock – I have no idea what religion any of the other people followed. However, the majority of Catholics would certainly have attended Mass on Sundays, and, as in England then, a good percentage of the Lutherans attended morning service. But once out of church there was no taboo of any kind on how they spent the rest of the day, and one form of gaiety was deliberately organised to meet youthful tastes.

This was the celebration on each Sunday by one or other of the villages along the valley of its patron saint's day. After lunch on Sundays Juli and Oscar, with a few friends and myself, would take the *Klingelbahn* along the river bank to

*Julius Kayser, 'Ready Money Wheatley', my
father and Max Seitlow at Koblenz, August,
1910*

Traben-Trarbach; the bridge in 1913 was made of narrow stone arches

Julius Kayser's cellars

DW (second from right)
tight after a students'
drinking party, with his
arm round the shoulders
of Carl Danz

(Below left) *Pia von*
Emert-Kohl
(Below right) *With my*
father (seated) and Julius
Kayser, 1913

Hilda Gosling

Barbara Symonds

whichever village was *en fête*. Arrived there, we went to the local inn and into a big barn-like room forming part of it that was opened for such occasions. Ranged endways against the walls there would be rows of trestle tables with benches on either side and people sitting drinking at them. A big space in the middle of the floor was left clear for dancing.

The band consisted only of an upright piano and a fiddler who played his fiddle while walking about among the dancers. When they struck up a man could walk up to any girl in the room he liked the look of, bow to her and ask her for the dance; and for her to refuse would have been considered most ill-bred, but he was expected to return her to her friends immediately the dance was over. Halfway through each dance the piano suddenly stopped, as in a game of musical chairs. The fiddler then went round with his hat and every male standing up on the dance floor had to put ten *pfennig* (one penny) into it. When he had completed his collection the piano started again and the dance went on.

There was no entrance fee to these village hops, but one was expected to buy wine or beer; and, indeed, dancing on a hot summer afternoon being thirsty work it would not have been much fun without them. But the local wines cost only five pence a bottle and for two pence or three pence more one could get a named wine from quite a good vineyard. To pay more was considered by my friends unnecessary and ostentatious; so, although on these occasions I always paid my share of our outing I was never embarrassed by the fear that I would not have enough money to do so.

My work in the cellars was the same as that of any of the other cellarmen. We racked wines with a hand pump through a large canvas hose from one cask to another; fined them to get them clear, sometimes filtering the more cloudy ones through a substance like blotting paper, bottled, corked, capsuled, labelled, wrapped and packed them. There was also quite a lot of pushing big wheeled trolleys about that were loaded with a gross or more of bottles, and of man-handling the great *Fuder* – as the hundred-gallon casks were called – so whenever I could I got myself put on to the lighter work of bottling, capsuling or labelling.

The labels used in those days were much more decorative

than those of today. Most of them had coloured pictures of the district from which the wine came, with a bend of the river, vine-clad slopes and a ruined castle, or of *Moselmädchen* and Bacchantes. But the names of the great vineyards remain unchanged and, to me, have a romantic ring that is all their own: Bernkasteler Doktor, Piesporter Goldtröpfchen, Enkircher Steffensberg, Ürziger Würzgarten, Zeltinger Schlossberg, Eitelsbacher Karthauser and Graacher Himmelreich.

Yet I cannot honestly say that I learnt much about wine – although I acquired a pretty good palate for it through drinking every quality from peasant growths to classic vintages. Herr Kayser never had me up to his penthouse when a tasting was in progress, and, apart from visits to his office when my father was in Traben I don't think I ever went there, except on one memorable occasion.

It happened that the swimming club was situated on the Trarbach side of the river only about a hundred yards from the Julius Kayser cellars. The bath consisted of a rectangular wooden structure floated on pontoons. On three sides of the enclosure so formed there stood rows of changing cabins; the fourth was simply a flat platform with a diving board upon it, so that the better swimmers who did not fear the current could dive off it into the open river.

The open side of the rectangle faced the cellars, so from the big windows of the packing floor there was an excellent view of anyone using the bath. Mixed bathing was not then allowed in Germany and as in the mornings every man was at work, from nine till twelve was reserved for the ladies. That meant the girls and women of families that I knew, and Pia among them. So I took to neglecting my work to watch them. Soon they spotted and recognised me, waved and shouted greetings.

One lovely summer day Pia and another girl were swimming in the open river just below the window from which I was watching them. Turning on her back Pia cupped her hands and called up to me, 'Come down and talk to us.'

Nothing loth I scrambled out of the big window, crossed the short length of railway line that served the cellars and went down to the river bank. After a few laughing exchanges

Pia cried, 'It's lovely in the water. Why don't you come in and join us?'

Of course, she was only joking, but it was the sort of dare that I could never resist. Next moment, fully clothed, I had plunged into the river and was swimming towards her. With screams of pretended fright the two girls turned and headed towards the bath; I followed. On the platform of the bath several other girls and women had been watching the scene, and some of them with manifest disapproval; for the more narrow-minded ones considered it immodest to allow a man to see them close up when clad only in a bathing-dress. As I approached these fled, with cries of angry protest, to their cabins and, poor silly creatures, locked themselves in.

I was by no means a strong swimmer and my water-logged clothes were weighing me down. I knew that I was too far out to turn back safely, so my only course was to swim on to the bath. I reached it and clung there panting while my girl-friends looked down at me with mixed amusement and uncertainty, not daring to help me up on to the platform from fear of the reaction of the staider women to this invasion of their privacy by a young, and clearly mad, Englishman.

I was rescued from my predicament by Herr Kayser. It chanced that he was crossing the river from his home to his cellars in his private punt. Taking in the scene, he diverted its course, picked me up, landed me and told me sternly to go home, change into dry clothes then report to him in his office.

Greatly chastened, and now fearing that his anger would lead him to inform my father how I had played truant from my work to perform this discreditable exploit, which might even lead to my being ordered home in disgrace, I did as he had ordered.

My surprise and relief can be imagined when I found him sitting among the roses on his roof garden drinking champagne with Pia and the girl who had been swimming with her. Bravely and generously they had dressed at once and come to Herr Kayser to take the blame for my exploit upon themselves. They told him that they had taunted me into coming in and that had I refused to do so I should have been branded as a coward. The Germans hold courage as the high-

est of all virtues, and Herr Kayser said that I had been guilty
of a most reprehensible social misdemeanour in invading the
bath during the ladies' hours, but in the circumstances I could
not have done otherwise without letting down my country.
He then gave me a kindly smile and a glass of champagne.

The affair did not altogether end there. One of the
middle-aged women who had taken refuge in her cabin was
a Frau Volkner. She complained about the incident to her
husband and he wrote an indignant letter condemning my
conduct to the local paper. But when it appeared I got my
own back on him by composing a doggerel verse in incredibly
bad German which I sang to the tune of one of Gertie Millar's
hits in *Our Miss Gibbs*. A line of the original chorus ran:

Folk don't do that up in Yorkshire-Yorkshire-Yorkshire.

My version went:

Man macht das nicht in Deutschland-Deutschland-Deutschland.

> *Zu schwimen mit Maidchen est Verboten dar*
> *Zu schwimen mit Maidchen est Schreclich! Forschpar!*
> *Herr Volkner hat so saght; so mus sein ganz var*
> *Man macht das nicht in Deutschland.*

The majority of the older people were more tolerant than the
Volkners so were amused when they heard about my exploit.
The younger ones were delighted with my nonsensical ditty
and, as it had a catchy tune, were soon singing it all over the
town. In consequence, instead of proving my ruin, the affair
brought me an increased popularity – particularly among my
student friends.

I suppose the cloven hoof that my father had always feared
from my resemblance to my wicked Uncle Johnny was now
coming out in me, but in my new surroundings it paid a good
dividend. My uninhibited delight in wine, song and laughter
had already led Juli and his boon companions to adopt me
as an honorary member of the Senior Students *Bund*, and my
prestige had been further increased by my showing them a
photograph of myself in the mess dress of an H.M.S.
Worcester cadet.

Most of them were a year or two older than myself so would

soon be leaving the *Gymnasium* to do their military service. At that time the period of conscription in Germany was three years, but was reduced to two for students such as these if they had passed certain examinations and, if their military service in the ranks was satisfactory they then passed out automatically as second lieutenants on the reserve of officers.

They were, of course, aware that we did not have conscription in Britain, but the photograph of myself in what appeared to be the uniform of a midshipman gave them the impression that by already having done voluntary service I had got several years ahead of them and, in the event of war, would at once become an officer of the Royal Navy.

I will admit that I did not go out of my way to undeceive them, and indeed, it was then my own belief that if Britain did have to go to war I should have no difficulty in obtaining a commission in the R.N.V.R. Anyway, as they all had the greatest admiration for the Royal Navy, the impression they acquired, that I was already on its reserve of officers, led them to regard me with far more respect than I would have received from young men in my own country had that actually been the case.

This was due to the intense interest they displayed in war and everything to do with it. They were convinced that war between Germany and France was inevitable and all of them were fanatically patriotic, their one great anxiety being that it might break out before they had done their military service with the result that they would be unable to participate in it. For, of course, they had no doubt at all that it would prove a walk-over for Germany and be over in less than six months.

Since Germany had beaten France to her knees in 1870, and taken Alsace-Lorraine from her, why they should still have felt such enmity towards France I never understood, but their hatred was so bitter that I heard many of them declare that they would die happy if it was with the knowledge that they had first killed one Frenchman.

They even carried this loathing of the French to the extent of including the Belgians, presumably on the flimsy grounds that in Belgium the French language was used. For some months while I was in Traben a young Belgian named Paul

Clemens was also there to learn German. He was the son of General Clemens who in August, 1914, most gallantly defended Liège, a charming young man of about nineteen. He was gay, well-read, had already had several mistresses and was far more a man of the world than any of his German contemporaries; so I found him interesting to talk to, and sometimes we went for long walks together at night. But he was barred from the clubs, never invited anywhere and completely ostracised, solely on account of his nationality.

For Britain and the British, on the other hand, with very few exceptions the Germans showed great admiration and friendliness. Again and again I was asked why we did not abandon our Entente with the decadent French and instead form an alliance with Imperial Germany. The somewhat ingenuous inducement was that together the German Army and British Navy could lick the world. It seems never to have entered their heads that in the event of their going to war with France Britain might prove hostile; so it is hardly surprising that they showed such shocked dismay, and felt that we had betrayed a friendship, when we carried out our treaty obligation to Belgium and entered the war against them.

Every occasion for military display was seized upon by them with avidity. All reserve officers kept their uniforms, together with equipment down to the last detail, packed away in tin trunks ready for *der Tag*. All of them, too, had precise instructions what to do in the event of mobilisation being ordered. Herr Kayser, for example, would within an hour or two have taken over from the regular officer who was station commandant at the important railway junction at Bullay, thus releasing him for more active duties. And on the Kaiser's birthday all reserve officers were entitled to wear their uniforms.

It was, of course, a national holiday and I was much amused to see a number of my older acquaintances strutting about the town booted and helmeted, chins in air, twirling their moustaches and clanking their swords. There were parades and martial music by the town band all day and the national anthem was sung again and again. Fortunately it had the same tune as 'God Save the King', so with an easy conscience I was able to join in by singing our anthem in English.

The centenary celebrations for the Allies' victory over Napoleon at Leipzig were also held while I was there. The *pièce de résistance* was a torch-light procession up the mountain to the old castle. As Juli informed me that a regiment of British Hussars had participated in the victory I felt no qualms about carrying a torch and taking part in the terrific drinking bout that followed.

Behind the Trarbach side of the Moselle lie the forest-clad mountains of the Hunsrück. On them several of the families had shooting and fishing rights, which brought delicious trout, and roebuck, which I had never before tasted, to their tables. But in the autumn a different kind of shooting took place up there. Thousands of rounds of blanks were fired from guns and rifles by the army on manoeuvres.

For a week or so a considerable contingent of troops was billeted on the town, and its inhabitants went wild with excitement. The billeting money was a pittance but even the poorest were eager to have a soldier as their guest, and there was most bitter competition to secure an officer. The quantity of wine consumed reached an all-time high and owing to that I narrowly escaped an unpleasant incident.

The Kaysers had as their billetee a tall and powerfully built Prussian lieutenant, and naturally they entertained him with the utmost lavishness. Late one night, long after Herr Kayser had gone to bed, and we younger people had had about as much wine as we could carry, the *Herr Oberleutnant* singled me out and began to bait me. I cannot recall the exact line he took but he made some very rude remarks about England and a disparaging allusion to my King. Juli, as host, was in a very difficult situation, since he and his friends regarded officers of the regular army as little less than gods, and to be deferred to in all things. Even so, he came over and did his best to change the conversation. But the big, ill-mannered brute would not be denied his fun. Pushing Juli aside, he stood, a good foot taller than myself, looming over me and, as he rocked back and forth on his feet, he blurted out fresh insults between belches.

I was in a horrible fix, for to take it lying down was utterly against all my instincts; moreover, to have done so would have been to lose face with my friends. Yet he was far too big for me to have any hope of knocking him down and, had I attempted to I could have been sent to prison for striking a German officer while wearing the Kaiser's uniform.

All I could do was to say, '*Herr Oberleutnant*, I'm sure you don't mean to insult my country. It's simply that you're too drunk to know what you're saying.'

'Drunk, am I?' he exclaimed angrily. 'I'll show you how drunk I am, you little English so-and-so!' Upon which he took a swipe at me.

By the grace of God the effort proved too much for him. With a final belch he heeled over and fell flat on his face on the floor, out cold. He was carried upstairs and put to bed still completely unconscious, and I felt that I was extremely lucky to have come so well out of the matter.

It was the only unpleasantness that I met with during my stay in Germany, except for a few rather embarrassing episodes with Herr Fritz Kayser, owing to that nasty-minded hunchback's acute jealousy of his pretty, if balloon-like, wife.

Whether it was because he was not well enough off, or too mean, to return hospitality, or because he was generally disliked, I do not know; but the Fritz Kaysers were rarely invited to parties and never had people to their house. Had they done so I have no doubt that he would have made the poor woman's life a misery by accusing her of wishing to be unfaithful to him after every social occasion on which some other man had shown her the least attention. As things were, the only outlet he could find for his obsession was to infer that I was having an affair with her.

His suspicions were, I suppose, based upon the fact that he must have known that she hated him and could not fail to be aware that she did everything she possibly could to make me happy and comfortable. Moreover, we always talked English together, and he probably suspected that we used that language to say pretty things to one another in his presence, and to make a mock of him, knowing that he could not understand us. For this last supposition he had some grounds, as when, after a few weeks, she had gradually confided to me her sad story, there were times at meals she would make remarks in front of him, such as, 'I cannot do so-and-so because he is too mean to pay for it'; and it may be that he understood more than we supposed.

The truth is, too, that she would have liked to have had an affair with me. By that I do not suggest that she was prepared to become my mistress; but she was so obviously yearning to be loved, and had I been willing to kiss and cuddle her while she poured out her woes she would have found that a great solace in her unhappiness. At times she even went so far as to show jealousy of my attachment to Pia, and hint that I could find a much more willing response to my affections in another quarter. But I always pretended not to understand her tentative advances.

I followed the same tactics with the unspeakable hunchback. He never got to the point of actually accusing me of trying to seduce his wife, but once a month or so during the latter half of my stay he would make unpleasant innuendoes and try to needle me with such questions as: 'Did I not think her good-looking? Would I not like to be in his shoes? As I was much nearer her age than he was, and we had so many interests in common, did I not consider that I made a much better companion for her than himself?' and so on.

In this one connection my idleness in learning German stood me in good stead. Even the Germans who spoke only a few words of English insisted on practising it when with me, and many of them spoke it fluently; so I could have got along quite well with a score or two of phrases for use with servants and my fellow cellarmen. Actually, after a while I could chatter away with ease in colloquial German, and even began to think in it; but to the end I remained totally ignorant of its grammar, and could read it only with considerable difficulty, so for all Herr Fritz knew my vocabulary, too, was extremely limited. In consequence, I was able to regard him with an asinine grin, and by shaking my head imply that I did not get his meaning. Unpleasant as these occasional domestic tensions were, they had their value in teaching me that tact and dissimulation provided the easiest way out of such awkward situations.

Even had there been no one like Pia living in Traben-Trarbach I think it unlikely that I should have allowed myself to be lured into a romance with Frau Kayser, for two reasons. Firstly, morals apart, I had taken very seriously my cousin Laurie's briefing that to play around with a married woman was to risk about the worst sort of trouble that any young man could get himself into. Secondly, I have never been emotionally drawn to any woman whom I did not regard as really beautiful. By that I do not mean that I have been less prone to brief sexual encounters than other normal men; but to engage my mind for more than a few hours the girl has had to be something very, very special.

I suppose this is a manifestation of the instinct which has always led me to secure, as far as I possibly could, the best in food, wine, clothes and everything which for many centuries was regarded as exclusive to the aristocracy. As far as women are concerned Kipling's observation that the Colonel's Lady an' Judy O'Grady are sisters under their skins contains an element of truth. It is certainly true to the extent that the most beautiful woman in the world *needs* some one to love every bit as much as the most ill-favoured of her sex; so why should her choice not fall upon oneself?

Applied personally, the above statement may sound extraordinarily conceited; but it is not so in fact, because the qualities that attract the two sexes are entirely different. Looks in a man count very little with women; the things they desire are, a display of intense devotion, a forceful and spectacular wooing, courage, generosity and an ability to make them laugh. Any man who is not cursed with incurable shyness can therefore enter the lists with a sporting chance, and if he observes the old dictum, 'Faint heart ne'er won Fair Lady', he may well be amazed at his own success. The chap who has the guts to go in over the garden wall is already halfway to her bedroom.

Naturally, the prettier the girl the greater the competition. But if one does overcome one's rivals, how magnificent the reward! Caesar and Napoleon, Rockefeller and Onassis, could obtain no more with their armies or their millions. Empires have been overturned solely for the hope of such victories. What other joy in life can possibly compare with that of having what to you is one of the loveliest creatures that God has ever made give herself happily to your embraces?

Perhaps the gods have been especially kind to me; but I certainly have no reason to regret my instinctive lack of desire for any woman who might be classed as second best. At seven periods in my life I have been desperately in love and only in two instances has my love not been returned. But I do not count my affaire with Pia as among those seven.

To start with, at the age of sixteen I still mentally divided girls into two distinct categories. Those in the lower classes were to be seduced without scruple, but I would have felt it to be demeaning myself to associate with them. And in this connection it must be remembered that generally speaking they were then, both in town and country little better than peasants. They were almost totally uneducated so to talk to, like moronic beings from some other world, could not afford hair-dos and pretty clothes, or the attentions of a dentist and rarely, if ever, took a bath. Those of the upper classes I had been taught to regard with a romantic idealism. The majority of them were then deliberately kept, as far as possible, in ignorance of sexual matters until they married. Even the idea that they might be subject to sexual urges was not to be thought of. Indeed, had one of them indicated an interest in such matters she would have lost caste in my eyes. In consequence it never entered my head to, as it is now termed, 'make a pass' at Pia.

Neither can it be said that in the real sense I was in love with her. I simply delighted in her beauty, enjoyed her gay companionship and sought every possible opportunity to be with her. Even more certainly it can be said that she was not in love with me. But she was flattered by my devotion to her and, I am sure, regarded me with considerable affection. I nearly always walked back alone with her from the *Tennisplatz* and on other occasions she was always happy to accept me as her escort. That, no doubt, was partly due to the fact that most of the young Germans in the town prided themselves on having a Spartan outlook, and considered it a weakness to show more than a passing interest in a pretty girl. In any case, while I was in Germany the lovely Pia filled for me the role that Hilda Gosling had filled for me during my *Worcester* days, plus a glamour that dear Hilda could not claim.

Pia was not only the undisputed belle of the town; in other ways she was quite exceptional. Her ugly but vivacious little mother was Dutch, and while the Dutch can hardly claim to be among the most elegant of peoples, Frau Emert evidently came out of their top drawer. She was connected by marriage in some way with the German Imperial Chancellor, Count von Bethmann-Hollweg, and to the envy of everyone else in the town, a year or so before I arrived in Traben-Trarbach, during a pleasure trip down the Moselle the Chancellor had broken his journey to take lunch at her house.

For an ex-*Worcester* boy the roasts of tender white veal, the *Leberwurst, Deutsche Beefsteaks* and other good plain German food was a pleasure to eat, but Frau Emert maintained a French cuisine that produced dishes that melted in my mouth, and in that house alone in the town champagne was served with every meal to which I was invited.

Pia, too, had been educated abroad in France and England and, in addition to her own and the language of those countries could also speak Italian and Spanish. More, she did not even buy her clothes in Germany; her tweeds and shoes came from London and her dresses from Paris. Among my papers I find a letter that I wrote to Beardsworth which, for some reason, was never sent. In it, during an eulogy of her I tell him that every season, spring, summer, autumn and winter, she had nine hats from Paris or Brussels and that she thought nothing of paying 150 marks (£7.50) for the best of them.

I find it almost unbelievable now that any hat should have cost so much, but I would hardly have been likely to say so if it was not reasonably credible. Even allowing for the grossest exaggeration on my part, it gives some indication o the scale on which this lovely girl lived, and my own extraordinarily good fortune in for nine months having such a beautiful, *soignée* and cultured girl as my intimate friend.

My mother wrote to me every week and I to her; and from her letters which I still have it is clear that we were still devoted to one another. In fact, I confided in her so fully that during my first weeks in Traben-Trarbach I was even fool enough to tell her about the drinking parties I had been to. Naturally she was much alarmed and I had a very decent letter from my father asking me only to go easy and urging me to be more discreet as he had had quite a job to resist my mother's pleas that I should be ordered home.

His other letters, alas, lacked that human touch and consisted mainly of exhortations to work hard, demands to know what I was learning and intimations that it would be the worse for me if he had any complaints from Herr Kayser about my conduct. He also referred frequently to the money he was laying out to give me advantages which his father had been unable to give him.

His memories of his hard life when my age no doubt justified his complaints that my letters to my mother led him to believe that I thought of nothing but pleasure – which was perfectly true – but my board at Fritz Kayser's cannot have cost him as much as had my school fees, and by this time he had fully recovered from the financial set-back he had sustained at the time I was expelled from Dulwich. Indeed, that summer my parents came out to Germany for what must have been a most expensive holiday, as throughout it they stayed at the best hotels and he spent money lavishly on giving my mother and myself a good time.

On 6 September 1913 I went to meet them in Cologne and we made a three weeks' tour of Düsseldorf, Bonn, Koblenz, Bingen, Rüdesheim, Frankfurt, Hamburg, Wiesbaden, Mainz, Heidelberg, Worms, Trier, Bernkastel, and so back to Traben-Trarbach.

My most pleasant memories of the trip were our stay at Wiesbaden and of being entertained by Karl Sichel at Mainz. September, after the tourists had left, was the smart season at Wiesbaden, and the town with its many de luxe hotels was full of wealthy people of many nationalities. Its *Kurhaus*, said to have cost a million sterling to build, was the most beautiful building I had ever seen. I might now think it over-ornate, but its great halls of marble and gold-encrusted carving filled me with wonder and admiration. It contained big gaming-rooms, the largest concert-hall in Germany, and a luxurious terrace-restaurant. Dining there one could watch the beautifully dressed women and many German officers in their colourful uniforms strolling up and down a wide

promenade between the terrace and a lake lit with chains of
fairy lamps, while listening to Viennese waltzes played by a
military band. The cost of a dinner was seventy-five pence
(the equivalent now being about £10) a head; but the chef
was a genuine Cordon Bleu, and it was there that I enjoyed
my first *omelette surprise*.

Karl Sichel was the head of one of the largest wine-
shipping firms in the Rhineland. He was also a rich, generous
and sophisticated Jew, and his ideas about entertaining were
much more on the lines of the *haut monde* than those of the
homely Herr Kayser. As an example of the difference in
their outlook, when Julius Kayser went to London he stayed
at a small comfortable private hotel, whereas Karl Sichel
always stayed at the Savoy and gave lavish parties there.

In Mainz he and his extremely smart wife entertained us
royally. Among other things they took us to see *Tannhäuser*.
It was my first opera, so I was naturally interested. But opera
has never appealed to me, mainly, no doubt, because I have
never learned to appreciate serious music, and also because,
as a natural storyteller, I become impatient and bored by
the slow development of its plots. Afterwards the Sichels
took us to supper at the Tavern of the Holy Ghost. This
occupied the strangest site of any restaurant I have ever
visited. It was in the crypt of a consecrated church still used
regularly for services.

It is an interesting comment on the German attitude to
Jews in the Kaiser's day that whereas, on the outbreak of war
Herr Kayser became the Colonel Commandant of an important railway junction, Herr Sichel, although he controlled a far bigger business, had to report for duty as a
sergeant, and throughout the conflict was never promoted
above that rank.

I returned with my parents to Traben for us to be just in
time to participate in a three-day junketing. In Germany it
was then a custom for families to keep in touch by holding a
Family Day, on which as many members of the family as
possible came together to exchange news and celebrate. This
year Herr Kayser was acting as host and fifty or sixty other
Kaysers of varying ages and states of prosperity had come
from all parts of Germany.

To entertain this big party the whole of the packing floor at the cellars had been cleared and long trestle tables set up, casks of several kinds of wine were broached and numerous other drinks such as peach and pineapple *Bowle* were provided. The latter is another delicious summer drink simply made by letting a tin of pineapple chunks soak for a short while in one bottle each of still and sparkling moselle that has been well iced.

Three nights running the family gorged itself there on huge supplies of food while innumerable speeches were made and innumerable toasts drunk. During the days we went on expeditions. For one Herr Kayser had had a small steamer brought up from Koblenz and we went down river to Marienburg. There a ruined abbey and a small hotel crowned a high neck of land only about half a mile wide where the Moselle nearly met itself after making an enormous loop of some twelve to fifteen miles. It was a famous beauty-spot and the view on both sides was magnificent.

As a guest of honour at these festivities they had an old gentleman who was famous for poetry he had written about the Moselle. He had a shock of white hair, a straggly white beard and pale blue eyes that so constantly watered as to give the impression that he was always crying. At no time did I hear him utter a single word and he appeared to me to be drunk from start to finish. Nevertheless they carted him about with them wherever they went, handling him with the greatest deference and filling him up with more wine at brief intervals.

When the big party was over my parents left for London. Juli accompanied me to the station to see them off and my father gave me twenty marks. Such was my irresponsibility about money that in spite of Juli's protests I insisted that we should stop at a *Weinstube* and spend five marks of it on a bottle of bubbly. Since it was early in the afternoon this was an absurd extravagance, but it was inspired by my feelings for Juli and that is why I mention it. He was a really fine young man, a good scholar and a fine all-round athlete. He was good-tempered but could be severe, high principled yet out for any fun and had a grand sense of humour. He was also the accepted leader of his student friends, and it was largely due to his example and advice that I owed my own popularity among them. In consequence I had a great admiration and affection for him and, I suppose, seized on this opportunity to stand him a much more expensive drink than we normally enjoyed.

My next excitement was the vintage. The vineyards of the Rhine and the Moselle are the most northerly in Europe, so it is only in exceptional summers, combined with freedom from early frosts, hailstorms when in blossom, and other disasters to which vines are subject, that the grapes ripen to perfection. The vintages of 1906 and 1908 were good and that of 1911 excellent, but 1912 and 1913 produced only wines of indifferent quality.

In 1913 the grapes had been allowed to hang late in the hope that they would acquire a little more sweetness, so vintaging did not take place in the Traben area until 18–26 October. During the day we all went out to gather the grapes and at night they were pressed in the cellars. In the old days, when only hand presses, like capstans, were in use the day's pickings far exceeded the capacity of the presses at night, with the result that large quantities of grapes had to be left unpressed for up to a fortnight. The juice of white and red grapes is the same colour if they are pressed within a few hours of picking, but after that they begin to take the colour of their skins. It was for this reason that in my youth one still often saw old German wines of a lovely deep golden colour; but by the time I arrived in Traben-Trarbach hydraulic presses had been installed in all the larger cellars. No doubt there is a good commercial reason for getting every picking pressed overnight, but the colour of a wine can add much to the enjoyment of a connoisseur, and to my mind the pale wines, which are universal today, have definitely lost something of their attraction through the modern procedure.

It was during or soon after the vintage that two English wine-merchants, one of whom was the buyer for the Army and Navy Stores, came as Herr Kayser's guests to Traben-Trarbach. He always put his visitors up at a small but pleasant hotel, called the Claus Fiest, on the Traben bank, and early one Sunday morning he sent for me to meet them there and accompany them on an expedition. It started with a brief visit to the cellars, at which we drank a bottle of wine. We then proceeded up the Trarbacher Schlossberg and at its top, to refresh ourselves after our climb, Herr Kayser declared, 'Here we must have *ein Glas Wein*': bottle number two. We then took a zig-zag course across the mountains for about five miles and down to Zeltingen. There we visited the cellars of two peasant proprietors at each of which we had *ein Glas Wein*: bottles three and four. Next we walked a few miles further, now along the river, to Kues, where at two more cellars we had *ein Glas Wein*; bottles five and six. We then crossed the bridge to Bernkastel where, at the charming Drei Könige Hotel, we had an excellent lunch washed down by two more bottles: seven and eight.

At that time there was a famous legal dispute in progress about the right to use the words 'Bernkasteler Doktor' on a label. The original vineyard, owned by a lady called the Widow Tranich, produced the finest and highest-priced of all the moselles. The great firm of Deinhard had purchased a neighbouring property and also claimed the right to use those golden words upon the wine produced from it. Frau Tranich had taken an action against them to protect her monopoly of the name, and Herr Kayser, who bought the greater part of her crop, was helping her to finance it. They were, therefore, the best of friends.

During lunch the matter was discussed and after the meal Herr Kayser said, 'I will now take you to meet the Widow Tranich.' With him we walked along the river bank to a house very similar to his own, with a charming vine-covered terrace. We went up the steps and along the terrace, Herr Kayser leading, the two wine-buyers next and myself bringing up the rear. At the far end of the terrace Frau Tranich was sitting with some friends, engaged in a very normal occupation for a Sunday afternoon; they were enjoying the contents of a big iced *Bowle*. Seeing this over Herr Kayser's shoulder the leading Englishman turned with a blanched face, and thrust his way back past his companion and myself, exclaiming, 'More wine! No; no! I can't manage it!'

His friend turned with him and they both fled; and as Herr Kayser was already bowing over the widow's hand, I was left to explain that they had both eaten something for

H

lunch which had suddenly disagreed with them. I was more than a little proud to think that although only sixteen I had stayed the course when two wine-merchants of long standing had had to throw in the sponge; particularly as I was able to keep the flag flying for my country while knocking back several glasses of Frau Tranich's excellent *Bowle*, and later drinking my share of yet another bottle of wine – this time the highly potent Bernkasteler Doktor – in her cellar.

The cellar was tiny, it held only ten casks, and all of them were full only when there had been an exceptionally good vintage; so each of them that held the indisputably authentic wine was worth a small fortune.

Later in the afternoon Herr Kayser and I collected our two truants from the hotel and went on to Trier. There we stayed at the Porta Nigra Hotel, which is opposite the great Roman arch that is the salient feature of the ancient city. The hotel, although of only medium size, was then quite palatial, and somewhat like Sacher's in Vienna, having huge rooms each protected from noise by tall double doors of baize. When I stayed there again forty-five years later it had suffered a sad decline. The lofty rooms had been cut up by partitions into twos or threes, making them like boxes, and the furniture was modern, hideous and scanty.

That night after dinner Herr Kayser took us to what would now be described as a night club. It had no dance floor or cabaret, but each table was set in a separate compartment formed from trellis-work adorned with a thick screen of artificial vines. In them one supped and drank while attended by pretty girls dressed in next to nothing, who sat on the knees of the visitors and helped them dispose of their champagne.

Herr Kayser invited both his guests to allow these lovelies to show them the upper part of the establishment, but both declined. As I was debarred by my principles from making sexual advances to girls of my own class and by my fastidious-ness from having anything to do with girls who lived in poor homes, I would have given my eyes to have been included in this invitation. One of them could have been the perfect answer to a need that I had long been feeling. But, alas, Herr Kayser evidently considered me still too young to in-

dulge in such delights; so I had to return, secretly suffering
from acute frustration and a virgin still, to our hotel. There
we said good-bye to his guests and, in spite of our punishing
day, he told me that I must be up and dressed for breakfast
at seven o'clock the following morning, as we were leaving
Trier by an early train.

I was far too awed of him to risk his displeasure by failing
to be on time, but we only just caught the eight o'clock train
and, to my surprise, it was not one back to Traben. It took
us up the Ruwer, on which some of the finest wines, popular-
ly classed as Moselles, are grown; and his object was a visit
to the cellars of the Kaiserlich Preussen Domain, where the
wines from the Kaiser's own vineyards (now owned by the
State) were made and bottled. All the wines emanating from
them are of the highest quality, a certain quantity are ear-
marked for use in the royal palaces, the remainder are distributed through merchants such as Herr Kayser, and there
was considerable rivalry among shippers to buy and handle
them. I was allowed to take part in a tasting there, and that
evening we returned to Traben.

With autumn tennis, bathing and boating had to be
abandoned so at the end of the vintage and parties to drink
the new-made must, as the fresh-pressed grape-juice was
called, we were entering a dull period of the year until
Christmas. Afterwards there would be ample snow on
the mountain slopes above the town for tobogganing and
ski-ing and the ice would be thick enough on the lakes up
there for skating. In the meantime some of the younger
members of the families amused themselves by getting up
amateur theatricals, and this, unfortunately, led to my blotting my copybook badly with Pia.

As the belle of the town and the most accomplished girl
in it she was naturally given the star part in the play that was
to be acted. In Traben-Trarbach there was no florist and
garden flowers were by then over, but somebody suggested
that it would be rather fun if at the end of the show I presented her with what would appear to be a bouquet but
actually contained a cauliflower.

Innocently I fell for this, and when she was called before
the curtain went forward to present my offering. Leaning out

over the footlights she took it from me with a charming smile.
As she stepped back both she and the audience realised that
it was a cauliflower. They gave a great roar of laughter;
she, poor girl, went as red as a beetroot and hurried off the
stage.

I realised at once that the joke had misfired, but not until
later its full implication. Although people in Traben-Trarbach normally ignored the prefix when speaking of the
Emerts they were entitled to put 'von' before their name, and
although I had never heard it used, their full name was
von Emert-Kohl. That they did not use it was hardly surprising because the latter word is the German for cabbage;
so I had been guilty of the frightful gaffe of presenting a
cauliflower to the cabbage.

The joke was the more biting because Pia was envied for
her beauty and the Emerts for their wealth, so her parents
were justifiably furious at the insult to her. But Pia herself
behaved with the sweetest forbearance. She had the generosity to appreciate that I had been guilty of no more than
what I believed she would take as a harmless piece of fun,
and that the real blame lay with the malicious people who
had wished to humiliate her by using me as their cat's-paw.

All I could manage to scrape together were a few rather
tatty late roses from some cottage gardens, but I took them
to her and my contrition at having hurt her was obviously
so heartfelt that she at once forgave me and persuaded her
mother, who had always been kind to me, to do the same.
Our reconciliation ended with *foie gras* and champagne.

About the end of October I received exciting news from
my mother. We were to move again and to a much larger
house. W.Y.B. had bought the freehold of it for her and its
redecorating was being put in hand at once. From then on
her letters were full of plans for getting into it, and about my
return to England. The idea was that I should spend about
a month at home, to include Christmas, then return to Traben
early in January to complete my German year.

Late in November there were very heavy rains, causing the
river to rise and to cascade in torrents under the arches of
the stone bridge. One night a discussion arose between some of
the senior students who belonged to the boat club on whether

it would be possible to take a skiff through one of the arches while the river was in spate. The general opinion was that the boat would be caught by the current, turned sideways on and, most probably, be smashed to pieces against one of the piers of the bridge.

I declared that there was no reason why that should happen if the boat's steerage way was maintained by the rower keeping it moving faster than the river, and if it was steered by a competent cox. Then, probably being tight, I volunteered to act as cox for anyone prepared to try it.

My stupid challenge was promptly taken up by a young man named Carl Danz. He was Juli's closest friend and had become a great friend of mine. In one eye he had a slight cast, which gave him a permanent vaguely amused expression; that apart he was always laughing, had a delightful wit, and was one of the gayest fellows I have ever known. Like myself, he had a lodging in Trarbach, so whenever we had spent evenings drinking on the other bank we always walked home together, which entailed a most courteous dispute upon which of us should leave the other actually at his door. Many a time, between two and three in the morning, we had walked arm in arm a dozen times up and down Trarbach's main street still reluctant to part and on several occasions, although my bed was less than a quarter of a mile away, I had gone in with him and slept on a couch in his room.

Carlchen was, too, a good oarsman, so I could not have had a more suitable companion for this dangerous venture. And dangerous it certainly was, for if an oar even grazed one of the piers that could be quite enough to overturn a flimsy skiff, and in the seething cauldron of water below the bridge we might easily drown before help could reach us.

The following afternoon our friends endeavoured to dissuade us from carrying out our attempt, but both of us felt that we could not possibly go back on what we had said we would do; so a skiff was carried up from the boat house below the bridge to about a mile above it, and duly launched. After that it was mainly up to me, as all Carlchen had to do was to put his back into it with a long, steady stroke and put his trust entirely in my judgment.

I had at least one considerable advantage over the boat club coxes. They took boats out only in calm summer weather, whereas, while in the *Worcester*, I had been at times used to coxing boats in rough water, and often with or against the racing tides of the Lower Thames in mid-winter. On the other hand the smallest of the *Worcester* boats had been solidly-built four-oared gigs. Now I was called on to handle a light skiff that floated high and was easily liable to capsize.

Taking the boat through the arch proved a tricky business, but we shot safely out on its far side to the rousing cheers of our friends and a considerable number of townsfolk assembled on the bridge above. As I had been the initiator of this folly, during my final fortnight in Traben I again became known as the mad Englishman, which, I will confess, did not displease me.

Instructions arrived from my father that I was to return home on 4 December, and with them money to give a party for the cellarmen and for my journey. As I had not been ordered to take any particular route I decided to go via the Hook of Holland, because the longer sea journey made it considerably cheaper and I would be able to keep the extra money to spend as I liked.

Expecting to see all my German friends again in the New Year, I bade them a cheerful farewell and set off. I changed trains in Cologne and on the way to the Hook did myself well in the dining car, washing down my dinner with half a bottle of champagne and topping off with a Grand Marnier. But the 4th is said to be an unlucky date for anyone whose astrological number, like mine, is an 8, and this one certainly proved so for me.

When I reached the Hook a storm was raging. The sea was reported to be so rough that nearly all the voyagers in the boat-train decided to cancel their passages and stay the night in the town. But the ship was a mail-boat, so she had to sail if possible, and at midnight I was one of the twelve passengers who sailed in her.

As I had never been seasick I imagined myself to be a good sailor. I am, for I have since travelled tens of thousands of miles without being seasick; but once we were out of harbour

I saw that I was to be called on to face something quite exceptional. The waves seemed mountains high, the steamer a mere cockleshell as alternately great wave crests crashed in a smother of foam over her fo'c's'le and she plunged into seemingly bottomless valleys between them. Imagining that there would be little hardship in dozing in the lounge all night, I had further economised on my journey by not booking a cabin; now the champagne I had bought on the train with that money was to cost me dear. It meant that I had to spend the whole night shivering with cold and in miserable discomfort, and although I managed to stick it out for two hours at the end of that time I could no longer stop myself from being sick.

It was not just a passing bout either. I was very, very sick indeed, so sick that for hours on end my body automatically continued its attempts to throw up from an empty stomach, and I prayed that there might come an end to my torment by the ship going down. The other eleven passengers were all sick, and quite a number of the crew. We were supposed to have docked at Harwich at eight o'clock in the morning, but it was after midday before we landed. The captain of the ship told me that it was one of the worst crossings he had ever experienced.

Never again was I fated to suffer in this particular manner, as even on bad crossings of the Bay of Biscay I have found it possible to stave off anything worse than queasiness by slowly drinking champagne and nibbling dry biscuits; but this awful night taught me just how terrible seasickness could be, and to show every possible sympathy and cosseting to those later travelling with me who suffered from it.

Decorators in those days must have worked with more speed than they do in these, for my parents had already moved into our new home. Following the directions I had been given, late in the afternoon I reached it, to receive a loving welcome from my mother, and soon forgot the horrors of the past night in the excitement of being shown over the house.

I did not return to Traben-Trarbach after Christmas. Why, I do not know. Perhaps my father tumbled to it that I was learning practically nothing there, in the sense he meant me to; but in fact I had left England a schoolboy and returned with the outlook of a man, so I had learnt a great deal about the things that really matter, as well as having had a wonderfully happy time.

15

LONDON 1914

MY new home was Clinton House, Palace Road, Streatham, S.W. Clinton occupied a piece of ground in a fork formed by the junction of Christchurch and Palace Roads.

However, the top of Brixton Hill and Tulse Hill, which adjoined it, was then a very select neighbourhood. Many of the houses were large enough later to be turned into nursing homes, boarding houses and schools. They all stood in their own gardens, some of which were two acres or more in extent, and Palace Road was actually a private road. It had a uniformed keeper, barriers each end that were closed one day in each year and no funerals – except those of residents – or other 'objectionable' traffic was allowed to pass along it. The road had received its name because looking up it from west to east one had a fine view of the distant Crystal Palace away on the heights of Sydenham.

Clinton was one of the smaller houses in the road, but it had a good, square central hall, three reception and six bedrooms, and its principal rooms were all large with big semi-circular windows at their western ends. It was also one of the most modern, built probably about 1900, with only two floors above stairs and no basement; so was easy to run. I had been given two rooms on the top floor, overlooking the garden, for my bedroom and a private sitting-room.

I never felt the love for it that I had had for Wootton, for although Clinton had a detached garage with a flat over for a chauffeur, it had no other outbuildings, potting sheds, lofts, etc., such as the much older house had had, and its garden, a triangle between the two roads, had neither the size, privacy nor attractiveness that had made old gardener Gunn's domain such a joy to me during my schooldays. Nevertheless, it was a great improvement on Becmead

Avenue, and made a very comfortable home. It also had the advantage of being within a quarter of a mile of the back gates of Aspen House garden.

As my parents had only just moved in I was temporarily placed at my mother's disposal to help her get things in order. At the same time I resumed all my old social activities with the Sharps, Goslings and other friends with whom I had kept up a correspondence while abroad. A fortnight sped by and we began to decorate the house for Christmas. In no time the Festive Season was upon us with lots of parties and I was again escorting Hilda to dances. Then, in the New Year, a new phase of my life opened. I became an employee in the family business.

My father went up by train from Streatham Hill Station to Victoria but I, presumably because it was cheaper, (the fare was, I think, only 3d.) caught a tram from the top of Brixton Hill to Victoria and from there a penny bus up Park Lane to Mount Street. Returning that way on winter nights could be far from pleasant, particularly the long tram journey. On the top deck one at least was spared from having strap-hangers lean over one, but the combination of cold fug and fog, the smell of stale sweat, cheap pipe tobacco and rainsoaked clothes was one that I was called on to endure for a long time almost daily. However, it is my good fortune that I have always had the ability more or less to ignore my surroundings and, having taken up reading again, I generally managed to concentrate on my book.

The 'office', as we always called 26/27 South Audley Street, was long but not very wide. The third of it nearest the street was a shop with a counter, and board floor on which fresh sawdust was scattered each morning. The middle section contained a five foot high partition behind which our manager worked on the ledgers, one tiny office just large enough to hold a desk and chair, and the stairs down to the cellar. The back part, which was somewhat wider, made a good big private office for my father. Except for this last the whole place was incredibly draughty owing to the shop having on its corner double swing doors which never closed completely, and, the office included, it was panelled from floor to ceiling with hideous shiny yellow pitch pine.

The first floor below-stairs was the wine-cellar. Under the office it consisted of alleys of bins and under the shop there was an open space where the capsuling, labelling and packing of the wines was done. This, too, was cold and draughty as it had always open doors on to the goods lift that came up in the pavement, and to the long area with its dozen or so subsidiary cellars in which empty bottles of various types were stored and washed. In the lower basement there was a scantling long enough to carry about six casks. It was there that the wines and spirits were bottled off. The whole of the rest of the lower cellar was given to storing cased wines, liqueurs, etc., and to stocks of beers, minerals and ciders.

Our upstairs staff consisted only of a rotund little Scot named Bonin, who rejoiced in the title of Manager, and a jolly chap named Archibald, who served behind the counter. When business was brisk Bonin popped out from behind his partition to assist, and I, too, served in the shop during the midday rush. My father, of course, saw all the most import-ant customers in his office, did all the buying and got out the accounts at the end of each month. He had no secretary and conducted all the correspondence of the business in his own hand, such copies as were needed being taken on oiled paper by a hand press. Belowstairs we had Hoskins, our only wine-cellarman, and Ted, who spent his days heaving crates of minerals and beers about. A driver for our one horse delivery dray completed the establishment.

From the above it will readily be seen that we were still not much more than an offshoot from old 'Ready Money Wheatley's' grocery business. Another twelve years were to elapse before I could issue from those premises – by then floored everywhere with thick pile carpet and with maho-gany-panelled walls – a catalogue listing only rare old brandies, which proclaimed that we had the honour to serve

THREE REIGNING SOVEREIGNS
TWENTY-ONE IMPERIAL, ROYAL, OR SERENE
HIGHNESSES
TWELVE BRITISH DUCAL HOUSES, and
THE LORD ARCHBISHOP OF CANTERBURY

However, we did already have a nucleus of fine customers;

the Joel brothers, Solly and Jack, who each bought 500 dozen of both Clicquot and Pommery whenever those famous champagne houses shipped a new vintage; old Nellie Liza Bass, Baroness Burton, who came in one day dressed like a charwoman to buy, for some reason, a single bottle of cooking brandy, and was so courteously treated by Archibald that she turned over to us all the business for her great mansion in Grosvenor Square; the joint millionaires Sir George and Lady Cooper who, like Nellie Liza, had been great friends of King Edward VII; and Mr. Frank Bibby, the head of the great shipping line, who had been my grandfather's first customer for wine.

There were numerous others, but the bulk of our wine business in those days consisted of small accounts with some of the less wealthy residents of Mayfair and single-bottle trade over the counter. What were then termed 'persons of quality' rarely came to my father's office. If they wanted to see him they sent for him; but far the greater part of their business with us was conducted by their stewards or butlers, and it was these who made up the majority of the people who called on my father. It was not really until the 1920s that, by his hard work, he had established the reputation of the firm as first class wine-merchants.

On the other hand we were the biggest suppliers of beers and mineral waters in the district. We had few serious rivals, for it was beneath the dignity of the great wine-merchants to handle such inferior liquors, and the situation of our premises gave us a big advantage. Our shop was almost exactly in the middle of the quadrilateral formed by Piccadilly, Bond Street, Oxford Street and Park Lane. Inside it, then, the only shops and offices were in North and South Audley Streets, Mount and Davies Streets, the lower end of Curzon Street and in Shepherd's Market. The only flats were above the shops in those streets and in three or four large blocks on the extreme edge of the area. The whole of the rest of it was occupied by big private houses, many of them as large as small palaces; as, for example, Sir George Holford's mansion which occupied the whole of the site now covered by the Dorchester Hotel, and the Duke of Westminster's mansion, with its courtyard entered by two

double, fifteen-foot-high wrought iron gates facing on Upper
Brook Street and at its back the tennis court and garden
upon which were later built the greater part of the Grosvenor
House Hotel. All these hundreds of houses were occupied by
wealthy families few of whom kept fewer than twelve servants
and many forty or more, so the consumption of beer and soft
drinks can be imagined. We also had many customers in
Belgravia, Bayswater, Kensington and Carlton House
Terrace.

To describe the business further would be out of place here
as I played little part in it until after my return from the
First World War, but I hope to record the more interesting
of my activities as a wine-merchant in the third volume of
these memoirs. For the time being my father made use of me
as a handy-man, mostly in the cellars, as I was already competent to assist Hoskins in bottling wines, labelling and
capsuling them and binning them away. Sometimes I washed
for re-use the dirty bottles returned by customers – a horrid
job as we had no bottle-washing machine and it had to be
done by hand. At others I dipped in hot wax newly bottled
Ports and Sherries, as these were then never labelled but their
types distinguished by a range of different coloured seals. At
midday I put off my leather apron to go up and help serve
in the shop at the beer counter, which was patronised daily
by numbers of lower servants, caretakers, porters, etc., who
lived nearby. Occasionally my father took me with him to
make a courtesy call on the steward of one of the big houses
we served, such as Lord Howard de Walden's mansion in
Belgrave Square, or Lord Rothschild's in Piccadilly.

In the superior business man's uniform of that age – a top
hat and grey cut-away tail coat – my father used to make
several such calls between ten-thirty and twelve o'clock each
morning. Indeed, it would be difficult for anyone who knows
Mayfair only as it has been for the past quarter of a century
to visualise how extraordinarily different its streets, their
traffic and the people using them looked previous to the
outbreak of war in 1914.

The average height of the buildings was much lower and
there were no big, many-windowed blocks at all. Apart from
the few shopping streets ninety per cent of the area consiste d

of the original houses built in Georgian times, when the centre of fashion shifted from Soho westward across the open fields to Hyde Park. From those remaining it would appear, owing to their comparatively narrow frontage, that, except for the isolated mansions, they were not very large; but in fact they had depth out of all proportion to their width, often with one or more interior courtyards, to give light to blocks of rooms remote from the street.

Motor cars had by then become numerous. Those used in Mayfair were lofty and roomy enough to seat five people comfortably, exclusive of the chauffeur and footman, who occupied a partitioned-off seat in front. A few very smart women went about in electric broughams, but the majority of ladies still preferred to do their shopping in carriages. The horses were plump, long-tailed and beautifully groomed; the paintwork and harness polished to a mirror-like brightness, and nearly all of them had a footman riding on the box beside the coachman, to jump down and open the carriage door. Both wore their master's livery and top hats with small, black fan-shaped cockades at the sides.

Quite a few people drove round in specially designed equipages, such as that of Madame Bischoffsheim. She was a very handsome old lady who always wore pale-coloured crinolines and wide-brimmed poke bonnets beneath which she displayed an aura of white curls. She went about in an open phaeton with a great hood, and sitting in it she looked like a pearl in a big oyster shell; while perched up behind the hood, rigidly erect in top hat and with folded arms sat a 'tiger' as juvenile footmen were called. Her house was a big stone-fronted mansion in South Audley Street, and there she maintained considerable state. In those days breakfast could still be a social occasion, and one day Sir Ernest Cassel invited her for it to his mansion in Park Lane, which later became the London home of the Mountbattens. At the door she was received by the major-domo and four footmen lined up on each side. This, apparently, annoyed her, as she had only six; so she promptly engaged another six, then invited Sir Ernest back to breakfast and had in her entrance hall the round dozen ready to bow as he walked in.

For social occasions footmen always wore buckled shoes,

white cotton stockings and gloves, black silk knee breeches, black and yellow striped waistcoats, tail coats of a colour in keeping with the livery of the family, and had their hair powdered. Of the above, for everyday service they retained only the white gloves and wasp-striped waistcoats, but with an ordinary coat over the latter they could often be seen hurrying on errands about the streets. Their masters mostly wore glistening toppers, high stiff white collars, wide cravats, spats, and carried Malacca canes. The era of the bowler and the rolled umbrella had not yet arrived, although occasionally one saw a brown bowler, and square-topped bowlers were popular with elderly gentlemen. The multi-millionaire, Sir John Ellerman, who lived in South Audley Street, always wore one, as also did W.Y.B.

Nearly all commercial traffic was still horse-drawn and the number of coal-carts in the area was prodigious. Few people had as yet installed gas fires and electric fires were, I think, still unknown. Coal was therefore used for bedroom fires as well as those in reception rooms, and the majority of people still cooked on coal ranges, so the quantity consumed in these big houses was vast.

The clientele of the few public houses in the neighbourhood was also very different from what it is today. I am told that now to lunch in the snack-bar at the Audley, on the corner of Mount Street, costs at least seventy-five pence; then no lady or gentleman would have dreamed of entering such a place and the charge for a cooked lunch there was 1/6d. It consisted of a cut off the joint and two veg., pudding, a wedge of cheese and a roll. My father and I used to have ours brought the hundred yards from the pub to the office on trays and the tip to the old boy who brought it was 1d.

That my father was pleased with the work I put in is shown by his walking into the office one morning towards the end of February after one of his visiting rounds and announcing that he had bought me a Triumph motor-bike. Actually it was a motor-bicycle and sidecar, and was the property of Lord Ashby St. Ledger's steward, a Mr. Atkinson.

His Lordship, who afterwards became Lord Wimborne, was another of our star customers, and was already living in Wimborne House, Arlington Street, which backs on to Green

Park and is next to the Ritz. On one occasion he asked my father to find him a first growth claret that had become very scarce – probably a Lafite or Latour of the great '64 vintage. My father found him a small parcel but when reporting it remarked, 'I'm afraid, though, your Lordship may think the price too high, as I shall have to ask you thirty shillings a bottle.' As in those days one could buy a very good château-bottled claret for five shillings, such a price was absolutely fantastic, and equivalent to at least £12 a bottle now; but Lord Wimborne retorted icily, 'Are you suggesting, Mr. Wheatley, that I cannot afford to pay thirty shillings a bottle for claret for my own drinking? Send it in.'

He could, of course, easily afford it, for he was immensely rich. The directors of the Ritz had long wished to increase the size of their hotel. As it has streets on two sides and Green Park on the third, the only direction in which they could possibly extend it was by buying and pulling down Wimborne House. After considerable deliberation they decided that it would be futile to make Lord Wimborne an offer which would do little more than enable him to buy another house of the same size. To ensure his accepting it must be really spectacular, so they wrote explaining the situation and offering him a million pounds. His Lordship replied refusing their offer. He added that he, too, had long wished to extend his property as it had no tennis court, and if the directors of the Ritz would sell him the western wing of their hotel, so that he could pull it down and make one, he would send them his cheque for a million pounds.

His steward, Atkinson, was a big, plump, youngish man who came from a better class than most upper servants. So that he could show me how to drive the machine, it was decided that we should both take a day off and go down to Brighton. He made a very pleasant companion so we had an enjoyable outing together, and after two lessons on quiet stretches of road, going and returning, I had mastered the machine sufficiently to take it over.

Unlike most young men of my age I had not the least interest in mechanics, so I made no effort whatever to understand the working of the engine and, I have no doubt, abused it horribly. However, I liked to picture myself as a demon driver and, to my own danger and that of the public, I was soon getting every ounce I could out of its three-and-a-half horse power.

My favourite sport was taking corners at maximum speed, although owing to the sidecar attachment I could not bring the bike over at an angle by throwing the weight of my body sideways. As it was only on Saturday afternoons and Sundays that I had long enough to drive out into the country most of my runs were made in the evening round about South London, and playing this game in built-up areas in which there was a lot of traffic several times nearly led me to disaster.

On one occasion I cornered at about forty miles an hour to find ahead of me a railway bridge that had three arches; a large central one spanning the road, and two only about six feet wide forming long tunnels over the pavements. To my horror I found that I could not pull the machine round sufficiently even to enter the line of the oncoming traffic. It was heading straight for the far pier of the bridge. There was only one thing to do, mount the pavement and enter the tunnel. I did. It was about forty feet in length. Some people had just entered the far end and were walking towards me. Fortunately, they screamed, turned and fled. The sight struck me as so funny that I never even thought of reducing speed, but burst into roars of laughter. Poor Douglas Sharp, who was in the sidecar, did not see the funny side of it, but as we shot out of the end of the tunnel and zig-zagged wildly through the oncoming traffic back to our own side of the road, I was literally weeping with mirth.

Looking back, it is obvious that I ought to have been heavily fined, or even been gaoled; but it was my good fortune that, although I had a number of minor accidents, I never injured any member of the public, one of my passengers, or myself.

On 28 April there was held at the Connaught Rooms the annual banquet of the Wine and Spirit Trades Benevolent Society, with Sir Joseph Lyons in the chair. My father was one of the stewards and took with him as his guests, W.Y.B., Tom Clements, a Mr. Awnyll, who was the under-manager of our bank in South Audley Street, and myself. Over five hundred of us sat down to dinner, among them the heads of all the great wine-shipping houses, and many of their principals from France, Germany, Portugal and Spain, who had come over for the occasion – also, of course, the whisky barons and the gin distillers.

There, for the first time I met many friends of my father who were later to become good friends of mine, among them the men who handled Pommery and Greno champagne. The agency was held by the Thellusson family who, as bankers, had achieved fame and fortune during the French Revolution. The partners were Lord Rendlesham and his brother, the Hon. Percy Thellusson. Their sales manager was a huge, genial Frenchman named André Simon, a name that was later to become a household word in Britain as that of the author of innumerable sound books about wine and, in the thirties, as the President of the Wine and Food Society. With them as their guest that night they had the owner of the Pommery vineyards and cellars, the Marquis de Polignac.

I single these people out for mention only because it was probably at this meeting that the course of my future was first mooted. The idea of my returning to Germany had been dropped but my father was anxious that I should continue to study wine-making in other countries; and by the early summer it had been definitely settled that my next sojourn abroad was to start in August with six months in Messrs. Pommery and Greno's cellars in Reims.

The dinner, typical of those lavish days, ran to twelve courses. We washed them down with 1908 and 1911 moselles and hocks, 1906 G. H. Mumm's Cordon Rouge, Château Lafite 1899, Graham's '97 Port and Martell's 40 year old Cognac brandy; so a good time was had by all.

Early in May we entered the busiest time of our year. The moneyed classes then had far more leisure than they do now and a high proportion of them migrated from place to place with the seasons. Soon after the New Year the smart place to be was in the gambling rooms or enjoying the sunshine on the Riviera. Scores of wealthy families owned villas there, many of them had private yachts and lived on them, cruising from harbour to harbour, hundreds more took rooms in the big hotels and the whole coast from Antibes to San

Remo swarmed with members of the British aristocracy. With the coming of the English spring they returned to enjoy the gardens of their stately homes. From the first week in May until the last in July they occupied their town houses for the London Season. In August those who had places in Scotland, and they were many, with those invited to join house parties there, went north to shoot grouse; while others went abroad to gamble at Deauville or Biarritz or visit the Rhineland, Belgium, Holland and Switzerland. September was the month for cures and saw thousands of the rich English in Baden-Baden, Vichy, Homburg, Carlsbad and Wiesbaden. In October they were back again on their estates to shoot the pheasants and partridges. November was the month of the Little Season, during which many of them again lived and entertained in London. In December, back to the country, for it was unthinkable to spend Christmas anywhere else.

Of course there were quite a number of peers and wealthy men whose official duties or commercial interests meant their living in London for most of the year, and the majority of dwellers in Mayfair kept their houses open with a skeleton staff, so that they could spend a few nights in them without inconvenience whenever they wished. But until the great redistribution of wealth began after the 1914–18 war there were quite a considerable percentage of houses that remained shuttered and occupied only by caretakers for eight or nine months every year; while in August Mayfair was so deserted that business came almost to a standstill, and the month of February was little better.

In the last week of April the shutters of the seldom-used houses were thrown back and the dust sheets removed from the furniture. Even families suffering from hard times, who felt that they could not afford to come up for the season, would have let their houses to rich Americans. The whole district began to pulse with a new vitality, and we worked overtime delivering wicker hampers, cases and crates containing drink of all descriptions.

Every night from early May onwards there were a score of dances and parties. The staffs of catering firms such as Gunter's, Searcy's, and our own Mayfair Catering Company were lucky if they got three hours' sleep in the twenty-four. Carriages and cars with their attendant footmen packed the big squares. From mansions in Grosvenor, Berkeley and Belgrave Squares, in Hill Street, Charles Street and Park Lane lights blazed until dawn and, counting also the innumerable smaller parties, London society could not have consumed less than five hundred dozen of champagne a night.

Meanwhile my private life continued much as it had before I went to Germany. Douglas Sharp remained my bosom friend, and Hilda Gosling, when she was on holiday from her school at Eastbourne, filled the role to me of a much-loved sister. The theatre was still the leading entertainment of its kind and we went to the Brixton Theatre to see such frightful melodramas as *The Rosary, Women of Paris,* and *The Royal Divorce.* But the cinema was rapidly gaining ground and one named the Golden Domes had been opened in Streatham.

The films of those days were very short, so the programme always contained about six items; the principal ones generally being an early Charlie Chaplin or Harold Lloyd, a Western, and an instalment of a serial film in which the beautiful, courageous, deceived, maligned, imprisoned and frequently threatened with 'worse than death' but always surviving and chaste heroine, was Pearl White.

It was at the Golden Domes one afternoon in July, that I first saw Barbara Symonds. She had an oval face, the bluest eyes I have ever seen, and rich gold hair that was slightly frizzy, so that when she stood with her back to the sun it made a golden halo round her head. She was my first great passion, but it lasted all through the 1914–18 war and did not reach its bitter end until 1919; so it is more appropriate that I should tell the story of it in the second volume of my memoirs.

My cousin Laurie also had a love affair that summer, and one that landed him in a packet of trouble. He took a great fancy to Dorothy, Douglas Sharp's elder sister, who in her early teens had taken me to kindergarten, and by this time was a pretty girl of about twenty-one. She fell in love with him and for some time they saw a great deal of one another.

As was liable to happen when a young man paid such marked attentions to a respectable girl, one night her father tackled Laurie and asked him his 'intentions'. Taken by surprise, Laurie replied that he had no thought of marrying yet, as he could not afford to do so. That was true enough for, though he later held an important post in the Foreign Exchange Department of J. Henry Schroeder and Co., the merchant bankers, he was then only a junior clerk there.

Whether Dorothy had asked her father to bring Laurie to the point or Mrs. Sharp had pushed her mild, retiring husband into doing so, history does not relate; but when Laurie's reply was made known to Dorothy she gave way to wild lamentations. Since Laurie had used lack of money as his excuse for refusing to become engaged, poor Mr. Sharp was then pushed into making a formal call on W.Y.B. They evidently thought that Laurie's rich 'uncle' would provide, and Mr. Sharp took the line that Laurie's attentions to his daughter had spoiled her chances with other young men. Regarding this as a form of blackmail, W.Y.B. refused both his assistance and to exert any kind of pressure on his 'nephew'; so Laurie escaped the noose, but only at the cost of some very unpleasant interviews.

By then, as I was seventeen, on our Sunday morning walks Laurie had taken to improving the theoretical side of my education on matters of sex, and describing to me the successes he had had with a number of girls while I was in Germany.

My code of morals being what it then was, I was naturally greatly shocked by his admissions; but Laurie only poked mild fun at the idea that one should regard well-bred girls as beings apart, never to be thought of in connection with the baser instincts. He pointed out the obvious, that if one saw two pretty girls in the nude, one of whom was a princess and the other a maid-of-all-work, but both with carefully done hair and manicured nails, one would not be able to tell t'other from which, and that having similar bodies women of all classes were subject to similar emotions where men were concerned.

He then went on to reveal a matter of which I had not previously been aware. I had believed that beautiful ladies finally surrendered to their lovers' pleas with great reluctance and only to reward their devotion. But Laurie assured me that this was not so; nine times out of ten they did it because they wanted to so badly that they could not help themselves.

To my amazement he told me that it was not only boys who masturbated, but girls as well, and that when it came to the sexual act women, if properly aroused, derived as much, if not more, pleasure from it than men. He added that girls were no better morally than ourselves, and their minds were constantly occupied with such matters; that the only reason for the respectable ones concealing it was their fear that if they admitted it to us we should cease to think so highly of them; and that once the ice had been broken by talking to them of such things any reluctance they showed to surrendering was nearly always due to the fear that they might be put in the family way.

As far as Dorothy was concerned, he maintained that he had never even mentioned marriage to her, had done her no harm, and that nothing but unhappiness could have resulted from his marrying her on his present salary. In that I am sure he was right, and now that I knew the facts I admired him for his courage in standing out against the Sharps and refusing, while still so young, to have a halter put round his neck. Dorothy, too, did far better for herself in the long run, as a few years later she married a very nice man of a suitable age who was rich enough to give her a house in one of the lovely terraces overlooking Regent's Park.

The London Season ran a similar course to that it had done for the best part of a century. At the Drawing Rooms held in Buckingham Palace the débutantes made their curtsey to Queen Mary, and the more favoured ones – my second wife among them – were also invited to a state ball at the Palace. Further down the Mall in St. James's Palace King George V held his levees at which young diplomats and officers in the Services were presented to him. Gay sparks in grey toppers and lovely ladies drove down in coaches to the Derby. There were the Royal Academy, Eton and Harrow at Lord's, Polo at Hurlingham, the Horse Show at Olympia, and Royal Ascot, with Henley, Goodwood and Cowes to follow.

When the news was published that on 28 June in Sarajevo the Archduke Franz Ferdinand and his wife had been assassinated no one thought much about it, for in those days anarchists quite frequently threw bombs, or shot at

royalties and presidents. But the crime had been inspired by
Serbians, and Austria demanded from Serbia reparations
and guarantees for the future that could not be granted
without humiliation.

For a month the diplomatic wrangling continued, Germany
backing Austria's demands and Russia supporting Serbia's
protests at their harshness, while the less bellicose powers
endeavoured to find a formula which would pacify Austria
while yet saving Serbia's face.

Still, few people took serious notice of the quarrel, but
among those few was Winston Churchill. On the excuse of
holding a naval review he concentrated the Grand Fleet at
Portsmouth and there, on 18 July, King George inspected
the greatest armada of steelclad warships that had ever sailed
the seas.

Another week and with appalling suddenness the people
woke to the fact that in a few more days, after forty years of
peace, the great nations on the Continent might again be at
war. Even then it was not thought by the public that Britain
would become involved. Yet important Germans in London
were already being secretly warned by their Embassy that
they ought not to risk being caught in an enemy country by
a possible outbreak of hostilities; so they should return to
their own without delay.

Among them was the Baron Goldschmidt von Rothschild.
He was a leading member of the German branch of the
family, but spent a great deal of his time hunting in the
English shires or living in his London mansion, 146 Piccadilly.
For some reason or other, on the morning of 30 July he
looked in at my father's office. Having done whatever business it was he came to do, the Baron threw a ticket on the
desk and said,

'That is for my box at Covent Garden, Wheatley. If you
and your wife like opera, perhaps you may care to use it.'

In those days the very rich took boxes for the whole
season; hence the Baron giving his away so casually for a
single night, even though he would not be able to occupy it
because he was returning to Germany. But, owing to this
fantastic chance my parents and I were present at the last
night of the Opera Season of 1914.

The box was on the ground floor tier, so we were only a few feet above the heads of the people in the stalls. Every man there was in white tie and tails; nearly every woman had bare shoulders and was wearing a tiara. The box was, also, far enough round for us to have a good view of the Royal Box in the centre of the second tier. This last night being a gala it was occupied by Queen Alexandra. With her, on one side, she had her sister, the Dowager Empress of Russia, on the other her sister-in-law, the Queen of Denmark. All three of these royal ladies positively blazed with diamonds.

The opera given was *Aïda*, but the spectacle on the stage was far outshone each time the lights went up by that of the auditorium. Every box was occupied and every stall. The hundreds of women were clad in every shade of silk and satin; some had velvet cloaks, others furs of ermine or Russian sable. Pearls which must have totalled thousands hung in ropes round their necks. Diamonds, rubies, sapphires and emeralds which must have been worth several million pounds glittered and scintillated from their hair, ears, necks, corsages and hands. It was a sight never to be forgotten.

It epitomised the old world of aristocracy, great private fortunes, luxury, elegance and leisure. Unknown to all of us that world had been struck its mortal blow even as we sat there. At that very moment hundreds of thousands of soldiers in Austria and Serbia were already on the march, millions more in Russia and Germany were to receive their mobilisation orders within a few hours. Before another week had passed Belgium, France and Britain would also be at war. And ten million men were to die before a gala performance would be held at Covent Garden again.

As our Foreign Secretary, Sir Edward Grey, was soon to tell the House of Commons, the Lights of Europe were going out and no man could say when they would be lit again. They never were; they never can be upon a similar scene to that I witnessed then. That world had endured almost unchanged since Waterloo, almost a hundred years; but on that night it passed never to return. To have seen the curtain come down upon it in such exceptional circumstances is a memory for which I shall be forever grateful.

INDEX

Compiled by Gordon Robinson

Dennis Wheatley's work has been **published in:**

Belgium	Switzerland
Brazil	Turkey
Czechoslovakia	The United States
Denmark	Yugoslavia
Finland	
France	
Germany	
Holland	*also in*
Hungary	Arabic
Italy	Armenian
Mexico	Flemish
Norway	Hindi
Poland	Maltese
Portugal	Russian
Rumania	Serbian
Spain	Slovene
Sweden	Thulu